Lackawanna and Western Railroad Company Delaware

Summer Excursion Routes and Rates

Lackawanna and Western Railroad Company Delaware

Summer Excursion Routes and Rates

ISBN/EAN: 9783337146412

Printed in Europe, USA, Canada, Australia, Japan

Cover: Foto ©Lupo / pixelio.de

More available books at **www.hansebooks.com**

SUMMER EXCURSION ROUTES

AND

RATES

DELAWARE, LACKAWANNA AND WESTERN
RAILROAD COMPANY

1897

W. F. HALLSTEAD
General Manager
Scranton, Pa.

PASSENGER DEPARTMENT
26 Exchange Place
New York

COPYRIGHTED BY
W. H. JOHNSON, COMPILER
1897

Unadilla Valley ~ ~

~ The Great Summer Resort

The Land of Song Birds
Flowers and Trout Streams

High altitude. Freedom from malaria, mosquitoes and insects. Warm days and cool nights.

The most economical and beautiful place in which to spend your vacation.

The Summer train service on the Unadilla Valley Railway will meet the needs of the Summer Residents.

This district is as good as the Adirondacks and much more convenient.

Richfield Springs, Cooperstown, Binghamton and Utica all of easy access.

There are numerous hamlets and villages at which board can be obtained at extremely reasonable rates.

For information and rates apply to ~ ~ ~ ~ ~ ~ ~
UNADILLA VALLEY RAILWAY CO.
80 BROADWAY, NEW YORK CITY, N. Y.

ELMIRA COLLEGE, ELMIRA, N. Y.
Oldest College in the World Devoted to the Higher Education of Women

The Telegram Printing Co.

Elmira, N. Y.

Engravers by all Modern Processes

Send for Samples of Work and Estimates

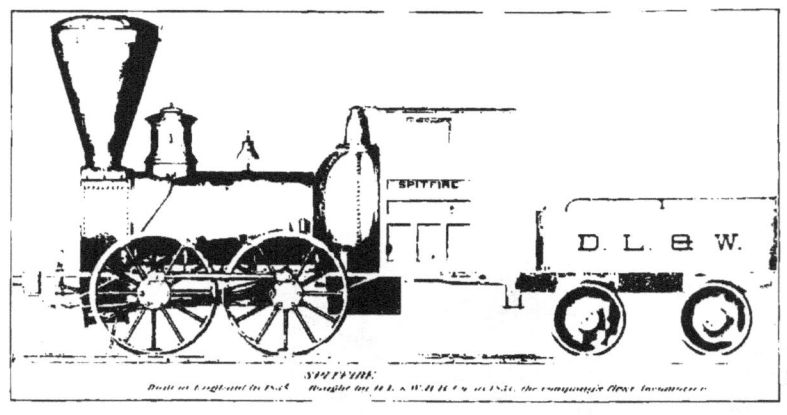

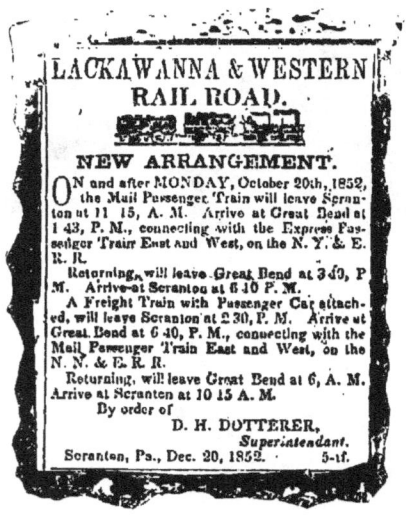

THE LACKAWANNA. —THEN, AND NOW.

FRONT FACING MT. WASHINGTON AND THE PRESIDENTIAL RANGE

The New : : :
Mount Pleasant
House, : : : :

In the Heart of the White Mountains.

Nearest Point from which to start for the ascent of Mt. Washington by the cog railroad and the nearest hotel to the north side ascent of the Main Pass of the mountains, the **Crawford Notch.**

Every interesting point in the mountains can be reached in one day's excursion from the Mount Pleasant House.

Through Parlor Cars to the Hotel grounds from New York, Boston, Portland, Quebec, Montreal, Ogdensburg and from Burlington, making an easy one day's trip from Bluff Point and other places on Lake Champlain.

A house thoroughly modern, with electric lights, private baths, and large music and dance hall; best equipped livery in the mountains; tennis courts built in most approved style on broken rock foundation; four fine bowling alleys; base ball diamond and golf links; *pure air, pure water* and the *grandest scenery in America east of the Rocky Mountains.*

Steam heat and log fires a feature of comfort in the fall.

ANDERSON & PRICE, Managers.
Also of HOTEL ORMOND, Florida.

Florida in... Winter.   The White Mountains in Summer.

ORMOND AND MOUNT PLEASANT.

THE HOTEL ORMOND, which has been spoken of throughout the resorts of Florida in unstinted praise of its table and the happy manner of entertaining its guests, has been, as it were, transplanted for the summer from the sunny ridge of the Halifax Peninsula to the rugged heights of New Hampshire, where, in its more luxurious summer garb as the "NEW MOUNT PLEASANT HOUSE," it continues to give refreshment and grateful shelter to the traveller. It is there the Mount Pleasant House, but in all that makes glad to tourists it is still the Ormond, as Messrs. Anderson & Price, with practically their entire force of skilled and efficient help, continue to be the living spirit within it.

It is a beautiful building, located on the edge of the great White Mountain Plateau, at the northern entrance to the main pass of the mountains, the "Crawford Notch." The famous peaks of the White Hills encircle it, and their crystal springs and streams and glorious atmosphere bring health and gladness to its guests.

The hotel caters for early and long season business, making rates to favor the early arrivals. The Mount Pleasant makes a specialty of entertaining travellers and tourists coming to the White Mountains to make the ascent of Mt. Washington, as it is the nearest house to the mountain, and the trains on the Mt. Washington Railway start from the very door-yard (after leaving the Fabyan station) to make the ascent, and it is the first hotel reached on the descent. From their own windows guests can see Mt. Washington from base to summit, and can decide in the morning whether to prepare for the ascent or await a more favorable day.

It is the terminus in the White Mountains of the Concord and Montreal Line from Boston, and it has a platform landing close to the house for passengers on through train from New York by Conn. R. Line, and from Boston and Portsmouth by the Boston & Maine R. R., and from Mt. Desert, Poland Springs, and Portland as well as from Burlington and Montreal by the Maine Central R. R. Thus, by its accessibility from the outside, having through parlor cars to its very doors from New York, New Haven, Hartford, and Springfield, and from Boston, Montreal, Burlington, and Portland, and the ease with which it is reached from all the neighboring resorts, it is a most desirable tourist centre.

It is a particularly favorable rendezvous for tourists going east from Saratoga, Lake George, Lake Champlain and the Adirondacks, as it is so easily reached from Burlington, the train leaving there at 10.30 A. M., via Montpelier, arriving at the station on the Mount Pleasant Hotel grounds at 4.05 P. M.

The Mt. Pleasant view of Mt. Washington and the "Presidential Range" is the grandest display of mountain scenery in America east of the Rocky Mountains.

The pure water of the Mount Pleasant spring, and the pure air of the White Mountain plateau, 1,700 feet above the sea level, make it one of the greatest health resorts in the world.

Driving is a great feature of the season at the Mount Pleasant, as, from its central location, all the drives of the mountains are tributary to its livery, which is the best equipped in the White Mountains. The party wagons are especially comfortable, and of a kind not elsewhere in use, except at Poland Springs, for which place they were originally designed, and have there proved a most popular success.

The house is striking in appearance architecturally, and is provided with every comfort and luxury of a thoroughly first-class hotel. Among the minor features are electric lights, steam heat, open fires, private baths, bowling alley, billiards, shuffle board, tennis court, base ball field, golf links, mountain paths, and, as a final attraction, the very best table that can be provided. An artesian well, drilled four hundred feet through solid rock, and supplying the purest, softest water, is a notable feature.

The orchestra is one of the finest among the New England resorts.

GLEN MOUNTAIN HOUSE   WATKINS GLEN NEW YORK

THE pure air of this mountainous region has proved so conducive to health, that an enchanting haven of rest, termed the Glen Mountain House, has been built on a clift in the life giving atmosphere of pines and hemlocks, where malaria is unknown, and to whose cool shades thousands annually repair for rest and recreation. It possesses all the modern conveniences; occupies an elevation of 300 feet above the village, and is the ONLY hotel connected with or in the immediate vicinity of Watkins Glen.

The Dining Room is in a Swiss Chalet across the Glen from the Hotel, whereby all heat and unpleasant odors arising from cooking, and noise and confusion occasioned by servants, are wholly avoided, rendering the Glen Mountain House one of the most delightfully cool and pleasantly situated summer hotels in the United States. A beautiful iron suspension bridge (covered), one hundred feet above the water, connects the two and fully protects the guests from sun and storm. It is a charming and somewhat novel idea and quite popular.

Apart from the hotel is the Amusement Hall, where all rational amusements, music, dancing, billiards, bowling, and rifles for ladies, can be enjoyed.

FREE admission to the Glen is enjoyed only by guests of the Glen Mountain House, notwithstanding publications of others to the contrary.

Satisfactory arrangements will be made, and every facility afforded for the accommodation of excursion parties, whether for the day or longer.

Popular rates will prevail at the hotel, and any information requested will be promptly furnished by addressing

W. E. ROBINSON, Prop.

GRAND HOTEL BROADWAY & 31st ST. NEW YORK

THE GRAND has been refitted with Electric, Ice and Refrigerating plants, modern plumbing, handsomely refurnished and decorated. No hotel is better located for family and transient patronage, and is in the heart of the theatre and shopping districts.

It is in every respect "up-to-date."

Army and Navy headquarters.

RATES FOR ROOMS, $1.00 AND UPWARDS
EUROPEAN PLAN

WM. G. LELAND, Proprietor

FORMERLY OF
LELAND HOUSE, SCHROON LAKE, N. Y.
HOTEL BENNETT, BINGHAMTON, N. Y.

Somerset Inn

THE SOMERSET INN, near Bernardsville, on the Delaware, Lackawanna & Western Railroad, is located among the highlands of New Jersey, in Somerset County (and in addition to the Inn there are for rent eight (8) handsome cottages, which cost to build $6,000 to $9,000 each, and are beautifully furnished). Appreciation of the healthfulness and charms of this section is shown in the many beautiful homes with which the hills are dotted.

The most important feature of this part of the country, however, is its healthfulness. The spring water, of which there is an unlimited supply, has been again and again analyzed, with the result that it has been pronounced by chemists the purest of waters. The dryness of the climate has proved especially beneficial to those suffering from rheumatism, neuralgia and weakness of throat and lungs.

Hard wood floors and trim, handsome new furnishings throughout, the best of beds, large, well-ventilated bed rooms and bath rooms, hot and cold water, gas, steam heat, open fire-places, spacious parlors, reading rooms, foyer hall and wide piazzas, make one's surroundings at Somerset Inn homelike and comfortable to a degree rarely found abroad.

Every convenience is maintained looking to the comfort of our guests; telephone, telegraph, post-office, good livery service, best accommodations for private turnouts, laundry, bowling alley, tennis court, golf links, billiard room, etc., while comfortable stages meeting the eight trains each way daily, make the Inn easy of access.

Better roads for driving and cycling, more picturesque drives and walks, better water, milk and air, can no where be found.

The country, lying as it does 800 feet above sea level, warm nights are unknown, and there are no nuisances, not even mosquitos. The grounds are tastefully laid out, and shade trees abound.

The children have not been forgotten. A fine play-ground in the pretty grove is arranged for their pleasure, and a play-room, for those days which must come now and then, when the little ones cannot go out of doors. Here they may enjoy themselves to their hearts' content, and annoy no one.

This is not an idealized picture of what we wish we could offer, but a plain statement of facts.

Where else, so easily reached, can such accommodations and environments be found? The Inn will open for guests June third and remain open during the fall months. Should further information be desired Mr. GEO. W. TUTTLE, the manager, may be found at the Inn, and will gladly accord every courtesy and attention to inquirers, either personally or by mail.

P. O. Address, **SOMERSET INN,**
SOMERSET COUNTY, N. J.

Train Service between New York and Bernardsville.

	A.M.	A.M.	M.	P.M.	P M.	P.M.	P.M.	P.M.	P.M.
Leave Barclay Street	7 10	8 50	12 00	S1 20	3 50	,4 30	4 50	5 40	S12 00
" Christopher Street	7 15	8 55	12 05	S1 25	3 55	4 35	4 55	5 45	S12 05
Arrive Bernardsville	9 03	10 26	1 37	S2 56	5 11	6 08	6 15	7 15	S 1 50
S Saturdays only.	A.M.	A.M.	P.M.	P.M.	P.M.	P.M.	P.M.	P.M.	A.M.

	A.M.	A.M.	A.M.	A.M.	P.M.	P.M.	P.M.
Leave Bernardsville	6 56	7 50	8 20	11 35	3 00	6 40	S 9 35
Arrive New York	8 20	9 20	9 30	1 20	4 40	8 25	S11 25
	A.M.	A.M.	A.M.	P.M.	P.M.	P.M.	P.M.

Contents.—Descriptive, Etc.

ROUTES AND RATES, ... Pages 123-168
FAMILY TICKET AND COMMUTATION RATES, . . "   170-171

Atlanta, N. Y.,	101	Mount Arlington, N. J., 42
Basking Ridge, N. J.,	28	Murray Hill, N. J., 28
Bath, N. Y.,	100	Newark, N. J., 21
Baldwinsville, N. Y.,	94	New Milford, Pa., 78
Berkeley Heights, N. Y.,	28	New Providence, N. J., 32
Bernardsville, N. J.,	31	Newton, N. J., 49
Binghampton, N. Y.,	79	Nicholson, Pa., 77
Bloomfield, N. J.,	22	North Brookfield, N. Y., 82
Boonton, N. J.,	41	Norwich, N. Y., 81
Brick Church, N. J.,	24	Orange, N. J., 24
Bridgewater, N. Y.,	83	Oswego, N. Y., 94
Bridgeville, N. J.,	53	Oxford, N. Y., 81
Budd's Lake, N. J.,	47	Oxford Furnace, N. J., 52
Buffalo, N. Y.,	108	Paris, N. Y., 82
Candor, N. Y.,	94	Passaic, N. J., 38
Cedarville, N. Y.,	84	Paterson, N. J., 38
Chatham, N. J.,	32	Phillipsburg, N. J., 52
Chester, N. J.,	42	Portland, Pa., 54
Chenango Bridge, N. Y.,	80	Port Oram, N. J., 41
Chenango Forks, N. Y.,	80	Pocono Summit, Pa., 63
Clark's Summit, Pa.,	75	Preble, N. Y., 88
Clifton, N. J.,	38	Richfield Springs, N. Y., 84
Conklin, N. Y.,	68	Rockaway, N. J., 37
Cortland, N. Y.,	87	Roseville Ave., N. J., 22
Crosco, Pa.,	60	Sanquoit, N. Y., 86
Dalton, Pa.,	75	Schooley's Mountain, N. J., 51
Dansville, N. Y.,	102-104	Scranton, Pa., 65-67
Delawanna, N. J.,	38	Sherburne, N. Y., 81
Delaware, N. J.,	53	Short Hills, N. J., 27
Delaware Water Gap, Pa.,	54-59	Sleeping and Parlor Cars, 15
Denville, N. J.,	37	South Orange, N. J., 25
Dover, N. J.,	41	Special Notice, 16
Earlville, N. Y.,	82	Spragueville, Pa., 60
Easton, Pa.,	52	Stanhope, N. J., 47
East Orange, N. J.,	24	Stirling, N. J., 28
Elmhurst, Pa.,	65	Stop-over Privileges, 18
Elmira, N. Y.,	96-99	Stroudsburg, Pa., 59
Fishing Points,	116	Summit, N. J., 27
Forest Park, Pa.,	50	Syracuse, N. Y., 90
Franklin, N. J.,	51	Tobyhanna, Pa., 63
Fulton, N. Y.,	91	Tully Lake Park, N. Y., 88
Game Laws,	117-119	Unadilla Forks, N. Y., 83
General Information,	19-20	Utica, N. Y., 86
Gillette, N. J.,	28	Washington, N. J., 52
Gladstone, N. J.,	31	Waterloo, N. Y., 48
Glen Ridge, N. J.,	23	Waterville, N. Y., 82
Gouldsboro, N. J.,	65	Watsessing, N. J., 22
Great Bend, Pa.,	78	Wayland, N. Y., 101
Greene, N. Y.,	80	West Winfield, N. Y., 83
Greigsville, N. Y.,	106	Wilkesbarre, Pa., 72
Grove Street (The Oranges),	24	Wyoming, N. J., 23
Hackettstown, N. J.,	51	Wyoming Valley, (The),
Harrison, N. J.,	21	Scranton, Pa., to North-
Henryville, Pa.,	80	umberland, Pa., 69-75
Highland Avenue, N. J.,	25	
Hopatcong, N. J.,	42-46	**Advertisements.**
Hubbardsville, N. Y.,	82	
Huntley, N. J.,	27	
Ithaca, N. Y.,	95	Adams, Jeannette, 180
Introduction,	17	American Bank Note Co., 182
Kingston, Pa.,	75	Ames, W. & C., 203
Kenville, N. J.,	46	American Ry. Supply Co., 192
Lackawanna & Montrose		Atlas Portland Cement, 176
R. R. (Alford to Montrose),	77	Bennett, The Hotel, 172
Lamsons, N. Y.,	91	Boarding House List, 180-181
Little Falls, N. J.,	38	Booss, F. & Bro., 9a
Lounsberry, N. Y.,	86	Bradley & Smith, 196
Lyndhurst, N. J.,	38	Briggs, T. & Co., 195
Lyons, N. J.,	28	Brown, N. Y., 194
Madison, N. J.,	32	Buffalo Wheel Co., 187
Manunka Chunk, N. J.,	53	Burnet Co., The, 202
Maplewood, N. J.,	26	Chautauqua, 168
Marathon, N. Y.,	87	Clyde, S. S. Co., 197
Milburn, N. J.,	26	Commutation Rates, 170-171
Millington, N. J.,	38	Dame & Townsend, 200
Montclair, N. J.,	23	Devoe & Raynolds, F. W. &
Morris Plains, N. J.,	37	C. T. Co.,
Morristown, N. J.,	33-36	Dickson Manufacturing Co., 193
Moscow, Pa.,	65	Dunby, Albert, 191
Mountain Station, N. J.,	25	East Coast Ry. & Hotels, 169
Mountain View, N. J.,	39	Eastman Kodak Co., 206-207
Mount Morris, N. Y.,	116	Elmira & Horseheads Ry., 172
Mount Pocono, Pa.,	61-63	Elmira College, 5
Mount Tabor, N. J.,	37	Ellsworth, The, 191

Fairchild House,	190
Fern Hall,	169
Fishing Ponds,	116
Fuller House,	186
Game Laws,	117-119
Gaze, H. & Sons,	121
Geneva Cycle Co.,	177
Germania Wine Cellars,	141
Gibson House,	190
Glen Mt. House,	7-9
Glenwood, The	115
Glen Island,	185
Gleason Sanitarium,	182
Gold Car Heating Co.,	198
Gould Coupler Co.,	199
Grand Hotel,	9
Grove Springs Hotel,	1
Gulick, W. A.,	191
Haggerty, J. Henry,	197
Harris, H. R.,	195
Hasting's Laundry,	194
Heller, M. B. & Co.,	188
Heft Lubricating Oil Co.,	175
Hirds, W. M. & Co.,	188
Holden & Sons,	90a
Hotel Gardner,	194
Jackson & Woodin Mfg. Co.,	198
Jefferson, The	188
Johns, H. W. Mfg. Co.,	203
Keuka Navigation Co.,	183
Kittatinny, The	114
Knowles Steam Pump,	193
Lappin Brake Shoe Co.,	202
Lozier, H. A. & Co.,	174
Manhattan Electrical Supply Co.,	204
Maurer, Henry & Son,	184
Millard, The	188
Miller's Hotel, 4th page of cover	
Minett Varnish Co.,	205
Maloney Oil & Mfg. Co.,	203
Monarch Cycle Co.,	110
Morris, Theo. W. & Co.,	196
Mountain View House,	192
Mt. Pleasant House,	7 & 8
National Ry. Spring Co.,	201
National Saw Co.,	173
Niagara Gorge Ry.,	187
Niagara River Line,	115
Nickel Plate Route,	90b
Nicks Tobacco Co., The	194
N. Y. State Fair, The	175
Osgood & Co.,	188
Packer Cycle Co.,	178
Passaic Rolling Mill Co.,	196
Plant System, The	111-113
Queen City Printing Co.,	195
Rathbun, Villas,	176
Robinson, M. W. Co.,	194
Roeblings, Jno. A. Sons Co.,	200
Rood, C. E.,	189
Sanatarium, The	120
Schaefer Bros.,	186
Skinner, Nathan,	189
Smith, D. & Son,	195
Somerset Inn,	10
Spring House,	186
Telegram Printing Co.,	5
Topping Bros.,	202
Turkish Baths,	208
U. S. Express Co., 2d p. of cover	
Unadilla Valley Ry. Co.,	4
Union Car Co., The	201
Vanderbilt & Hopkins,	197
Vanderbilt Hotel Syracuse,	2
Vose & Cliff Mfg. Co.,	201
Wabash Railroad,	
Webber, Jos. F.,	195
Westcott Exp. Co., 3d p. of cover	
Wiscasset, The	122
Wyckoff, A. & Son,	196
Wyoming Shovel Works,	202
Yost Mfg. Co.,	170
Zimmerman, F. L.,	188

PULLMAN VESTIBULE BUFFET PARLOR AND LIBRARY CARS.

EXCURSION ROUTES AND RATES,

AND

INFORMATION RELATIVE THERETO MAY BE OBTAINED OF

- **CHAS. L. HACKSTAFF,** GENERAL EASTERN FREIGHT & PASSENGER AGENT, 429 Broadway, New York.

- **M. L. SMITH,** DISTRICT PASSENGER AGENT, Scranton, Pa.

- **W. C. BRAYTON,** GENERAL AGENT PASSENGER DEPARTMENT, Globe Block, Syracuse, N. Y.

- **HOWARD J. BALL,** GENERAL WESTERN PASSENGER AGENT, 289 Main St., Ellicott Square Building, Buffalo N. Y.

- **FRED. P. FOX,** TRAVELLING PASSENGER AGENT, 152 Baldwin Street, Elmira, N. Y.

ALSO OF THE FOLLOWING:

New York, (Barclay St Depot)............C. H. GOVE	Wyoming, Pa.................................H. H. ANTRIM
" (Christopher St. Depot)....A. R STILSON	Kingston, " ....J. J. MULLEN
" (14 Park Place). ....F. STILES	Wilkes Barre, Pa ....G. SMITH
" (4th Ave., cor. 12th St.)....W. J. MANGIN	Plymouth, " ....G. H. LAWRENCE
" (942 Broadway)..................S. BEDELL	Nanticoke, " (Depot)..............B. C. KISTLER
" (53 West 125th St.) ....N. F. GUYER	" (City)..................J. B. SCUREMAN
" (235 Columbus Ave.).........M. F CLARK	Shickshinny, " ....E. W. GARRISON
Brooklyn, (338 Fulton St.).............WM WISERT	Berwick, " ....DUVAL DICKSON
" (720 Fulton St.)............OSCAR SEYMOUK	Espy, " ....J. H. MILLER
" (106 Broadway).....GEO. E. SUTHERLAND	Bloomsburg, " ....W. R. KOCHER
Hoboken, N. J......................W. H. JEFFERDS	Rupert, " ....G. W. MEARS
Paterson, " ....F. M. BARR	Danville, " ....A. M. GEARHART
Boonton, " ....F. E. BLOXHAM	Northumberland, Pa.....................R. G. SCOTT
Newark, " (Depot)............C. A. PALMER	Greene, N. Y. ....E. H. JACKSON
" (182 Market St.).......F. T. FEAREY	Oxford, " ....G. P. MEAD
Orange, " ....W. T. ATNO	Norwich, " ....W. S. WAGNER
Summit, " ....J. J. LANE	Sherburne, N. Y..........................H. H. TUCKER
Chatham, " ....J. P. RUSK	Waterville, " ....C. H. GRAVES
Madison, " ....C. R. HOPKINS	Richfield Springs, N. Y. ....C. C. MERRILL
Morristown, " ....W. R. M. FREGANS	Utica, N. Y. (City).......................J. H. MACGARRITY
Dover, " ....A. M. McFALL	Chenango Forks, N. Y................O. L. HARDING
Stanhope, " ....M. VAN HORN	Whitney's Point, " ....L. N. ENGLISH
Waterloo, " ....W. N. GRAY	Marathon, " ....C. BURGESS
Newton, " ....Z. H. SNYDER	Cortland, N. Y. (Depot)..............W. E. WOOD
Hackettstown, N J............W. M. EVERITT	" (City)..................W. T. BUSHBY
Washington, " ....W. SHIELDS	Homer, " ....J. H. STARIN
" ..Ass't Ticket Ag't, H. S. GROFF	Syracuse, " (Depot)...............W. S. CUMMINGS
Oxford Furnace, " ....W. J. AXFORD	" (Globe Block).........W. C. BRAYTON
Bridgeville, " ....R. H. KINNEY	Fulton, " (Depot)...............E. J. HOGAN
Delaware, " ....HARRY PETERS	" (Village)...............F. A. HOGAN
Portland, Pa ....H. LOVE	Oswego, " ....W. B. PHELPS
Water Gap, Pa ....D. C. STAPLES	Owego, " ....W. H. COREY
Stroudsburg, Pa..................A. C. LODER	Ithaca, " (Depot) ....M. A. QUICK
Spragueville, " ....P. M. ARNOLD	" (City).................F. W. PHILLIPS
Henryville, " ....C. HOWARD	Nichols " ....A. B. KIRBY
Cresco, " ....W. D. YOTHERS	Waverly, " ....E. S. WHEELER
Mount Pocono, Pa ....HARRY SMITH	Elmira, " ....W H. PETERS
Pocono Summit, Pa............W. A. MILLER	Big Flats, " ....S. C. LEONARD
Tobyhanna, " ....D. C. YOTHERS	Corning, " (Depot)................H. E. ELWOOD
Gouldsboro, " ....S. S. HAGER	" (City).................D. C. McKEE
Moscow, " ....J. S. LATOUCHE	Painted Post, N. Y......................D. M. SAYLES
Elmhurst, " ....E. W. DAVIS	Savona, " ....C. D. DAVIS
Scranton, " (Depot)...........M. L. SMITH	Bath, " ....G. H. PARKER
Clark's Summit, " ....W. P. LITTS	Kanona, " ....C. C. COOK
Glenburn, " ....JAS. EDWARDS	Avoca, " ....W. H. THOMAS
Dalton, " ....H. W. HAGER	Wallace, " ....JAS. E. COOK
Factoryville, " ....H. L. HARDING	Cohocton, " ....C. C. CUFF
Nicholson, " ....E. D. BELL	Atlanta, " ....E. W. LENT
Foster, " ....O. D. ROBERTS	Wayland, " ....R. C. NEILL
Kingsley, " ....W W. ADAMS	Perkinsville, " ....J. E. SCHU
Alford, " ....J. M. DECKER	Dansville, " ....C. A. SNYDER
Montrose, " ....W. B. B. BAST	Mount Morris, " ....J. A. MUNYON
New Milford, " ....D. W. HAGER	Leicester, " ....W. J. RANDOLPH
Great Bend, " ....C. C. SIMMONS	Buffalo, N. Y. (Depot)...............G. A. PRESTON
Conklin, N Y. ....F. P. BADGER	" (289 Main St.)........G H. STAGG
Binghamton, N. Y...................A. E. KENT	" (377 Main St.).......C. W. MILLER
Pittston, Pa...........................T. F. BURKE	

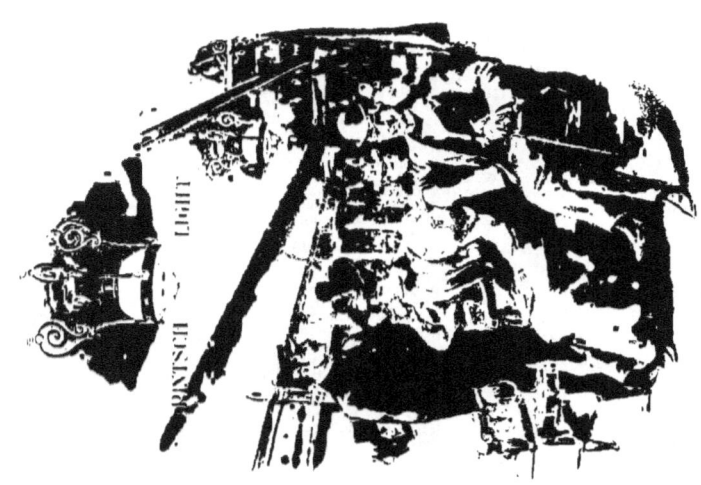

D. L. & W. STANDARD COACH AND PULLMAN SLEEPER.

PULLMAN PARLOR AND SLEEPING CAR SERVICE.

Vestibuled Buffet Parlor Cars, daily except Sunday.
NEW YORK, HOBOKEN AND BUFFALO.

Train 3 (Café Car).	Train 6 (Café Car).
Leave New York................10.00 A. M.	Leave Buffalo.................9.30 A. M.
" Hoboken...................10.15 A. M.	Arrive Hoboken................7.19 P. M.
Arrive Buffalo..................8.00 P. M.	" New York..................7.25 P. M.

Vestibuled Buffet Parlor Cars, daily except Sunday.
NEW YORK, HOBOKEN AND OSWEGO.

Train 3 (Café Car).	Train 4 (Café Car).
Leave New York................10.00 A. M.	Leave Oswego.................7.30 A. M.
" Hoboken..................10.15 A. M.	Arrive Hoboken................1.48 P. M.
Arrive Oswego..................7.00 P. M.	" New York..................1.55 P. M.

Vestibuled Buffet Parlor Cars, daily except Sunday.
NEW YORK, HOBOKEN AND RICHFIELD SPRINGS.

Train 3 (Café Car).	Train 6 (Café Car).
Leave New York................10.00 A. M.	Leave Richfield Springs........10.35 A. M.
" Hoboken..................10.15 A. M.	Arrive Hoboken................7.19 P. M.
Arrive Richfield Springs........7.10 P. M.	" New York..................7.25 P. M.

Vestibuled Buffet Parlor Cars, daily except Sunday.
NEW YORK, HOBOKEN AND ELMIRA.

Train 5 (Café Car).	Train 2.
Leave New York................1.00 P. M.	Leave Elmira.................6.00 A. M.
" Hoboken..................1.15 P. M.	Arrive Hoboken................2.47 P. M.
Arrive Elmira..................9.15 P. M.	" New York..................3.00 P. M.

Buffet Parlor Cars, daily except Sunday.
NEW YORK, HOBOKEN AND PLYMOUTH.

Train 171.	Train 172.
Leave New York................4.00 P. M.	Leave Plymouth................7.10 A. M.
" Hoboken..................4.15 P. M.	Arrive Hoboken...............12.07 P. M.
Arrive Plymouth................9.40 P. M.	" New York.................12.20 P. M.

Vestibuled Buffet Sleeping Cars, daily.
NEW YORK, HOBOKEN, BUFFALO AND ITHACA.

Train 7.	Train 10.	Train 8.
Leave New York....7.00 P. M.	Leave Buffalo......4.30 P. M.	Leave Buffalo......7.30 P. M.
" Hoboken......7.15 P. M.	Arrive Hoboken....6.25 A. M.	Arrive Hoboken....7.18 A. M.
Arrive Buffalo......7.00 A. M.	" New York....6.40 A. M.	" New York....7.30 A. M.

NOTE.—Passengers arriving at Hoboken on Train 10 may remain in car until 7.30 A. M.

Vestibuled Buffet Sleeping Cars, daily.
NEW YORK, HOBOKEN, BUFFALO AND OSWEGO.

Train 11.	Train 9.	Train 8.
Leave New York....8.30 P. M.	Leave New York....9.30 P. M.	Leave Oswego......9.00 P. M.
" Hoboken....8.45 P. M.	" Hoboken....9.45 P. M.	Arrive Hoboken....7.18 A. M.
Arrive Buffalo......8.00 A. M.	Arrive Oswego.....8.30 A. M.	" New York....7.30 A. M.

Vestibuled Buffet Sleeping Cars, daily.
NEW YORK, HOBOKEN, BUFFALO AND ITHACA.

Train 9.	Train 12.
Leave New York................9.30 P. M.	Leave Buffalo.................10.00 P. M.
" Hoboken..................9.45 P. M.	Arrive Hoboken................9.26 A. M.
Arrive Buffalo.................11.20 A. M.	" New York..................9.40 A. M.

Vestibuled Buffet Sleeping Cars, daily.
NEW YORK, HOBOKEN AND RICHFIELD SPRINGS.

Train 9.	Train 8.
Leave New York................9.30 P. M.	Leave Richfield Springs,........8.50 P. M.
" Hoboken..................9.45 P. M.	Arrive Hoboken................7.18 A. M.
Arrive Richfield Springs........8.05 A. M.	" New York..................7.30 A. M.

Vestibuled Buffet Sleeping Cars, daily.
PHILADELPHIA AND BUFFALO.

Trains Penna.R.R. 54 and 570, D.,L.& W. 7.	Trains D., L. & W. 12 and Penna. 567.
Leave Philadelphia, Broad St. Station..7.02 P. M.	Leave Buffalo.................10.00 P.M.
Arrive Buffalo..................7.00 A. M.	Arrive Philadelphia,Broad St.Station 10.00 A.M.

Pullman Parlor Cars, daily, except Sunday.

Stanhope Special.	Washington and New York Express,
Train 79.—LEAVE.	Train 86.—LEAVE.

New York...4.20 P.M.	Mt. Arlington.5.57 P.M.	Washington...7.02 A.M.	Boonton.... 8.17 A.M.
Hoboken .. 4.36 P.M.	Hopatcong.....6.00 P.M.	Hackettst'on .7.21 A.M.	Paterson....8.40 A.M.
Paterson....5.05 P.M.	ARRIVE	Hopatcong ....7.44 A.M.	Hoboken....9.07 A.M.
Boonton....5.30 P.M.		Mt.Arlington.7.51 A.M.	ARRIVE
Dover........5.46 P.M.	Hackettstown.6.25 P.M.	Dover .... 8.02 A.M.	New York...9.20 A.M.

NO. 3 QUEEN CITY VESTIBULED SPECIAL.

Special Notice.

SUMMER EXCURSION TICKETS herein described are sold from June 1st to October 1st, and are good for return until October 31st, except when otherwise noted, and have all the privileges of first-class tickets, including stop-over at any point on the "LACKAWANNA," and on all lines permitting stop-over.

Should passengers desire to leave a train or boat, they should notify the conductor or other proper official, who will issue a stop-over check or endorse the ticket, if stop-over is allowed on that line.

Tickets reading *via* Fall River Line of steamers are good for stop-over at Newport, R. I., in either direction, on application to Purser.

Tickets reading *via* Richelieu & Ontario Navigation Company's Steamers between Toronto or Alexandria Bay and Montreal do not include meals or berths between these points, when going East; going West from Montreal both are included. Between Montreal and Quebec meals and berths are extra in both directions.

Tickets reading *via* New York Central and Hudson River Railroad, between Canandaigua or stations East, and Niagara Falls will be accepted for passage either *via* Lockport or Buffalo.

Through tickets *via* the New York Central & Hudson River or West Shore Railroads will be accepted for passage between Albany and New York by the Hudson River Day Line or People's Line Steamers without extra charge.

Through tickets *via* the Hudson River Day Line Steamers will be accepted for passage on the New York Central & Hudson River or West Shore Railroads between Albany and New York on payment of $1.10.

Tickets reading *via* Delaware & Hudson Canal Co.'s Railroad will be accepted for passage between Plattsburgh and Port Ticonderoga, on Lake Champlain Steamers.

Children, between five and twelve years of age, half fare; over twelve, full fare.

One hundred and fifty pounds of baggage checked free on each full ticket, and seventy-five pounds on each half ticket.

Coupons between Richfield Springs and Cooperstown *via* Otsego Lake Steamboat and Stage Co. are good for passage only; baggage is charged extra.

As many of the steamer and stage lines cease running, or make irregular trips about October 1st, passengers should consult the proper advertising matter on the subject. Summer excursion tickets to local points mentioned herein are good for continuous passage only. Agents not supplied with regular tickets will use blank Excursion Tickets, Form 418, Limited to October 31.

Agents in New York, Brooklyn, Hoboken and Newark will use *Form "U" 418* to all stations (except Dansville, to which they will use Form 418, limited to October 31st).

Introduction.

THE DELAWARE, LACKAWANNA AND WESTERN RAILROAD COMPANY, in issuing its Summer Excursion Book for 1897, feels that it again places before the travelling public a book that will be found useful. The complete register that is given of all the available rural or urban spots along its line between New York and Buffalo, cannot but help the tourist, the vacationist and the holiday seeker in the selection of a resort, wherein the summer months can be spent to an advantage.

A glance at the following pages will suffice to show that many of the most famous resorts in the States of New Jersey, Pennsylvania and New York are directly on the Lackawanna Line, so that special allusion to them here is unnecessary.

A description of each place is given, much space being devoted to such among them as rank as summer resorts of national fame.

The illustrations herein contained are reproductions of photographs taken from scenes along the railroad, and are of a miscellaneous character.

A feature that will commend itself at once is the exhaustive list of *routes* and *rates* that is given, and which can be utilized in connection with tickets purchased *via* the Lackawanna Road.

Those in search of rest, of recreation, or of sport have only to glance through these pages, and from among the many mountain, lake and river resorts described, or from those where wealth and fashion reign supreme, select a place to their taste. The Lackawanna penetrates a section of country so diversified and so picturesque, that any person with an appreciation for the Creator's handiwork, as displayed through almost the entire region traversed by this road, will be apt to reflect before making a choice.

Great care has been taken in the compilation of this book to guard against errors, and it is offered to the public as a reliable guide and a work replete with interesting reading.

The Company feels assured that the public will appreciate the effort that has here been put forward, and presents it to that public with the compliments of the Passenger Department.

Stop-over Privileges
ON SUMMER EXCURSION TICKETS.

❦

NOTE. It should be understood that the stop-over privileges extended by the several lines (as noted below) require passengers to take such trains or boats as make stops regularly at the desired stopping-place. These stop-over privileges do not apply to tickets limited for continuous passage.

BOSTON & ALBANY R. R.	Stop-over allowed for 10 days on notice to conductor.
BOSTON & MAINE R. R.	Stop-over for 10 days allowed at any station (except between Salem or Reading and Boston) on notice to conductor.
CANADIAN PACIFIC R'Y	Stop-over allowed on notice to conductor.
CANANDAIGUA LAKE STEAMBOAT CO.	No stop-over allowed.
CENTRAL VERMONT R. R.	Stop-over allowed at any station on notice to conductor.
CENTRAL R. R. OF NEW JERSEY	Stop-over allowed on notice to conductor, except on New York & Long Branch R. R.
CHAMPLAIN TRANSPORTATION CO. (STEAMER ON LAKE CHAMPLAIN)	Stop-over allowed on notice to purser.
CONCORD & MONTREAL R. R.	Stop-over allowed at any station on notice to conductor.
CONNECTICUT RIVER R. R.	Stop-over allowed at any station on notice to conductor.
COOPERSTOWN & CHARLOTTE VALLEY R. R.	Stop-over allowed at any station on notice to conductor.
DAY LINE STEAMERS (ON HUDSON RIVER)	Stop-over allowed on notice to purser.
DELAWARE & HUDSON CANAL CO. R. R.	Stop-over allowed at any station on notice to conductor.
DELAWARE, LACKAWANNA & WESTERN R. R.	Stop-over allowed at any station on notice to conductor.
FALL BROOK RAILWAY	Stop-over allowed at any station on notice to conductor.
FALL RIVER LINE (OLD COLONY S. B. LINE)	Stop-over allowed at Newport, R. I., in either direction, on notice to purser.
FITCHBURG R. R.	Stop-over allowed on notice to conductor.
GRAND TRUNK R'Y	Stop-over allowed at any station on notice to conductor.
HUDSON RIVER DAY LINE	Stop-over allowed on notice to purser.
KINGSTON & PEMBROKE R'Y	Stop-over allowed on notice to conductor.
KNOX & LINCOLN R. R.	Stop-over allowed on notice to conductor.
LAKE GEORGE STEAMBOAT CO.	Stop-over allowed on notice to purser.
LEHIGH VALLEY R. R.	Stop-over allowed at any station on notice to conductor.
MAINE CENTRAL R. R.	Stop-over allowed at any station on notice to conductor, except on excursion tickets which are limited to continuous passage in each direction.
MONTPELIER & WELLS RIVER R. R.	Stop-over allowed at any station on notice to conductor.
MT. WASHINGTON R. R.	No intermediate stops.
MUSKOKA & GEORGIAN BAY NAVIGATION CO.	Stop-over allowed.
NEW BEDFORD, MARTHA'S VINEYARD & NANTUCKET S. B. LINE	Stop-over allowed for 10 days on notice to purser.
NEW YORK CENTRAL & HUDSON RIVER R. R.	Stop-over allowed at any station on notice to conductor.
NEW YORK, NEW HAVEN & HARTFORD R. R.	Stop-over allowed on notice to conductor.
NEW YORK, PROVIDENCE & BOSTON R. R.	Stop-over allowed on notice to conductor.
NIAGARA NAVIGATION CO.	Stop-over allowed on notice to purser.
NORWICH LINE (NORWICH & N. Y. TRANSPORTATION LINE)	Steamers make no intermediate landing.
OLD COLONY R. R.	One stop-over allowed at any station on notice to conductor.
OLD COLONY STEAMBOAT LINE (FALL RIVER LINE)	Stop-over allowed at Newport, R. I., in either direction, on notice to purser.
OTTAWA RIVER NAVIGATION CO.	Stop-over allowed at Carillon, Grenville and Caledonia Springs—at other points on notice to purser.
PENNSYLVANIA R. R.	Stop-over allowed at any station on notice to conductor.
PEOPLE'S (NIGHT) LINE STEAMERS (ON HUDSON RIVER)	Steamers make no intermediate landing.
PHILADELPHIA & READING R. R.	Stop-over allowed at any station on notice to conductor.
PORTLAND, MT. DESERT & MACHIAS STEAMBOAT LINE.	Stop-over allowed at any landing on notice to purser.
PORTLAND STEAM PACKET LINE.	Steamers make no intermediate landings.
PROFILE & FRANCONIA NOTCH R. R.	Stop-over allowed at any station on notice to conductor.
PROVIDENCE LINE	Steamers make no intermediate landing.
PROVIDENCE & WORCESTER R. R.	No stop-over privileges.
QUEBEC CENTRAL R'Y	Stop-over allowed on through tickets, reading between Quebec & Sherbrooke, on notice to conductor.
RICHELIEU & ONTARIO NAVIGATION CO.	Stop-over allowed on notice to purser.
ROME, WATERTOWN & OGDENSBURGH R. R.	Stop-over checks issued on notice to conductor.
ST. JOHNSBURY & LAKE CHAMPLAIN R. R.	Stop-over allowed on notice to conductor.
ST. LAWRENCE RIVER S. B. CO.	Stop-over allowed at any landing on notice to purser.
STEAMERS ON CAYUGA LAKE (CAYUGA LAKE STEAMBOAT)	Stop-over allowed at any landing on notice to captain.
STEAMERS ON SENECA LAKE (SENECA LAKE S. N. LINE)	Stop-over allowed at all landings.
STONINGTON LINE (PROVIDENCE & STONINGTON S. S. LINE)	Steamers make no intermediate landing.
THOUSAND ISLAND STEAMBOAT CO.	Stop-over allowed for 30 days.
VERMONT VALLEY R. R.	Stop-over allowed at any station on notice to conductor.
WESTERN NEW YORK & PENNSYLVANIA R. R.	One stop-over allowed on notice to conductor.
WEST SHORE R. R.	Stop-over allowed at any station on notice to conductor.
WHITEFIELD & JEFFERSON R. R.	Stop-over allowed at any station on notice to conductor.

General Information.

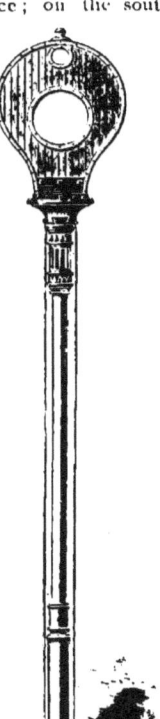

FERRIES.

ON leaving New York, the traveller by the DELAWARE, LACKAWANNA & WESTERN RAILROAD is carried across the Hudson by well appointed, double-decked ferry-boats, equipped with spacious upper and lower cabins, and lighted with electricity.

Barclay Street. The ferry from the foot of this street makes the trip to Hoboken in twelve minutes.

Christopher Street. The trip across is made in five minutes.

Hoboken. Here is located the terminus of the Company's road, the depot being a model of artistic beauty. The station is Gothic in design, with long sloping roofs, and on the northern side has a high, narrow tower, which adds greatly to its attractiveness. The general waiting-room is both large and airy. On the east side is the ticket office; on the south side is a room for ladies and a smoking room for gentlemen. On the north side are entrances for Hoboken patrons, as well as for those who cross from New York by the two ferries. A good restaurant, where a buffet lunch can be obtained, is provided in the waiting-room, and confectionery, fruit, etc., is obtainable at the counter adjoining.

The baggage-room is on the north-west corner, and passengers and others will always receive prompt and polite attention and answers to inquiries from the employees in that department.

The United States, the *only Express Company operating* over the Delaware, Lackawanna & Western Railroad, *has an office located* near the baggage-room, where its patrons can secure the benefits of its *superb service.* Its *Order and Commission Department* can be called upon to procure for the *Summer Guest* or others all that is needed either from the *city* or the *country.*

Experienced and well-informed ushers are stationed at the doors through which passengers pass to the trains. These men give the inquirer any information concerning the arrival and departure of trains, and, before the departure of each train, call out the names of all the stations along the route at which stoppage will be made.

The above-stairs portion of the station contains the headquarters of this railroad's branch of the Young Men's Christian Association, which are fitted up attractively. The conductors have a comfortably appointed room adjoining, and a furnished reception room. Baths, hot and cold, are provided. There is also a room in which all the men can meet for social intercourse, reading, playing games, etc.

THE HALL BLOCK SIGNAL.

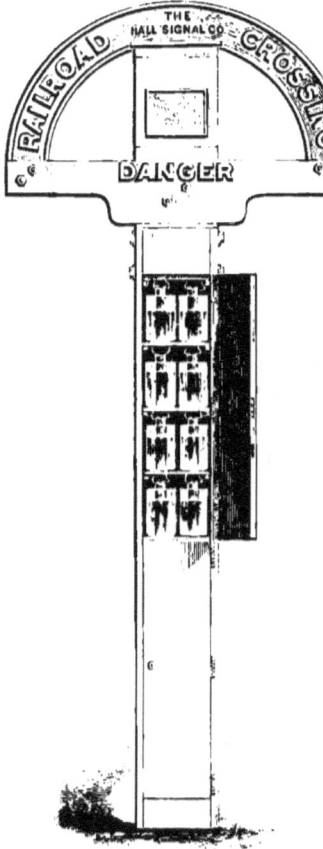

The large train-shed contains nine tracks, all of which are occupied the greater part of the time by the incoming and outgoing trains.

It has been the policy of this Company to abandon regular train service on Sundays, and this has been found to work to the best advantage. Only newspaper and milk trains are run on Sundays, and this cannot very well be avoided.

The motive power and rolling equipment of the Delaware, Lackawanna and Western are of the most approved types. The locomotives are built for speed, and with a view to hauling capacity. Spark arresters and extension fronts are being applied to all of those engines that were built prior to these innovations in modern mechanics, and all new engines are fitted with these appliances when built. In addition each engine is equipped with the "Blizzard" engine lamp for classification service.

The exteriors of the cars are painted in the Company's standard color, dark green, while the interiors are finished in polished mahogany. The Company has adopted the Pintsch system of car lighting. Each car is fitted with globes containing four burners, from which a clear, white, brilliant light is obtained, which enables passengers to read in any part of a car without straining the eyes.

It is the opinion of experienced travellers that no railroad in this country runs better equipped, or has more easy riding cars than these; and all trains are protected at the rear by two *utility* side tail lamps, well elevated, thus securing the longest possible range for the rear danger signal.

On all through express trains the modern vestibule attachment is used, and Pullman's best drawing-room and sleeping-cars are run.

The Lackawanna is a double-track line to Buffalo, and is the shortest route running between New York and that city. The road-bed is heavily ballasted with gravel and sand and is of unusual firmness. The heaviest steel rails are used to accommodate the additional weight of the constantly improving motive power and rolling stock.

By reason of these improvements travelling on this line is accompanied with all available elements of comfort and ease. The enjoyment of this result of skillful engineering and car building, is materially increased by the using of anthracite coal in the locomotives.

"BLIZZARD."

"UTILITY."

Morris and Essex Division.

From HOBOKEN the Morris and Essex Division extends westward. One line runs by way of Morristown, taking in the most beautiful and healthful resident section of Northern New Jersey. The Boonton Branch diverges in a northerly direction after leaving the big Bergen tunnel at West End, touching at Paterson and Boonton, crossing the former line at Denville and again connecting with it at Dover,

Photo. by H. A. Henckel, N. Y.
DELAWARE, LACKAWANNA & WESTERN R. R. STATION AND FERRY, HOBOKEN, N. J.

from which places both lines are operated westward as one to Washington, Warren County, N. J., seventy miles from Hoboken. The first station in New Jersey, beyond Hoboken, is

HARRISON.   *Altitude, 29 ft.*

7.17 miles from New York ; Single ticket, 15 cts.; Excursion ticket, 25 cts.

This town, formerly known as East Newark, is situated in Hudson County, and borders on the Passaic River. It is principally known for its manufacturing industries.

NEWARK. *Altitude, 38 ft.*

7.69 miles from New York ; Single ticket, 15 cts.; Excursion ticket, 25 cts.

This city is the commercial metropolis of New Jersey. It is situated on the west bank of the Passaic River, upon which craft of all kinds ply, and affords important communication with New York through Newark Bay and Staten Island Sound.

Newark is one of the oldest cities in the State. It covers a large area in Essex County, and ranks as one of the most important manufacturing centres of the United States. Its iron and leather industries being among its chief industries.

The population is over one hundred and eighty thousand.

Broad Street, running north and south through the city, is one of the most attractive thoroughfares in the country, containing many great business houses, elegant residences and churches. Washington and Military Parks, with their numerous stately elms, are the pride of Newarkers. High Street is famous for the architectural beauty of its numerous costly dwelling houses.

The extreme northern, southern and western sections of the city are largely occupied by residences, and Newark lays just claim to having throughout clean and well-maintained streets.

The famous Passaic River course, where the National Association of Amateur Oarsmen occasionally settle their contests is situated here, and the course is known as one of the best for rowing used. It is decidedly picturesque on the Kearney side of the river, and at intervals, along both shores, the boat-houses of the various clubs are located.

All conveniences of a first-class city can be had here. These include gas, electric light, fine hotels and boarding-houses, good street car systems, theatres, athletic clubs and churches of every denomination. The drives in all directions are pleasing.

Newark, too, is a healthful and well governed city. Its death rate is low, and epidemics seldom prevail. Several first-class daily papers supply the news.

The society of the city includes a number of the most famous families of New Jersey.

ROSEVILLE AVENUE. *Altitude, 143 ft.*

9 miles from New York ; Single ticket, 15 cts ; Excursion ticket, 25 cts.

Formerly Roseville was a suburb of Newark, but the phenomenal growth of that city absorbed it. It is wholly a residential section, and stands high and dry at the summit of the heaviest grade on the division. The houses are tastefully built, nearly all of them being surrounded by gardens. Roseville Avenue is destined to become the most thickly settled part of the city, and residences are increasing with a rapidity worthy of a Western boom. At this station the Bloomfield Branch leaves the main line. The first stop is at

WATSESSING. *Altitude, 135 ft.*

10.95 miles from New York ; Single ticket, 23 cts.; Excursion ticket, 40 cts.

Here there is but a small settlement and a few farms. This is a congenial spot for quietude, and the residents have all the desirable elements of sociability. An important and progressive village just beyond it is

BLOOMFIELD. *Altitude, 124 ft.*

11.58 miles from New York ; Single ticket, 25 cts.; Excursion ticket, 45 cts.

The history of this town is associated with Revolutionary times, and it is among the best known places in the State. Although the enterprise of modern civilization has imprinted itself in every section, yet there are some old-fashioned houses and other landmarks which serve to remind one that Bloomfield was on record a century ago. At the head of the park stands the old church, a sacred pile, that for more than one hundred years has stood to the glory of God. For many years Bloomfield has been the favorite resort of summer visitors. It is rich in its arboreal growth, has fine roads, good society, and all the elements that arise from thrift and progressiveness. It is the home of many prominent business men, and the residences, in many instances, are both sumptuous and costly.

Adjoining Bloomfield, and but one mile beyond it, is

GLEN RIDGE. *Altitude, 170 ft.*
12.22 miles from New York; Single ticket, 27 cts.; Excursion ticket, 47 cts.

It can be consistently said that this is one of New Jersey's beauty spots. Built, as it is, upon a hill, which commands a charming view of the surrounding country, an attractiveness is given it that favors but few places in this region. Ten years ago Glen Ridge was little more than a wooded slope. Wealth and enterprise have developed the available acres, and the work of improvement is still progressing. This is a village of handsome residences, grassy lawns, park-like estates, and fine roads. The residents, for the most part, are New Yorkers, and these have all the push that characterizes the wide-awake Gothamite.

Glen Ridge is a pleasant and a convenient spot in which to spend a summer. The last station on the branch is

MONTCLAIR. *Altitude, 239 ft.*
13 14 miles from New York; Single ticket, 30 cts.; Excursion ticket, 50 cts.

Montclair (often called the Athens of New Jersey), lying on the eastern slope of the Orange Mountains, is unsurpassed for beauty of situation and healthfulness in the vicinity of the metropolis.

The majority of the residences command magnificent views of New York harbor and the surrounding country.

The population is ten thousand, and the town is growing rapidly in a very substantial way. The public schools are excellent, and there is a military academy and several private schools.

The churches represent all the denominations. The water supply is excellent, and the town enjoys all modern improvements. Three newspapers record all local matters of interest.

Mountain Avenue, running at the base of the mountain from the Orange line to Upper Montclair (3½ miles), dotted by magnificent residences, is said to surpass any avenue or street in the vicinity of New York.

Montclair cannot be seen, to be appreciated, in an hour or two. One must penetrate its by-ways and shaded avenues to realize how much nature has done for this terraced hamlet.

About two-thirds of the roads are macadamized, and it will only be a matter of a few years when they will all be so.

This town may be recommended as desirable in every way, as a place of residence.

Verona and Caldwell

are villages beyond Montclair, which are not on this line of railroad, but communication with them is attained by a stage route that connects with all Lackawanna trains at Montclair. The stage fare is 10 cents.

Mention is made of these places, as they are widely known and appreciated for their remarkable health-possessing qualities, and the picturesqueness of the surrounding country, together with their adaptability for summer residence.

Returning again to the main-line, the next station beyond Roseville Avenue is

GROVE STREET, EAST ORANGE. *Altitude, 153 ft.*
9.65 miles from New York ; Single ticket, 20 cts.; Excursion ticket, 30 cts.

A town of phenomenal growth and rich with pretty homes. The streets are uniformly laid out, paved, curbed, and have flagged sidewalks. A feature of the place is that the houses, for the most part, are built separately, and have spacious lawns, neat gardens, and beautiful shade. The streets, too, are lined with spreading shade trees. There are churches of all denominations within easy reach. The nearness to Newark and New York makes Grove Stteet a particularly desirable place of residence or temporary sojourn.

EAST ORANGE. *Altitude, 172 ft.*
10.04 miles from New York ; Single ticket, 25 cts.; Excursion ticket, 35 cts.

The same may be said of East Orange as has been said of Grove Street. In reality the former may be called the town proper, as many of the large stores that supply residents are located here. No more bustling little place exists on the line. It has all the elements of enterprise, including water, electric light, etc., schools, churches, social clubs, etc.

The Orange Athletic Club, known the country over, has fine grounds located here in the vicinity of the railroad station, and the drives which extend in all directions are as delightful as they are varied.

BRICK CHURCH. *Altitude, 180 ft.*
10.63 miles from New York ; Single ticket 25 cts.; Excursion ticket, 40 cts.

Years ago, before the Oranges gained the enviable distinction they now possess as places of residence, the old brick church marked the place surrounding which this delightful town has been built. The name, therefore, for some reason, has clung to it. Years ago the name may have been appropriate, but to-day it has no special significance beyond that it recalls memories of times gone by. Brick Church may be said to be in the heart of the Oranges. There are but few luxuries obtainable in a large city not available here, and this town long since established for itself a reputation for being a most desirable one for residence. Here, situated on Prospect Street, is the beautiful home of the Orange Club, the principal social organization of the Oranges, and also the Orange Athletic Club House, which is both spacious and artistic in design.

ORANGE. *Altitude, 185 ft.*
11.36 miles from New York ; Single ticket, 25 cts.; Excursion ticket, 40 cts.

The city is located on a plain, almost level, and in all New Jersey no more delightful one can be found. Along the main avenue stores of all kinds do a thriving business. Electric and other street cars run to nearby points, arrangements in this respect being most convenient. The streets of the city are uniformly laid out and delightfully shaded. The private residences have spacious lawns about them, and many of the structures are marvels of architectural beauty. Electric lights and good water are among the luxuries. The city supports an opera house, and two or three uswspapers. Churches of all denominations raise their spires in every part of the town. The system of schools is as perfect as can be found anywhere. A charm about the city is the high mountain range that skirts the western boundary. The range is called Orange Mountains, and is a spur of the Blue Ridge. It runs toward the northeast, and slopes gracefully toward the valley in which the city is partly located. At the summit of the mountain is located Llewellyn Park, laid out with every elegance of taste and effect in artistic landscape gardening. It contains the homes of wealthy people, and is acknowledged to be the most magnificent spot in New Jersey. Nearby, from Eagle Rock, a view of 25 miles around the country can be had. Thomas Edison, the "wizard of electricity," has a fine home in the park, as also had the late Gen. McClellan. The side of the mountain is flecked with imposing residences and finely laid out grounds; among the oldest and finest being that of the Essex County Country Club, whose historic house and beautiful grounds make it one of the most charming country clubs in America.

HIGHLAND AVENUE. *Altitude, 182 ft.*
12.23 miles from New York; Single ticket, 30 cts.; Excursion ticket, 50 cts.

A few years ago this section of the Oranges was called "Valley Station," because the business portion lies in a valley. The name, in a sense, was misleading, because the side hills afford a most beautiful residence section. In addition to being a most desirable place in which to reside, Highland Avenue has a commercial importance. Its hat industry is very extensive, and the quality of the hats made ranks favorably with those manufactured elsewhere. An incline railway near here conveys passengers to the summit of the Orange Mountains, and a ride on it is an enjoyable experience.

MOUNTAIN STATION. *Altitude, 156 ft.*
13.08 miles from New York; Single ticket, 35 cts.; Excursion ticket, 55 cts.

There is a vast difference between this and its nearest neighbor. While Highland Avenue is realy a very busy place, Mountain Station is the opposite. Essentially a town of homes it is picturesque in the extreme. Nature has been allowed to hold sway to a very large extent, and the feature that will impress the visitor most favorbly is the magnificent shade that makes the summer months congenial. To the north the valley reaches until it meets the mountains, and is dotted with pretty residences. To the south the hill rises gradually from the railroad station, and residences with park-like grounds are to be seen in all drections, and extend along westward until they unite with

SOUTH ORANGE. *Altitude, 139 ft.*
13.84 miles from New York; Single ticket, 40 cts.; Excursion ticket, 60 cts.

The Oranges terminate here after occupying five miles of territory. South Orange is an important place, because it is the terminus of a number of express and accommodation trains to and from New York. Like the other towns it is famous as a place of residence. Churches and schools are plenty, and good local government is a feature that recommends it. The drives about South Orange are romantic, and good roads are the rule. The "Field Club," an organization that needs no introduction, is favorably known wherever outdoor sports are discussed and indulged in. The club-house and beautifully laid out grounds, between Mountain Station and South Orange, are in plain view of passing trains, and here the wealth and beauty of the united Oranges meet in season to enjoy some of the best contests of the State.

The club-house is equipped with all the appurtenances of a first-class club, together with the necessary conveniences of one devoted so largely to field sports.

The grounds, twelve acres in extent, include a quarter mile bicycle track, three baseball diamonds, eight tennis courts, two football fields, croquet grounds, quoit courts, shooting traps, etc.

From early summer till late in the fall, open tournaments are held in all out-door sports, in which the prominent amateur athletes of the country participate, and the bicycle and foot races, tennis and trap shooting contests, attract widespread attention.

A most interesting feature connected with the Field Club is the opportunity it affords to all its members for indulging in out-door sports and games. "Business men's" contests in baseball, tennis, quoits, etc., take place during the season, and those only are allowed to compete who have never acquired much skill in such sports. The prominent athletes have their opportunity in the open tournaments. Further, the children of members have exceptional facilities for innocent and healthy amusement in the grounds, and are afforded every protection by the keepers in charge.

The Field Club is essentially a family club, and is readily taken advantage of by all who are attracted to South Orange and its vicinity, and as a family summer resort it is very popular. In winter part of the grounds are flooded, and good skating is enjoyed.

MAPLEWOOD. *Altitude, 131 ft.*
15-36 miles from New York ; Single ticket, 45 cts. ; Excursion ticket, 65 cts.

A very pretty place for persons who delight in beautiful scenery is Maplewood. Its location, at the base of the mountain, gives it a wild charm. As yet the village has not developed to any great size, but it has several very pretty cottages situated on well-made streets, and there is plenty of shade. It has excellent water, fine drives, and pure mountain air. For a summer vacation spot it ranks among the most desirable.

WYOMING. *Altitude. 160 ft.*
16-39 miles from New York ; Single ticket 50 cts. ; Excursion ticket, 70 cts.

Wyoming is a delightful little town, situated right on the side of the mountain. At this point the "first mountain" turns directly northward. Here are many beautiful homes, with spacious grounds, in the midst of a high-wooded slope, where all is wild and picturesque. The scenery around Wyoming is charming, and never grow tiresome. There is not an objectionable feature in the town or neighborhood. It is essentially a home-spot, and persons who go there never regret it.

MILBURN. *Altitude, 148 ft.*
17.01 miles from New York ; Single ticket, 50 cts. ; Excursion ticket, 75 cts.

This is an old-fashioned town with quaint houses, whose style of architecture suggests a half-century or more ago. It even possesses the conventional mill-pond, which adds to its antiquated appearance. Milburn has always been a popular place for summer boarders. It is surrounded by farms, and has good boarding-houses in town. An excellent supply of water is one of the essential features of the place, and its well-cared-for roads are known all over the State. The terminus of the Milburn bicycle course is here, and in the season wheeling never ceases.

SHORT HILLS. *Altitude, 206 ft.*
17.86 miles from New York ; Single ticket, 55 cts. ; Excursion ticket, 80 cts.

Short Hills can be especially recommended as a charming place of residence. Situated in a large park, the residences, all of which are palatial, occupy plots, around which wind smooth macadamized roads. There are no fences round-about, and every house has a well-appointed stable attached. The aim of the individual who established Short Hills has been carried out well. It is for homes only, and not a single place of business is connected with it. A few years ago this delightful spot was but a wooded slope. Enough of the grand old forest trees have been preserved to afford a pleasing shade, that in summer almost hides the houses from view.

HUNTLY. *Altitude, 306 ft.*
19.11 miles from New York ; Single ticket, 55 cts. ; Excursion ticket, 80 cts.

A little station on the mountain, established to accommodate the few people who reside there. A fine view of the valley can be had, and on a clear day New York Bay is visible.

SUMMIT. *Altitude, 385 ft.*
20.14 miles from New York ; Single ticket, 55 cts. ; Excursion ticket, 80 cts.

There is no place on this line that can lay claim to more advantages than Summit. As its name implies it is situated on the brow of the second mountain, and is reached after the hard climb of a grade that begins at Milburn.

This village has developed solely on its own merits. Its growth has been strong and so far shows no signs of abating. Backing the development of Summit are men of wealth and thrift. The houses that are in course of erection are attractively laid out, and its macadamized streets, of which there are over fifty, are of the finest and most elaborate kind. Owing to its altitude Summit is a bracing spot in which to spend the summer. The air is always fresh and salubrious, and on that account persons afflicted with pulmonary troubles have made it their permanent home. In summer the population generally doubles. All the hotels and boarding-houses, of which there are many of the first-class, are well patronized, and the place in summer presents a lively appearance. Many of the permanent residents rent their homes for the season, and the demand often exceeds the supply. Looking northward from Summit is a magnificent view of the Passaic Valley and Blue Ridge Mountain and towards the southeast, Brooklyn, New York Bay and Staten Island can be seen. The drives through the valleys and over the mountains are magnificent.

Churches of the Episcopal, Methodist, Presbyterian, Baptist and Catholic faiths abound. The social centre is the Casino Club, to which is attached a theatre, bowling alley, etc. The Club is composed of the prominent men of the place and is well patronized. The Fresh-Air Home, so well known, and with which many benevolent women of Summit are identified, is situated on Stony Hill, south of Summit. The town is lighted with gas, and has a new and excellent sewerage system ; it is also supplied by the Commonwealth Water Company with pure water drawn from springs in the mountain.

At Summit the Passaic and Delaware Branch diverges toward the west and runs for 21 miles through a valley of unsurpassed beauty and loveliness. The first station is

WEST SUMMIT. *Altitude, 340 ft.*
21.83 miles from New York; Single ticket, 65 cts.; Excursion ticket, 95 cts.

A small settlement of quiet homes. The surrounding country is given up to agricultural pursuits.

MURRAY HILL. *Altitude, 251 ft.*
23.40 miles from New York; Single ticket, 70 cts.; Excursion ticket, $1.00.

The ridge that skirts the village on the east is from whence the place is named. Several elegant homes of New Yorkers are situated here and the view is extensive and very fine. The country is fertile and studded with many prosperous farms.

BERKELEY HEIGHTS. *Altitude, 226 ft.*
25.77 miles from New York; Single ticket, 75 cts.; Excursion ticket, $1.10.

Until very recently this place was unimportant. A company having purchased a tract of land, has parcelled it out in building lots and laid out streets, and Berkeley Heights is soon destined to become a thriving spot.

GILLETTE. *Altitude, 213 ft.*
27.15 miles from New York; Single ticket, 85 cts.; Excursion ticket, $1.15.

A quiet settlement surrounded by hills and containing charming patches of scenery. It is a fine farming country and a healthful place for summer boarders.

STIRLING. *Altitude, 221 ft.*
28.51 miles from New York; Single ticket, 90 cts.; Excursion ticket, $1.20.

This place is associated with revolutionary history by having been named after Lord Stirling. Along the ridge of Long Hill are several pretty residences. The view of the valley for miles east and west is one of the best in Morris County. Many of the residents find employment at a silk mill near by. Aside from this, agriculture is the principal pursuit.

MILLINGTON. *Altitude, 274 ft.*
30.16 miles from New York; Single ticket, 95 cts.; Excursion ticket, $1.25.

This is one of the most picturesque spots on the branch. The Passaic River here seen winds around big bluffs and through fertile meadows and gives a charm to the surroundings seldom met. Several persons have taken advantage of the picturesqueness of the place to build handsome houses. The drives about Millington are interesting and the roads good.

LYONS. *Altitude, 305 ft.*
31.74 miles from New York; Single ticket, $1.00; Excursion ticket, $1.30.

Lyons and neighborhood is devoted to agriculture. Though small and of little commercial importance, it is a splendid place wherein to spend a summer, as the surroundings are healthful and farm life can be enjoyed without stint.

BASKING RIDGE. *Altitude, 373 ft.*
33.63 miles from New York; Single ticket, $1.05; Excursion ticket, $1.40.

This old town with its odd buildings, quaint people and general air of antiquity is widely and favorably known. In the church-yards are headstones dating back over

Photographed by H. C. Pyle, N. Y.
IN AND ABOUT BERNARDSVILLE AND SOMERSET INN, ON PASSAIC & DELAWARE BRANCH.

Photographed by H. C. Pyle, N. Y.
IN AND ABOUT BERNARDSVILLE AND SOMERSET INN, ON PASSAIC & DELAWARE BRANCH.

a hundred years, and many of the descendants of those they eulogized live in the vicinity. For the summer resident Basking Ridge is full of interest, with an additional attraction in its bracing atmosphere.

BERNARDSVILLE. *Altitude, 430 ft.*
34.75 miles from New York; Single ticket, $1.10; Excursion ticket, $1.45.

This attractive place, situated as it is in the midst of the Somerset County hills, is frequently alluded to as the "Alps" of New Jersey, and the name is not misapplied. Being beyond the first range of mountains (the Oranges) west of New York, the distinct change from the dampness of the ocean to dry mountain air is at once felt. The entire section abounds in wild scenery, changing from a very extensive outlook over and beyond fertile valleys to byways through gorges, alongside of mountain streams amidst luxuriant foliage. The mountain roads are hard and always smooth and lead in all directions through pretty villages and an extremely prosperous farming section. Since its first settlement by New Yorkers many years ago Bernardsville has been the most popular of New Jersey resorts until now its population is represented largely by summer residents, whose beautiful and costly residences dot the hills and appear at every turn in the landscape. Near here is situated "Round Top," the beautiful home of Frederic P. Olcott of New York City, comprising one thousand acres of land, and the most extensive breeding farm in the East. It is worth a day's journey to visit this estate. Its miles of shaded drives are always open to the public. The Bernardsville-Mendham district has long been famous as a health resort to those suffering from Rheumatism and complaints of a Malarial origin; there is no marshy ground in this section of mountain and valleys, and Mosquitos are unknown.

Situated in the hills between Bernardsville and Mendham is the "Somerset Inn," surrounded by eight cottages especially well built and finished for the accomodation of the guests of the hotel, it is the best equipped mountain hotel within 100 miles of New York. The Inn has recently been enlarged and refitted and affords accommodations that can be favorably compared with any other first class hotel in the country. Special fast train service brings Bernardsville within one hour of New York by rail. The Inn accommodates 250 guests.

MINE BROOK. *Altitude, 215 ft.*
37.38 miles from New York; Single ticket, $1.20; Excursion ticket, $1.60.

FAR HILLS. *Altitude, 160 ft.*
38.87 miles from New York; Single ticket, $1.25. Excursion ticket, $1.65.

PEAPACK. *Altitude, 190 ft.*
41.26 miles from New York; Single ticket, $1.35; Excursion ticket, $1.80.

GLADSTONE. *Altitude, 230 ft.*
42.19 miles from New York; Single ticket, $1.40; Excursion ticket, $1.85.

The general character of all these places is similar. The region, on account of the lack until recently, of railroad facilities is undeveloped, Peapack notwithstanding. The Rockaway Valley Railroad touches here on its way between Whitehouse and Mendham, and these two lines are destined to build up this spot. Gladstone is an old place with a new name, and is a town that has made great strides since it obtained railroad facilities. The region is well adapted to summer recreation, as the drives are good, and many interesting places are near by.

Returning to the main line the next station beyond Summit is

NEW PROVIDENCE. *Altitude, 271 ft.*
21.69 miles from New York ; Single ticket, 60 cts.; Excursion ticket, 95 cts.

The village lies back about a half mile from the station. It is a farming region and quite popular with city people, who find it a pleasant spot in which to spend the summer season.

CHATHAM. *Altitude, 231 ft.*
23.33 miles from New York; Single ticket, 65 cts.; Excursion ticket, $1.00.

This ancient town has always been held in high esteem by many who return every year to spend the summer. It has much to recommend it. The Passaic River flows through it, and affords good fishing and boating ; the drives through the valley and over Long Hill are delightful. The Chatham Fish and Game Protection Association, which has recently erected a handsome Club House here, looks after the fish and game in the vicinity.

STANLEY, situated south of Chatham on the Eastern slope of Long Hill, is a settlement of pretty homes, and, from its location, a grand and ever-changing panorama of the valley of the Passaic spreads out before the eyes. On account of the scenery from Long Hill, this locality has become popular.

MADISON. *Altitude, 245 ft.*
25.55 miles from New York ; Single ticket, 70 cts.. Excursion ticket, $1.10.

This enterprising town has for the past three years been prospering under a borough government. It has a Mayor and Town Council at the head of its affairs; it also possesses excellent water and electric light systems, and all the comforts of a large city are available. Building is very active and promises so to continue. Madison rejoices in four churches and the Webb Memorial Chapel, an imposing edifice, built and presented to the town by James A. Webb, Esq., a prominent and enterprising citizen. This place has been known as a health resort for a long time, and on that account, may well be recommended. It is noted for the number of its elegant residences, many of which are surrounded by large estates. Mr. H. McK. Twombley has laid out, at an enormous cost, over 200 acres as a park, and the work will result in one of the finest estates in New Jersey. The town itself is in a valley, and on both sides of the long sloping hills pretty homes are located. The view from these hills across the Passaic Valley is one of the features that captivates the seekers of suburban homes.

Drew Theological Seminary, in the immediate vicinity is well known and is visited by persons from all parts. Good roads and picturesque drives make Madison a pleasant resort for city people during the summer months.

CONVENT. *Altitude, 379 ft.*
27.62 miles from New York ; Single ticket, 75 cts.; Excursion ticket, $1.15.

The Convent of St. Elizabeth, a large educational institution conducted by Sisters, is located in plain view of the railroad, and from this the station derives its name.

Photo. by H. A. Henckel, N. Y.

AWAITING TRAIN, MORRISTOWN STATION.

MORRISTOWN. *Altitude, 326 ft.*

29.70 miles from New York ; Single ticket, 80 cts.; Excursion ticket, $1.25.

This old town, so prominently identified with the history of the Revolutionary War scarcely calls for any introduction.

Its fame was established when it was first chosen by Washington as the headquarters of the Continental Army, and the associations of those stirring times of our nation's history are still cherished by the descendants of many of the gallant soldiers who took up arms and fought for their independence under the leadership of General Washington.

Not the pages of history alone point to Washington's association with Morristown, for his headquarters, situated on an eminence in the northern part of the city, have been preserved, and since they came into the possession of the State, more land which has been laid out in beautiful grassy lawns, and broad paths skirted by shade trees has been reserved about them. Cannon that have, from time to time, been used in defence of the nation, and which were individually presented, are mounted and frown threateningly around the quaint old building. The national emblem is spread to the breeze daily, not only to indicate the spot, but to show that the patriotism of our fathers is still ablaze in the breasts of their descendants. To quote from the address of Hon. Theodore F. Randolph, on opening of this building to the public, July 4, 1875 : " During the summer of 1873, this property, so long and widely known as the old headquarters of Washington, was offered for sale. A few gentlemen concluded to purchase it, and having done so, formed a society known as the Washington Society of New Jersey, the principal object of which is to perpetuate this house with its great historic associations, and to gather within these walls so large and interesting a museum of articles connected with the Revolutionary and other history of the Colonies, that this old mansion, rendered immortal by the name of Washington, shall become a Mecca towards which all Americans will turn their

WASHINGTON'S HEADQUARTERS, MORRISTOWN, N. J.

steps and obtain, as from a fountain, inspiration to patriotic life and purpose. Under this roof have been gathered more characters known to the military history of the war of the Revolution than under any other roof in America—a fact not generally known. Here, the elegant and brilliant Alexander Hamilton lived during the long winter of 1779, and here he met and courted the lady he afterwards married, the daughter of General Schuyler. Here, too, were Green, the splendid fighting Quaker, as he was, and the great artillery officer Knox, the noble La Fayette, the stern Steuben, the polished Kosciusko, the brave Schuyler, gallant Light Horse Harry Lee, old Israel Putnam, mad Anthony Wayne, and that brave soldier, but rank traitor Benedict Arnold. Here, too, from time to time, gathered prominent members of the Continental Congress and statesmen of that day. This dwelling was also for many months, the home of Martha, the wife of George Washington. Within these rooms, with quiet dignity and grace, she received her husband's guests. Never idle, she sat a constant example of thrift and industry. In front of this house, in yonder meadow, lay encamped Washington's body guard—originally a selected troop of about one hundred Virginians. Day and night they kept watch and guard over these headquarters and the precious lives it contained. Many were the plans, and several were the attempts by the enemy to pierce to this old house and to the powder-mill in its rear, and thus at one blow destroy all hope of successful revolution. Had this house been once successfully attacked, and its inmates taken, America's Revolution would, in all probability, have been known to history as America's Rebellion. But, among these hills of Morris no Briton's foot ever trod in Revolutionary times save as a prisoner.''

Fort Nonsense, where Washington's guns were planted, is at the summit of the highest hill in town. There a survey of the valley and surrounding country was made and a careful watch was kept for the appearance of the enemy. The site of the old fort is marked by a slab bearing a suitable inscription.

Morristown may justly claim not to have rested solely on its past record. It now has a population of nearly 10,000 and is governed by a Mayor and Common Council. Every convenience that other cities afford is here available. The avenues are broad, delightfully shaded, and well maintained. Some of the most magnificent residences in the country are located here, and they may be found in all parts of the city, on the neighboring hills, and in the suburbs. This entire region is a sanitarium, and no more healthier spot can be found. The population is made up largely of wealthy New Yorkers, and in summer it is the most sought-after resort within the same distance of New York. Manufacturing is not permitted within the city limits. The Green is a public park occupying an entire square. It is shaded by stately elms, and is divided into fine walks. An elegant soldiers' monument stands on the west side of the Green.

The drives for miles around are most beautiful. Pocahontas Lake is a pretty sheet of water within the city limits, and contains bass and pickerel. It affords good sport for the angler, and the catches are often large. Speedwell Lake is another pretty spot, situated about a mile outside of the city toward Morris plains, and offers inducements to fishermen who wish to try their skill.

MENDHAM is seven miles from Morristown, and stages connect with all trains to carry passengers there. It has the distinction of being located in the heart of the mountains, and there is scarcely a cooler or more bracing spot in all New Jersey. It is renowned for its health giving qualities, and also for the long extended view over valley and lower mountain. The place is nothing but an old-fashioned village, filled with quaint houses, honest people, fertile farms and perpetual happiness. If Mendham had first-class railroad facilities it would prove a dangerous rival to all other

WASHINGTON'S HEADQUARTERS, MORRISTOWN, N. J.

places in the State within the same distance from New York. In the warmer months it is filled with summer boarders, and its attractions are almost without limit.

MORRIS PLAINS. *Altitude, 403 ft.*
32.01 miles from New York ; Single ticket, 90 cts. ; Excursion ticket, $1.35.

Many people regard Morris Plains as being the most beautiful spot along this line. It derives its name from the fact that the town is built on a high plateau, surrounded on the north and west by mountains. Summer here is delightful, on account of the breeze having a clear sweep across the plain. The soil is sandy, and within an hour after a heavy shower is very often as dry as though there had been no rainfall. For this reason the entire section is remarkably healthful. The roads are splendidly kept and driving is a luxury. A mile back from the station is the imposing building of the State Hospital for the insane. Morris Plains is composed nearly entirely of fine buildings, owned and occupied by well-to-do citizens. There is a small lake within the village limits, where boating and fishing can be enjoyed.

MOUNT TABOR. *Altitude, 531 ft.*
35.66 miles from New York ; Single ticket, $1.00 ; Excursion ticket, $1.40.

Mount Tabor has become famous on account of the annual gathering of the Methodists, who hold their camp meeting exercises here, and enjoy a quiet sociable time in accord with their religious precepts. It is one of a number of picturesque peaks that jut out from the Blue Ridge Mountains. The mountain slope is dotted here and there with pretty cottages owned by members of the Methodist faith, and occupied by them nearly all summer. Life here is calm and enjoyable, and the place is restricted against all nuisances and disorder.

DENVILLE. *Altitude, 520 ft.*
36.33 miles from New York ; Single ticket, $1.00 ; Excursion ticket, $1.50.

This is a quiet farming district, with few inhabitants. To those who enjoy farm life and its attendant luxuries of fresh eggs and milk, it may be well recommended. A short branch road connects Denville with Boonton, and the run between these points occupies but fifteen minutes.

ROCKAWAY. *Altitude, 556 ft.*
38.05 miles from New York ; Single ticket, $1.05 ; Excursion ticket, $1.60.

A good deal of life is to be found in this bustling little village of manufacturing industries. Rockaway is prettily situated, partly in a valley and partly on a hillside. The Rockaway River flows through it, lending to the picturesqueness of the place. The village boasts several good stores, and in summer is a favorite vacation resort.

The attention of the reader is now directed to the Boonton Branch, which meets the Morris and Essex division at Dover, the next station beyond Rockaway, where both lines continue westward as one.

After leaving Hoboken, the first station west of the Hackensack River, is

KINGSLAND. *Altitude, 25 ft.*
7.12 miles from New York ; Single ticket, 25 cts.; Excursion ticket, 35 cts.

Noted principally for being the place at which the Company's machine shops are located. The village is thrifty and of steady growth. It contains many farms and some pretty cottages.

LYNDHURST. *Altitude, 34 ft.*

8.24 miles from New York; Single ticket, 30 cts.; Excursion ticket, 40 cts.

The country about here is attractive, and the pretty village that is growing about the railroad testifies to its healthy popularity. A very pleasant summer can be spent here in driving and roaming about the country.

DELAWANNA. *Altitude, 53 ft.*

9.38 miles from New York; Single ticket, 35 cts.; Excursion ticket, 45 cts.

A quiet spot, of great beauty, and few inhabitants, bordering on the Passaic River, which at this point assumes a picturesqueness that at once charms the newcomer. Boating, bathing and fishing are among the pleasures of this place.

PASSAIC. *Altitude, 97 ft.*

10.91 miles from New York; Single ticket, 40 cts.; Excursion ticket, 55 cts.

Passaic is one of the three important cities on the branch. It contains a population of over 20,000, and is a thriving city, where enterprise carries everything before it towards prosperity. The city contains many miles of broad, well-shaded streets, and is famous for the large number of its elegant residences. No city in New Jersey has enjoyed a more rapid and continued growth. Here are churches of all denominations, a theatre, athletic clubs, etc. Although Passaic is a city, it attracts hundreds of city people each recurring summer.

CLIFTON. *Altitude, 121 ft.*

12.15 miles from New York; Single ticket, 45 cts.; Excursion ticket, 65 cents.

The village of Clifton lies to the eastward of the railroad, and is as pretty and well laid out as any in the State. It is noted for the number and variety of its shade trees, and the quiet character of its inhabitants.

PATERSON. *Altitude, 188 ft.*

14.68 miles from New York; Single ticket, 50 cts; Excursion ticket, 70 cts.

Paterson is called the "Lyons of America," on account of its immense silk industries. It is one of the largest cities in New Jersey, and in the importance of its industries, principal among which is the building of locomotives, probably ranks second. The Delaware, Lackawanna & Western Railroad runs along the western section of the city, and plays an important part in its commercial welfare. A tour of the manufactories is not only interesting but instructive. The high falls of the Passaic, famous throughout the country, are also worthy of a visit on account of the great beauty of Nature's handiwork.

WEST PATERSON. *Altitude, 188 ft.*

15.64 miles from New York; Single ticket, 50 cts.; Excursion ticket, 70 cts.

A suburb of Paterson, just outside the city limits.

LITTLE FALLS. *Altitude, 187 ft.*

18.25 miles from New York; Single ticket, 65 cts.; Excursion ticket, 80 cts.

This pretty little village, the honors of which are divided between manufacturing and agricultural pursuits, can be cheerfully recommended as a resort, at once pleasing

Photo by H. A. Heuckel, N. Y.   PASSAIC FALLS.

and refined. Here all the comforts of country life await the stranger, and the fertile farms that dot the valley supply vegetables, milk and eggs in abundance. Little Falls turns out a great amount of carpeting every year, the falls here being the attraction for the manufacturer. The angler, too, can enjoy himself, and if fortune favors, may find good luck in casting his line in the Passaic, for at this point black bass fishing is excellent. The angling grounds are above the falls.

MOUNTAIN VIEW. *Altitude, 175 ft.*

20.84 miles from New York ; Single ticket, 70 cts.; Excursion ticket, 90 cts.

The name of this spot originates from the fact that it is in full view of the Blue Ridge mountains. It is a farming country whose chief attraction is pure air, beautiful scenery and good drives.

LINCOLN PARK. *Altitude, 174 ft.*

22.93 miles from New York ; Single ticket, 75 cts. Excursion ticket, 95 cts.

WHITEHALL. *Altitude, 221 ft.*

25.10 miles from New York ; Single ticket, 80 cts.; Excursion ticket, $1.05.

Photo. by H. C. Pyle, N. Y. ROCKAWAY RIVER, AT BOONTON, N. J.

MONTVILLE. *Altitude, 309 ft.*
27.79 miles from New York; Single ticket, 80 cts.; Excursion ticket, $1.15.

These three villages have the same character as Mountain View, and are all desirable places in which to spend the summer months.

BOONTON. *Altitude, 411 ft.*
29.63 miles from New York; Single ticket, 80 cts., Excursion ticket, $1.25.

Boonton is among the oldest towns in the State. It is beautifully situated on a mountain side, and commands a magnificent view extending over 15 miles across the Passaic Valley. There is a grandeur about the Rockaway River as it flows down the mountain through the town and then breaks into foaming cascades as it tumbles along the ravine, winding in many directions descending the valley. The Rockaway River at Boonton affords wild views that are seldom equalled within the limits of civilization. Boonton was at one time a great iron manufacturing centre, but of late years this industry has fallen into decay. As a place of residence it is superb, the society is good, the surroundings are salubrious, and the air is permeated with the odor of pine from the mountains. As a summer resort, this town is too well known to need recommendation, and the city people who spend the hot months here do not seem to be able to get back again soon enough.

DENVILLE, where the Boonton Branch tracks cross the M. & E. Division, is 35 miles from New York by this line. After a run of four miles around the base of a high mountain, both lines meet at

DOVER. *Altitude, 573 ft.*
41.61 miles from New York; Single ticket, $1.10; Excursion ticket, $1.75.

On entering Dover, one finds a busy centre surrounded by high hills and delightful scenery. The large shops of the Delaware, Lackawanna & Western are located here, and a small army of men are kept at work the year round building new cars and repairing the old. Several other thriving manufacturing industries are also here. Dover is a great mining centre, the adjacent mountains being filled with a fine deposit of iron. The U. S. Government powder works are located at Picatinny, and are one of the attractions to visitors. The city has fine schools, churches of all denominations, and an opera house. The mountain drives in this section are peculiarly inviting. The Rockaway River and Morris Canal both flow through the city. In summer, Dover is one of the liveliest cities in New Jersey.

PORT ORAM. *Altitude, 642 ft.*
43.40 miles from New York; Single ticket, $1.15; Excursion ticket, $1.80.

A quiet little farming hamlet which derived its name from being a station on the Morris Canal.

After leaving Port Oram the Chester Branch runs eleven miles westward through a country famous for its rugged mountain peaks, green valleys and brisk streams. This entire section of Morris County ranks among the most healthful portion of New Jersey. There is no limit to the pastoral beauty of the scenery north, and the advantages Port Oram has for vacation enjoyment are numerous. The fertile farms offer every inducement to lovers of rest and quiet, and the hotels and boarding-houses cater especially for city boarders. In fact, all of the villages overflow with city people during the summer months. The water is pure and of good quality, the drives delightful, and the air remarkably bracing. The villages on the Chester Branch are

KENVIL (formerly McCAINSVILLE). *Altitude, 712 ft.*
46.73 miles from New York; Single ticket, $1.25; Excursion ticket, $1.95.

SUCCASUNNA. *Altitude, 724 ft.*
48.02 miles from New York; Single ticket, $1.30; Excursion ticket, $2.00.

IRONIA. *Altitude, 699 ft.*
50.18 miles from New York; Single ticket, $1.35; Excursion, ticket, $2.05.

HORTONS. *Altitude, 693 ft.*
51.72 miles from New York; Single ticket, $1.40; Excursion ticket, $2.10.

CHESTER. *Altitude, 682 ft.*
54.74 miles from New York; Single ticket, $1.50; Excursion ticket, $1.25.

Returning to the main line, the next station is

MT. ARLINGTON. *Altitude, 995 ft.*
46.36 miles from New York; Single ticket, $1.25; Excursion ticket, $1.95.

Mount Arlington is the station from which Lake Hopatcong is reached by wagon for stage, and was established by enterprising citizens of Lake Hopatcong as a convenience in reaching trains. From this station to Lake Hopatcong Country Club, formerly the Hotel Breslin, an electric railway will be run.

HOPATCONG STATION (Lake Hopatcong). *Altitude, 926 ft.*
48.86 miles from New York; Single ticket, $1.30; Excursion ticket, $2.05.

On alighting from the train the prospective sojourner expects to have his craving for a glimpse at this silver pool in the mountains satisfied at once. But in this he is mistaken. Instead, a little steamboat of the Lake Hopatcong Steamboat Co. awaits him at the landing, adjoining the station on the Morris canal, and runs by a rather unusual and interesting route to all important points on the lake to deliver passengers.

One of the novelties of the trip is a pleasant ride of a mile up the canal to the lock. On reaching the latter point the boat is "locked in" and raised up several feet, and when the surface is reached, Lake Hopatcong, with its clear green water, irregular shores and numerous rock-bound, wooded islands, presents itself with such suddenness as to completely enrapture all who are contemplating a loiter of more or less lengthy duration on its sloping shores. And at the Lake Landing, one hundred and fifty feet north of the station, are also other steamers—the latter belonging to the Hopatcong Steamboat Company—which carry passengers to all points on the Lake. The boats of the Hopatcong Line are comfortably appointed side-wheelers, and at the present comprise the "Hopatcong," the "Musconetcong," and a steam launch, the "Nariticong." In addition to these, a new steamer has been launched.

The lake itself is partly located in Morris and partly in Sussex county. Its altitude is 1,027 feet above the sea level, and 36 feet above the Delaware River, 35 miles westward. The water, which rises from crystal springs, is transparently green, very deep, and teems with game fish. Black bass and pickerel of enormous size are caught every season, and catfish of good weight are also taken. Hopatcong is the rendezvous of expert fishermen and fisherwomen, and it is the rare sport thus provided that attracts many an angler here each season. Howard P. Frothingham, Esq., Mayor of the borough of Mount Arlington, himself an enthusiastic fisherman, is the fish warden for Lake Hopatcong. He enjoys his office, because, as a true sportsman, he likes to see game fish protected. Woe be to those caught by him fishing out of season, or in season, for that matter, using nets, fikes or any other unlawful means of trapping the

Photo. by H. A. Henckel, N. Y. APPROACHING LAKE HOPATCONG, N. J.

fish. Persistent effort on his part has driven these scalawags out of his jurisdiction, so that legitimate fishermen who go to Hopatcong can count on having good sport and happy catches for their trouble.

In this limited space it would be impossible to describe or do justice to the famed beauties of this lake. It so closely resembles Lake George that it is frequently alluded to as the "Lake George of New Jersey." This allusion is justified, although Lake George is so much larger as to make the comparison hardly fair. Lake Hopatcong (1,027 feet above sea level), however, has an advantage of 685 feet in altitude over its rival, and in the beauty of its scenery its equality is unquestioned.

Indian tradition is closely associated with both lakes, although Hopatcong never had a Cooper to weave that subtle charm about it that will always cling to the "Horicon," as a result of the ingeniously constructed plots and charming description of Central New York given by the famous writer of "The Leatherstocking Tales."

There is such a variety to the everchanging scenery of Lake Hopatcong, or "Hopachung," as the red men called it when they settled on its shores. When the water is ruffled by the slightest breeze, its depth appears to lessen, and at sunset when the surface becomes mirror like, the shadows of the mountain seem to sink fathoms in its sparkling depths.

About the middle of June the influx of visitors commences, and from that time until September one round of gaiety succeeds another. The hotels and boarding-houses are full, the lake becomes dotted here and there with pleasure craft of all descriptions, from the frail canoe with sail and paddle to the costly steam launches. The Lake Hopatcong Country Club, formerly the Hotel Breslin, at Mt. Arlington, will be the abode of fashion and culture. The grounds surrounding it are terraced, and handsomely laid out with blossoming shrubs and flowers. The view from the long piazza over the lake comprises many pretty patches of scenery.

For camping out this place excels all others. The wooded shores offer the finest kind of seclusion; the bathing is good, and fishing adds materially to the pleasures of camp life. Not the least interesting feature of an evening on the lake is to watch the camp fires gleaming here and there along the opposite shores, and listen to the frequent camp cries of "rival" parties blending with song and accompaniment.

The little hamlet of Mount Arlington is a collection of neat cottages bordering on the lake, and on the hill above it. One of these, the cottage of Miss Lotta Crabtree, the actress, deserves particular mention, because its interior is not only gorgeous in its appointment, but in the extent of its artistic arrangements it has been praised by every connoisseur in decorative art.

The walks and rambles are as numerous as they are beautiful, and while out on a tramp anyone fond of exercise is likely to run across an extraordinary number of people, and wonder whence these folks came. Anyhow, everyone there is out for pleasure or rest and each makes the best of his opportunity.

A peculiar freak of nature here is Floating Island, at the southern extremity of the lake near Shippenport. The island never appears over one foot above the surface of the water, and is covered with tamarack, spruce and wild flowers of a curious growth in great variety.

Raccoon Island is on the eastern boundary of Henderson's Cove and is covered with a heavy growth of timber. From the fact that human bones have been unearthed on the island, it is supposed that the Indians buried their dead there.

Halsey Island, opposite Nolan's Point, is artificial. Many years ago the Canal Company, with proper authority, flooded the lake and this caused the water to rise to a sufficient height to flood part of the main land peninsula, thus forming several islands, of which this is the largest.

The River Styx, an arm of the lake that empties into it back of the mountain, is quieter than any place around. It is a romantic spot, and on account of the solitude that prevails is a favorite abode for such birds as herons, which stand in the water on one leg, heedless of all that surrounds them.

Henderson's Cove is probably the most beautiful spot on the lake; it is made so by the rugged bluffs that overhang it, which are covered by a hardy growth of oak and hemlock. Trips by boat to the cove are one of the fascinating pleasures of life here.

The lake finds its outlet by the Musconetcong River, which flows in an irregular course and empties into the Delaware, 40 miles distant. At times the Canal Company utilizes the water as a means for feeding the Canal, and at such times the lake surface recedes two feet or more.

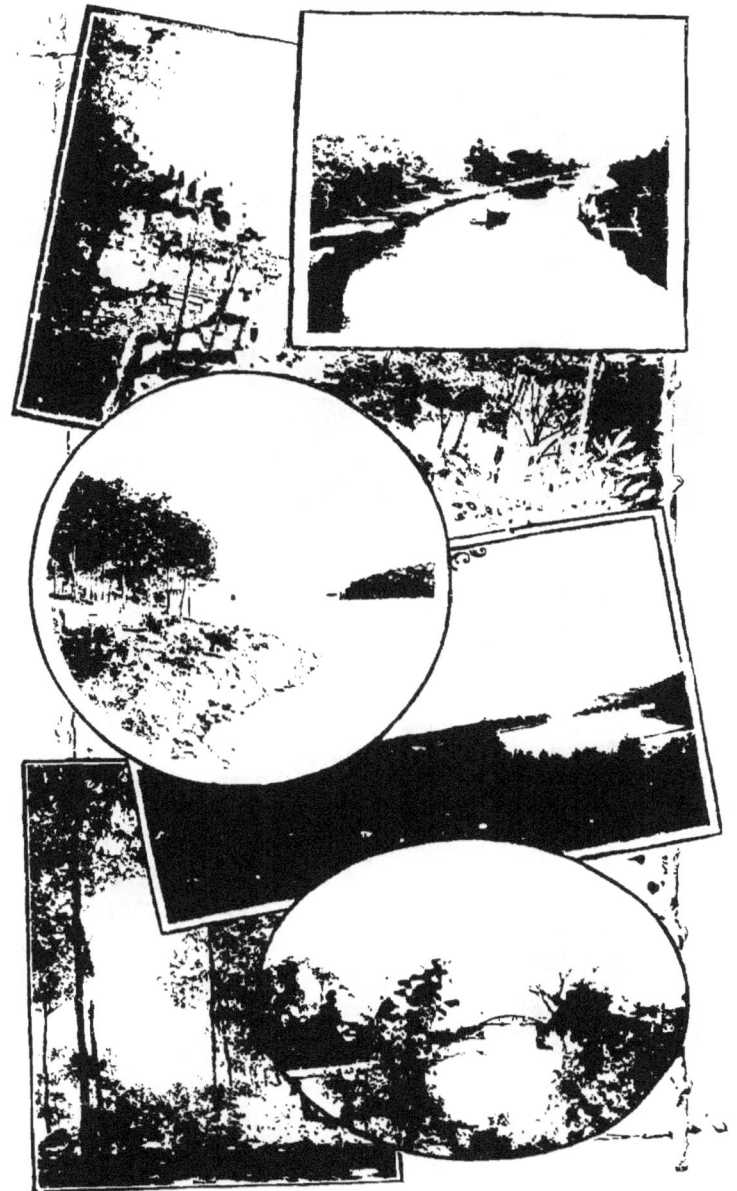

SCENES IN AND ABOUT LAKE HOPATCONG.

STANHOPE.

Altitude, 871 ft.

51.32 miles from New York ; Single ticket, $1.40 ; Excursion ticket, $2.10.

Stanhope has become known, not on account of its iron-smelting industries, but by reason of its general thrift. It has several churches and schools ; has stores of all kinds, and rejoices in one weekly paper. Passengers alight here to be staged through the mountains to

BUDD'S LAKE.

Altitude, 933 ft.

Distance from Stanhope, 3 miles.

" Restless and sparkling, its silvery sheen,
Reflects the bold hills in a setting of green."

This pretty sheet of water, almost circular in shape, boasts of being one of the most delightful lakes near New York. It is the resort of many people who love to enjoy the summer season surrounded by pleasant associates in an atmosphere of pure, health-giving air. The beauties of Budd's Lake are always enjoyable, and there is no monotony in a sojourn there. The man who likes fishing, here may gratify his whim by dropping in his line and hauling out vigorous black bass or pickerel. Both these voracious varieties are ready to meet the angler half-way and take the alluring bait. The wonderful stillness of the water, especially at evening, attracts the holiday maker, and boating is much indulged in. The conventional hammock can find no more delightful place to swing in than above the ruffled wavelets, as, under the influence of a cool morning breeze, they ripple on the pebbly shore. Everybody comes here in happy expectancy, and unless hypercritical and difficult to please, they are not disappointed, except, perhaps, at the too short summer which gives way to breezy autumn when the inevitable "good-bye" to the mountains has to be spoken. The sportsman

AT ANCHOR, BUDD'S LAKE, N. J.

can linger longer and be well repaid for his pains. He may have enjoyed himself thoroughly and been fortunate with rod or gun, but the inducement of bagging a few ducks from the lake, where they congregate every fall, often proves an attraction too strong to be resisted.

WATERLOO. *Altitude, 716 ft.*

51.52 miles from New York ; Single ticket, $1.50 ; Excursion ticket, $2.25.

Here, at the gateway of the rugged hills of Sussex County, begins the Sussex Railroad. The road is 26 miles long, and traverses a very picturesque country. It is wild, full of little lakes, ponds and silvery streams, that furnish excellent fishing.

Photo. by H. C. Pyle, N. Y. ON THE SUSSEX BRANCH.

On account of the mountainous character of the neighborhood, game of all sorts abounds. The partridge is frequently seen along the highways, and, during the fall —

> "Up from the stubble gets the quail,
> I hear the partridge drumming."

Bears, too, are not strangers in Sussex, and scarcely a season goes by that some one does not have to recount the destruction of one or more of these furry creatures. The summer sojourner, of course, is not as eager to kill bears as to roam about at will and avoid them. There is no danger, however, of meeting bruin in the summer months, as it is only in winter that he ventures within the bounds of civilization to forage for his provisions, and when satisfied with a pig or two, he returns quietly to his lair.

As there are innumerable farms and plenty of good hotels and boarding-houses, the region through which the Sussex Railroad runs is particularly inviting to summer vacationists. In fact, any person who appreciates a mountain summer, with pleasant surroundings, can make no mistake in giving any of the places mentioned a season's trial. On leaving Waterloo, the first station is

ANDOVER. *Altitude, 635 ft.*

60.66 miles from New York ; Single ticket, $1.75 ; Excursion ticket, $2.65.

Is a picturesque village of about 600 population, at an altitude of 650 to 763 ft. Among the mountains and lakes, along the line of the Sussex Branch of the Lackawanna, at junction of the Lehigh and Hudson Railroad, 60 miles from New York City.

It is noted for its neatness, healthfulness and grand scenery. From Hill-top, five minutes walk from depot, a view surpassed by none in the State of New Jersey, overlooking the Blue Mountains for 55 miles, including Jennie Jump, Delaware Water Gap, Culver's Gap, High Point, as well as Sparta, Panther and Allamuchy Mountains.

Among the 44 lakes that surround the village in a radius of eight miles are Lake Hopatcong, Swartswood, Panther, Cranberry, Auble, Stag, Turtle, Roseville, Bear, White, Slater, Gardner, Iliff, Goodale and Burkmire, all of which afford excellent bass and pickerel fishing, several of the above being near the village. The drives in all directions are exceedingly attractive. The lakes and mountains remind one of Switzerland. The Methodist church is a model, the Presbyterian very neat. Six daily trains to and from New York City. Morning papers, 8 a. m.; evening papers, 6 p. m. Mosquitoes almost unknown. Excellent board can be obtained at reasonable prices.

The Standard Musical String Co. send goods to all parts of the country. Two excellent physicians to attend those indisposed.

NEWTON. *Altitude, 599 ft.*

65.53 miles from New York ; Single ticket, $1.90 ; Excursion ticket, $2.95.

Newton, the county seat of Sussex, is considered one of the prettiest, as well as most prosperous, towns in North Jersey. The altitude ranges from 580 to 800 feet above mean tide at New York. The population is about 3,500, and the locality one of the healthiest in the State. The town has two shoe factories, employing over 500 persons, besides other manufactories. Its streets are lighted by arc electric lights, and water has been introduced into the town. Gas is also at command for lighting and heating. The principal streets are macadamized, and the sidewalks are flag and granolithic. As the nights are invariably cool, the daily range of 15° to 25° brings refreshing sleep, and mosquitoes are rarely seen. It has two newspapers, which are known far and wide as compendiums of local news. With prompt and convenient train service, there is no more desirable place in the Jersey Highlands. Business men traveling between town and city are favored by trips in the cool of the day, the average running time being two hours, and on some trains without change of cars. New York morning newspapers reach the town at 8.30 A. M. The drives in the neighborhood are noted for their beauty, and the proximity to Swartswood, Culvers, Hopatcong, and other lakes, render a summer residence a matter of comfort as well as pleasure. There is a Sunday train to and from New York.

LAFAYETTE. *Altitude, 654 ft.*

70.20 miles from New York ; Single ticket, $2.05 ; Excursion ticket, $3.25.

AUGUSTA. *Altitude, 495 ft.*

73.27 miles from New York ; Single ticket, $2.20 ; Excursion ticket, $3.45.

BRANCHVILLE. *Altitude, 576 ft.*

74.95 miles from New York ; Single ticket, $2.25 ; Excursion ticket, $3.50.

BEAUTY SPOTS ON THE SUSSEX BRANCH.

FRANKLIN.   Altitude, 552 ft.

77.84 miles from New York; Single ticket, $2.35; Excursion ticket, $3.60.

Returning again to the main line the next station is

HACKETTSTOWN.   Altitude, 561 ft.

60.10 miles from New York; Single ticket, $1.65; Excursion ticket, $2.45.

This is one of the oldest towns in New Jersey. It is situated in the midst of pleasant surroundings, and is an enterprising village of pretty homes and well shaded streets. It has a Mayor and Council and its municipal government is good. The Hackettstown Collegiate Institute, known throughout the country as a prominent seat of learning, is situated here. During the summer season the town is very active on account of the influx of the city people who come to obtain recreation and wholesome air.

Schooley's Mountain.

Like an immense forest, lying some distance back from the town, is Schooley's Mountain, a resort almost too well known to require detailed description. The mountain when viewed from a distance, resembles a long plateau, so even is its summit, and it is covered with a rich growth of forest trees. Nature has been so unusually kind to this romantic spot that many wealthy gentlemen have selected it as their summer home. Among these are Alfred Sully, Esq., the well-known railroad magnate, and Mr. E. D. Stokes. The Sully abode is palatial in its appointments, and the grounds are laid out in bright flower beds, arbors and shrubbery. Mr. Sully takes great pride in his valuable assortment of grapes, and has one of the choicest graperies in the State. The air on the mountain is cool and bracing and is favorable for all

JUNCTION OF MAIN LINE AND M. & E. DIVISION AT WASHINGTON, N. J.

pulmonary affections and asthma. There are no mosquitoes here, and slumber at night should always be between a pair of warm blankets. The Heath House and "The Dorincourt" are the most prominent summer hotels on the mountain.

PORT MURRAY.   *Altitude, 585 ft.*
66.46 miles from New York ; Single ticket, $1.85 ; Special ticket, $1.70 ; Excursion ticket, $2.75.

WASHINGTON.   *Altitude, 503 ft.*
69.88 miles from New York ; Single ticket, $1.90 ; Special ticket, $1.70 ; Excursion ticket, $2.85.

This is the most important city in Warren County and is noted for the number of its manufactories, principal among which are the piano and organ industries. The town is located at the base of Pohatcong Mountain and the valley is one of wonderful beauty and fertility. The city is noted for its fine hotels and summer boarding houses and for that reason is well patronized by out-of-town folks.

BROADWAY.   *Altitude, 373 ft.*
74.77 miles from New York ; Single ticket, $2.05 ; Special ticket, $1.85 ; Excursion ticket, $3.05.

STEWARTSVILLE.   *Altitude, 372 ft.*
78.90 miles from New York ; Single ticket, $2.05 ; Special ticket, $2.00 ; Excursion ticket, $3.20.

PHILLIPSBURG.   *Altitude, 218 ft.*
83.63 miles from New York ; Single ticket, $2.05 ; Excursion ticket, $3.25.

This city, one of the largest in the State and an important railroad centre, is the last in New Jersey on the line of this road. It is situated on the Delaware River. In mentioning Phillipsburg it is sufficient to indorse it as a city where can be had all conveniences other places of its size afford. The manufacturing industries are important and represent vast wealth. But Phillipsburg is most important as a railroad centre.

EASTON, PA.   *Altitude, 218 ft.*
84.24 miles from New York ; Single ticket, $2.10 ; Excursion ticket, $3.30.

Easton is situated just across the Delaware River from Phillipsburg, and is connected with it by a long bridge. This city, being one of the largest in Pennsylvania, needs no description here ; in limited space justice could not be accorded it. This is the seat of Lafayette College.

Returning again to the main line, which continues westward from Washington, the first station beyond is

OXFORD FURNACE.   *Altitude, 436 ft.*
74.39 miles from New York ; Single ticket, $2.05 ; Special ticket, $1.85 ; Excursion ticket, $3.05.

If this little town were referred to as a small edition of Sheffield, it should not be considered as inappropriate. The iron industry is all that is recognized here. The Oxford Steel and Iron Company controls the immense plant that turns out nails famous the country over. Nearly all the inhabitants depend on this industry for a living. The town was founded by a Scranton family, and its great success is principally due to their energy. Blairstown, the home of the Hon. John I. Blair, one of New Jersey's iron kings, is within a few miles of here, and is well worth a visit.

BRIDGEVILLE. *Altitude, 486 ft.*

78.39 miles from New York ; Single ticket, $2.15 ; Special ticket, $1.95 ; Excursion ticket, $3.20.

Just across the little Pequest River, connected by a three-arch stone viaduct bridge, is this quiet town. The attraction here is fishing, and the waters that furnish it are the Pequest River, Beaver Brook, and several small ponds. Among the natural attractions is Jenny Jump Mountain, close by. The region hereabouts is one of delightful simplicity, and profitable farming is largely conducted.

MANUNKA CHUNK, N. J.—JUNCTION OF BELVIDERE DIVISION PENNSYLVANIA R. R. FOR TRENTON, PHILADELPHIA AND THE SOUTH.

MANUNKA CHUNK. *Altitude, 511 ft.*

80.14 miles from New York ; Single ticket, $2.20 ; Special ticket, $2.00 ; Excursion ticket, $3.30.

At this point the road connects with the Belvidere Division of the Pennsylvania Railroad for Philadelphia, Baltimore, Washington and all points south and southwest. The place is small, and agricultural pursuits are the principal industry.

DELAWARE. *Altitude, 290 ft.*

82.64 miles from New York ; Single ticket, $2.25 ; Special ticket, $2.05 ; Excursion ticket, $3.40.

Delaware is located among the hills of northern New Jersey, and on the banks of the Delaware River. The surrounding country is hilly, almost mountainous. Numerous roads lead to places of varied interest, affording delightful drives. Several picturesque and romantic spots in the vicinity invite the rambler, while the river is a source of entertainment for the boatman and fisherman. The Gap, and other attractions within easy reach, are the object of frequent picnics and excursions during the season. In summer the population generally doubles. A number of good boarding-houses are located in the vicinity, and Delaware is quite a popular summer resort.

PORTLAND, PA. *Altitude, 292 ft.*

85.64 miles from New York ; Single ticket, $2.35 ; Special ticket, $2.15 ; Excursion ticket, $3.50.

This pretty little village is reached by crossing the Delaware River on a 1,200-foot bridge. The river view afforded from trains at this point is very fine. Portland has several commercial industries and is an important town in this region.

DELAWARE WATER GAP. *Altitude, 390 ft.*

90.64 miles from New York ; Single ticket, $2.55 ; Special ticket, $2.35 ; Excursion ticket, $3.70.

Of all the resorts along the line of the Lackawanna, none is more strikingly beautiful than this great handiwork of Nature. Its praises have been sung for generations, and one never wearies of them. From the time that the Redskin ruled the domain the popularity of this grand chasm through the mountains has been established, and each year the demand for hotel accommodations continues to increase. There is a peculiar rugged picturesqueness about the scenery that attracts the attention of the observer, and holds it until it is so firmly imprinted on the mind as never to be forgotten. Residents love to tarry by the clear water of the grand old Delaware, and enjoy the pleasures of boating and fishing, and the transient visitor is willing to journey any distance, if it is only to spend a day here. Many excursions are run to Water Gap from different points during the summer months, and so popular have these become that they are booked for months in advance at the Company's passenger department office.

A critical review of this region, and the Delaware River, cannot fail to be of interest to the readers.

The Delaware River rises 200 miles northward, in two lateral branches flowing from the western slope of the Catskill Mountains, 2,000 feet above the sea level. The western branch passes through a lake near its source, retaining, strange to say, its quaint aboriginal name "Utsayantha." This is described as a circular sheet of transparent water covering an area of 70 acres and having an elevation of 1,888 feet ; a mirror of beauty in the wooded wilderness, so secluded that few, save the red men, have ever gazed upon its serene solitude. In its course, the river hugs the base of the grand old mountains, older in date of upheaval than the snow-clad "Alps," which once formed a barrier to its passage, and rolled back the flood of waters, submerging for a long time the lesser hills and swelling plains that now, clad in verdure, adorn its borders.

The character of the rocks in this portion of the Blue Ridge is that of gray and red sandstone and conglomerates, containing white quartz pebbles of large size. The escarpment at the point of dislodgment is more bold on the New Jersey portion of the mountain, the means of the angle for the entire elevation of 1,600 feet being about 70 degrees, while projecting cliffs, as seen from the gorge, exhibit sections of perpendicular descent. On the Pennsylvania mountain the general slope from the summit to the river is less precipitous ; a mass of talus having been detached from the crest by the frost of winter, and pouring like lava down its sides, has covered the surface to the depth of many feet, concealing the rugged projections that characterize the face of the opposite mountain.

From both the summits—Mount Tammany in New Jersey and Mount Minsi in

DELAWARE, LACKAWANNA & WESTERN R. R.   55

Pennsylvania—views of great extent and beauty are obtained, but it is difficult to do them justice by mere description; they must be seen to be fully appreciated. One overlooks, to the south, a scene of vast breadth, comprising mountains and hills,

DELAWARE WATER GAP, LOOKING SOUTH.

villages and farmhouses, cultivated fields, groves of woodland and primitive forests —the river on its sinuous journey filling up the picture. It was upon the summit of Minsi, that, over a quarter of a century ago, a romantic young lady lost her way, and was exposed for a greater part of a night on the ledge of a cliff, to which she had fallen, and from which she was rescued with much difficulty. On the way to Mount Minsi to the settled portion of the Gap, a fine view is obtained from

PROSPECT ROCK.—This bare platform, though much below the summit, enables

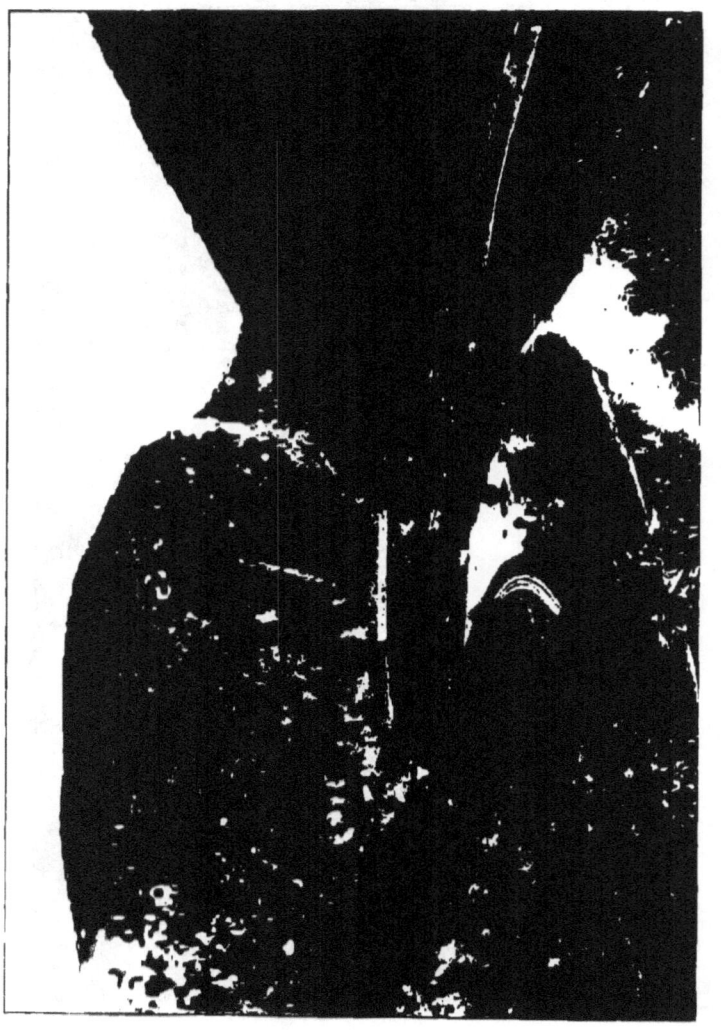

DELAWARE WATER GAP, LOOKING SOUTH

the visitor to enjoy one of the finest pieces of scenery on the Delaware. The view up the river extends beyond the islands to the distant hills and mountains, through which the river winds its tortuous course and glides smoothly along the base of the precipice from which you are gazing. Near Prospect Rock is

THE HUNTER'S SPRING.—A wild secluded spot where many Lenape huntsmen as well as those of modern time, have been refreshed, and have lain in wait for the deer as they came panting for the cooling waters. It is at the head of a wild ravine

MARSHALL'S FALL, DELAWARE WATER GAP.

and the source of Eureka Creek, which tumbles over the rocky bed in its rapid descent to the river, and in which are found Moss Cataract and Rebecca's Bath. Near by is

DELAWARE WATER GAP, FROM THE SOUTH

THE LOVER'S LEAP.—This is the artist's favorite spot and is made memorable as the scene where the Indian Princess "Winona" and her lover took their fatal step.

CALDENO CREEK.—This is a noted spot. It has its rise high up the side of Mount Minsi. Dashing and foaming in its descent, it flows at length into the valley, and after gladdening the inmates of several farm houses, changes its course and runs close by the ruins of an old saw mill, which at one time it made busy as the machinery was put in motion by the splashing of the water over a big wheel. From the old mill the stream flows across a green meadow and loses itself in an entanglement of forest, from which it again emerges at Moss Cataract, dashes over its mossy bed, fills Diana's bath afresh, gives a leap over the falls of its own name and hastens on to lose its identity in the broad waters of the Delaware.

TABLE ROCK AND COOPER'S CLIFF.—Both are situated on an extended rocky platform of about 300 feet in elevation, overlooking the river and the cultivated hills in the distance. The confused mixture of forest and hills, and the cultivated land below the cliff on which one stands, form a beautiful foreground to the finely developed proportions of the gorge in the distance.

SUNSET HILL, rises only a few rods to the northeast of the apparently undisturbed stratification of Table Rock, and is a confused, disjointed, irregular mass of rock from base to apex.

We have given a tolerably fair idea of the general character of the scenery and views of Water Gap, but its attractions, if they begin, certainly do not end there. There are numerous walks besides those we have named, and drives which we have not mentioned at all—long drives to the beautiful falls of Winona and Bushkill, and short drives to romantic places with commonplace names: Fox Hill, the Knob, Lake of the Mountain and a dozen others. Stroudsburg is but four miles distant.

The air about here is pure and appetizing, and while the days are not hot nor humid, the nights are so delightfully cool that sleep of the kind that rests and invigorates is assured. The Water Gap is famous for its fine hotels. The drinking water, from Caldeno Creek, is very pure.

STROUDSBURG AND EAST STROUDSBURG, PA.

Altitude, 400 ft.

94.89 miles from New York ; Single ticket, $2.70 ; Special ticket, $2.50 ; Excursion ticket, $3.85

These two towns are delightfully situated on Brodhead's Creek, the former being the county seat of Monroe. They have a combined population of 5,000 inhabitants, and, are noted for their beauty and the magnificent scenery surrounding them. For more than half a century people have been attracted to this section on account of its wild grandeur, its remarkable healthfulness, and its clearness and dryness of air. The State Normal School of the fourth Pennsylvania is located at East Stroudsburg ; it is thoroughly equipped and is one of the

noted educational institutions of the state. George P. Bible, A. M., is principal. The following are among the widely known places of interest near these two towns: Delaware Water Gap, Highland Dell, The Sanitarium, Silver Lake, Buttermilk Falls, Sambo Falls, Bradley's Falls, Mosier's Knob, Marshall's Falls, Lake of the Mountain, Winona Falls, Lake Poponoming, Bushkill Falls, Dingman's Falls and Forest Park.

STROUDSBURG STATION

FOREST PARK.
BUSHKILL, PIKE COUNTY, PENNSYLVANIA.
15 miles from Stroudsburg.

It comprises about sixteen thousand acres of land, diversified by mountain and valley, lakes and streams.

Its mountain streams, fed by bubbling springs, are the lurking places of countless trout, and the lakes are the abiding places of the gamy black bass and the sun-loving perch.

In the forest, much of which is in primeval state, deer and bear, partridge and pheasant, grouse, quail, woodcock, foxes, rabbits and squirrel abound.

SPRAGUEVILLE. *Altitude, 524 ft.*

99.14 miles from New York ; Single ticket, $2.85 ; Special ticket, $2.65 ; Excursion ticket, $4.05.

Spragueville is an attractive village surrounded by many hills, which give it a picturesque appearance. It is the summer home of several wealthy persons whose residences are costly and beautiful. Like its larger neighbor, Stroudsburg, it is located on Brodhead's Creek, which at this point is decidedly pretty, and is famous for the fine trout fishing it affords. The Analomink streams, both celebrated for their trout, are near the village. The drives are magnificent for miles around and pleasure afforded by them coupled with riding and walking keep tourists busy enjoying themselves.

HENRYVILLE. *Altitude, 784 ft.*
MONROE CO., PA.

102.64 miles from New York ; Single ticket, $2.95 ; Special ticket, $2.75 ; Excursion ticket, $4.20.

If you were anxious to spend all day Saturday catching fine brook trout—beauties that run up to a pound and three-quarters—you could not do better than take the short trip on the D. L. & W. necessary to reach Henryville, a little town prettily situated on a mountain side. At the station you will find a spanking team of farm horses and a good springy buckboard ready to take all comers over the mountain to Parkside. Here you are surrounded by some of the most prolific brook trout streams in America—East and West Branch, Brodhead, Cranberry, Heller, Paradise and Devil's Hole—all famous. Parkside, on the banks of the Analomink, is a beautiful little rural retreat, not more than three hours' ride from New York. The Park House is situated in the centre of beautifully laid out grounds, with the river at one side and the mountains on the other. The altitude of the place gives it perfect freedom from mosquitoes and malaria, and in summer the temperature is delightfully cool.

The ride over the hills from the station will furnish an appetite alone worth the trip. And the food! Food that is sweet and fresh, food that is free of a city smell, food that has a natural ring to it—butter, cream, eggs, milk, vegetables, and all sorts of things, right from the farm. Lounge about the farm Friday evening, smoke your pipes or cigars and listen to the yarns about the big fish you will have to battle with in the morning. When you retire for the night sleep will not be difficult to woo, and you can peacefully close your eyes with the cheering knowledge that a refreshing breakfast will be ready when you open them again. After that go forth to flail the wooded streams, and your basket will be heavy with fine-sized fish on your return. Sunday resting about the farm, eating delicious fruit, and breathing the invigorating mountain air until night falls again, will fill the day with restful memories. The early morning train may be taken on Monday, and—the city reached all too soon. The points of interest within easy riding or driving distance are the Water Gap, Red Rock Glen, Prospect Ledge, Silver Cascade, Pocono Summit, Point Lookout and one or two others of less fame.

CRESCO. *Altitude, 1,203 ft.*

108.14 miles from New York ; Single ticket, $3.15 ; Special ticket, $2.95 ; Excursion ticket, $4.45.

Cresco is situated in the highlands of Monroe County close to the Delaware River. It can be safely said that the forests and streams about here give more pleasure than the average sportsman can find time to enjoy. A region of woodland and water, it attracts them every season, and has attained for itself a well deserved reputation.

WISCASSET POOL, MOUNT POCONO.

MOUNT POCONO. *Altitude, 1,824 ft.*

114.14 miles from New York ; Single ticket, $3.35 ; Special ticket, $3.15 ;
Excursion ticket, $4.65.

The Pocono Mountains cross the northeastern counties of Pennsylvania and are spurs of the same great chain that crosses the Atlantic section from the Catskills in New York to the Black Mountains in North Carolina.

The extensive panoramic view that spreads before one's gaze emphasizes the fact that Mount Pocono is very nearly the highest point of the mountains. In the foreground, the few clearings give a touch of cultivation ; further down is the wood-covered valley, and beyond, the pine-clad hills roll back, dotted here and there by a farm

TRINITY CHURCH, MOUNT POCONO, PA.

house or a clearing, the horizon bounded by the long line of the Blue Ridge, standing out like a huge rampart. A little to the right, Pocono Knob raises its rock-bound summit two thousand, six hundred feet above the level of the sea. On the left, through the famous Delaware Water Gap are seen the hills and mountains of New Jersey. Over all the moving cloud shades cast their ever changing tinge of light and shade.

The atmosphere is wonderfully dry, pure and pine-laden, far more so than at an equal altitude along the main Alleghaney Range. The many persons to whom mountain breezes are as a sparkling cordial, will find here on the spurs of the Pocono, all that need requires or fancy seeks.

The thermometer registers on an average from ten to fifteen degrees lower than in the cities of New York and Philadelphia. The nights are cool and the air soft and balmy. There are no mosquitoes. The climate here is almost a specific for malarial diseases and can be equally recommended to those suffering from debility due to overwork, over-worry or other causes. The altitude is not so great as to increase nervous conditions as is the case in higher altitudes.

Here all throat and chest troubles are benefitted and weak lungs are made strong. To hay-fever and asthmatic subjects this locality is a blessing. In a word, this Pocono region is second to no eastern locality for all of the requirements of a typical health resort.

As a proof of the dryness of the atmosphere, it is stated that as a rule, the grass will be entirely free from dew on summer nights as late as eleven o'clock.

The success of the Mount Pocono region as a health resort is fully assured and there are now ample hotel and cottage accommodations within a few miles of the station.

Some of the hotels have every modern convenience, steam-heat, enabling one to enjoy cool weather, the laurels and rhododendrons of June as well as the changing foliage of the invigorating autumn days without the discomfort of an improperly heated house; rooms en suite with private bath, ample parlors, billiard rooms, porches, and all other modern conveniences.

THE WISCASSET.

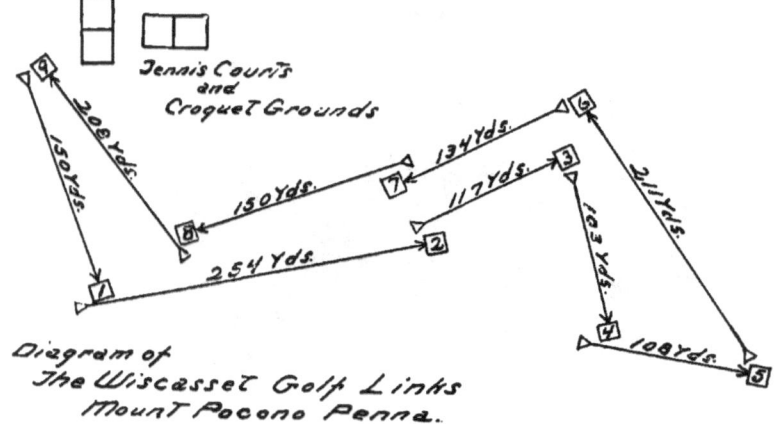

Diagram of
The Wiscasset Golf Links
Mount Pocono Penna.

There are numerous walks and drives, the roads being exceptionally good for a mountain district. The Indian Run drive on the grounds of "The Wiscasset" is especially romantic. The various streams in the neighborhood are easily accessible and give good sport with the rod. There is also good hunting in the autumn. The popular games, notably golf, tennis and croquet are amply provided for.

The rhododendron and laurel should be mentioned as an especial attraction in the spring and early summer. Late in June the rhododendron is in its glory and the thousands of bushes covered with delicate blossoms, each as it breaks open its pink shaded treasure of bloom forming a perfect boquet in exquisite contrast to the wealth of dark green behind, makes a dainty picture, worthy the brush of the most ambitious painter.

The water in this region is of the purest quality. Minerals being scarce, it naturally carries a minimum quantity of these substances and there is no region that can boast of purer water than the Pocono Mountain region.

Some of the hotels are supplying their guests from springs situated at a distance, beyond the possibility of contamination, bringing the water in rustless, tasteless pipes to properly located cement reservoirs, from which in turn it is piped to the hotel as pure, sweet and sparkling as when it rushed forth at the spring.

THE WISCASSET RESERVOIR.

POCONO SUMMIT. *Altitude, 1,961 ft.*

116.64 miles from New York ; Single ticket, $3.45 ; Special ticket, $3.25.
Excursion ticket, $4.75.

This paradise of the sportsmen does not differ in character from Mount Pocono. The doors of the few hotels are open to welcome the season's guests, and every facility for comfort and enjoyment is offered. The engineers of western-bound trains are always glad when they reach the summit that they may take matters a little easier in the descent that follows.

TOBYHANNA. *Altitude, 1,929 ft.*

121.30 miles from New York ; Single ticket, $3.60 ; Special ticket, $3.40 ;
Excursion ticket, $4.95.

Tobyhanna is a mountain village of about 800 inhabitants, and is prettily situated on the western slope of Pocono, about equal distance from Stroudsburg and Scranton.

VIEW FROM SUMMIT OF MOUNT POCONO.—WATER GAP IN DISTANCE, 23 MILES AWAY.

NORTHERN APPROACH TO PARADISE TUNNEL.

Several industries are established here and the outlook is promising. The air being pure, cool and bracing, the place is becoming famous as a resort for people affected with pulmonary diseases.

GOULDSBORO. *Altitude, 1,970 ft.*
126.64 miles from New York ; Single ticket, $3.80 ; Special ticket, $3.60 ;
Excursion ticket, $5.15.

A small town named after the late Mr. Jay Gould, who, in the early part of his life, established a tannery here. It is a pleasant, healthy spot, and is growing in favor as a summer resort.

MOSCOW. *Altitude, 1,887 ft.*
134.89 miles from New York ; Single ticket, $4.10 ; Special ticket, $3.90 ;
Excursion ticket, $5.50.

This is quite a thriving town and one of the prettiest west of the mountains. It is also a fine agricultural region, and in summer is gay with the cheery voice of happy vacationists. The walks and drives about here are among the most attractive features.

ELMHURST. *Altitude, 1,100 ft.*
137.89 miles from New York ; Single ticket, $4.20 ; Special ticket, $4.00 ;
Excursion ticket, $5.60.

A quiet colony that has become known as an excellent place to spend a vacation. It is healthful, and the scenery in the neighborhood is very attractive.

Elmhurst, nine miles from Scranton towards New York, has in the last few year, come into deserved prominence as a place of resort. It is noted for its pure waters, pure air and beautiful scenery.

Hotel Elmhurst is replete with every modern improvement, including gas and electric bells in every room, and is supplied with pure spring water, with thorough plumbing and drainage. The broad porches command an extended view of mountain, lake and woodland. The hotel grounds comprise four acres and contain croquet and lawn tennis courts, and are made doubly attractive by the flowers and shrubbery and well-kept and verdant lawns.

Elmhurst is brought into close communication with Scranton by the Nay Aug Falls and Elmhurst boulevard, just completed, which provides a magnificent driveway second to none in the country. From the heart of the city the road emerges into beautiful Nay Aug Park and after spanning Nay Aug gorge with a steel bridge 350 feet long and 125 feet above the water, winds around the mountain peaks in graceful curves and with easy grades, disclosing at every turn grand and far reaching mountain views, which makes this beautiful drive without a peer for scenic effect.

SCRANTON. *Altitude 740 ft.*
147.89 miles from New York ; Single ticket, $4.55 ; Special ticket, $4.35 ;
Excursion ticket, $6.00.

Scranton is the capital of Lackawanna County, Pa. Its coal and iron industries have placed it in the foremost rank of manufacturing cities. Millions of people annually pay tribute to the output of coal from the Scranton region ; and the steel rails that thread this continent from ocean to ocean, and from the Canadian border to the Gulf, are to a very large extent produced in the rolling mills within plain view of the Lackawanna trains that speed by.

MOSES TAYLOR HOSPITAL, SCRANTON, PA.

WOODWARD BREAKER

Scranton with its 100,000 population is a metropolis of Northeastern Pennsylvania, and the third city in the state. Being located in the famous Lackawanna-Wyoming Valley, and on the Lackawanna River, it occupies a succession of hills and eminences, important among which is Hyde Park Hill, from which a magnificent view of the city and surrounding country may be obtained.

The city is supplied with good water, and claims to be one of the best lighted places in the country. The hotels are good and well maintained. There are churches of all denominations, literary societies, social and athletic clubs, and excellent street-car facilities. Several railways connect here, making it an important railroad centre as well as manufacturing town. Not the least interesting feature of the city is a

DINING STATION, SCRANTON, PA., WM. HANLEY, PROP.

visit to the rolling mills and giant coal breakers, which when the busy season is at its height, crush and prepare for shipment fifty-five thousand tons a day. A visit to the subterranean coal galleries in the mines will prove an entertaining experience and one worth the trouble.

Despite the immense amount of manufacturing done here, the city, unlike many others, is not permeated with smoke and gases, as might be expected. On the contrary the air is pure, and the city is a very pleasant place to visit or remain in at any season of the year. In fact, Scranton contains as many magnificent residences and public buildings as any city of its size in the United States, and this bears the best testimony to its healthfulness that can be given.

Among the resorts within a short distance is Carbondale, with its great switchback and gravity road to Honesdale. Numerous lakes in the surrounding mountains afford good fishing, black bass and pickerel being plentiful.

IN THE WYOMING VALLEY.

In the Wyoming Valley.

The Bloomsburg Division.

FOLLOWING the Susquehanna River along the greater part of the division, the view from the train is particularly fascinating. This portion of the Wyoming Valley abounds in historic interests as well as in some of the wildest scenery that can be found on the line. For the latter reason it has grown rapidly in favor as a region for summer resorts.

The first station beyond Scranton is

BELLEVUE. *Altitude, 723 ft.*

149.27 miles from New York; Single ticket, $4.60; Special ticket, $4.35;
Excursion ticket, $6.05.

TAYLOR. *Altitude, 723 ft.*

150.90 miles from New York; Single ticket, $4.65; Special ticket, $4.35;
Excursion ticket, $6.10.

LACKAWANNA. *Altitude, 637 ft.*

154.28 miles from New York; Single ticket, $4.75; Special ticket, $4.35;
Excursion ticket, $6.30.

DURYEA.

154.97 miles from New York; Single ticket, $4.80; Special ticket, $4.35;
Excursion ticket, $6.35.

PITTSTON. *Altitude, 572 ft.*

156.97 miles from New York; Single ticket, $4.85; Special ticket, $4.35;
Excursion ticket, $6.40.

At this point the railroad crosses the Susquehanna River. Among many interesting places are Campbell's Ledge, a high and picturesque bluff, which, in early history, was used by the Indians as a point of observation.

SUSQUEHANNA AVENUE. *Altitude, 579 ft.*

157.48 miles from New York; Single ticket, $4.90; Special ticket, $4.35;
Excursion ticket, $6.50.

WEST PITTSTON. *Altitude, 570 ft.*

158.23 miles from New York; Single ticket, $4.00; Special ticket $4.35;
Excursion ticket, $6.50.

WYOMING. *Altitude, 588 ft.*

160.24 miles from New York; Single ticket, $4.95; Special ticket, $4.35;
Excursion ticket, $6.60.

This town became noted as early as 1778, through being the scene of a massacre by Indians, now better known as the Wyoming Massacre. The spot where the butchery occurred is an interesting place to visit.

FORTY FORT. *Altitude 558 ft.*

162.16 miles from New York; Single ticket, $5.00; Special ticket, $4.35;
Excursion ticket, $6.65.

BENNETT. *Altitude, 553 ft.*

163.79 miles from New York; Single ticket, $5.00; Special ticket, $4.35;
Excursion ticket, $6.70.

At Bennett's connection is made with the Harvey's Lake Branch of the Lehigh Valley. Harvey's Lake is a pretty sheet of water high up in the mountains, which has long been famous as a resort for excursionists and sportsmen.

AT MOUNT LOOKOUT COLLIERY, (300 FEET BELOW THE SURFACE) WYOMING, PA.

KINGSTON. *Altitude, 562 ft.*

164.90 miles from New York; Single ticket, $5.00; Special ticket, $4.35;
Excursion ticket, $6.80.

At Kingston, connection is made with Wilkes-Barre, one mile distant. A line of electric cars runs between the two places. The Delaware, Lackawanna & Western's workshops occupy a large plot of ground here and contribute largely to the prosperity of the town. Coal operations are also extensively carried on, and the company's largest coal breaker is in use here.

Here is situated the celebrated Methodist Episcopal Seminary, which was originally erected in 1844 at the modest cost of $5,000. This great institution flourished until 1853, when the original building was burned, but soon after another and far handsomer building took its place. The popularity of Wyoming Seminary as a Christian school and educational establishment has so extended that it now comprises some half a dozen or more buildings.

WILKES-BARRE. *Altitude, 550 ft.*

167 miles from New York; Single ticket, $5.00; Special ticket, $4.35;
Excursion ticket, $6.85.

Wilkes-Barre is one of the most prosperous cities of Pennsylvania. It is beautifully situated in the Wyoming Valley, and owes its prosperity to the rich and extensive anthracite coal fields in the vicinity. One of the great veins is thirty feet in thickness.

On account of the supply of coal, so close at hand, many industries have sprung up here and capital has been heavily invested. The citizens have been generous in their outlay of money, and in consequence the natural attractions of the city have been much improved. The society is refined, and as a summer resort the city offers many inducements.

PLYMOUTH. *Altitude, 535 ft.*

168.05 miles from New York; Single ticket, $5.05; Special ticket, $4.45;
Excursion ticket, $6.90.

AVONDALE. *Altitude, 530 ft.*

170.12 miles from New York; Single ticket, $5.10; Special ticket, $4.50;
Excursion ticket, $7.00.

NANTICOKE. *Altitude, 538 ft.*

171.52 miles from New York; Single ticket, $5.15; Special ticket, $4.55;
Excursion ticket, $7.05.

Connection is made here with the Pennsylvania Railroad.

HUNLOCKS. *Altitude, 531 ft.*

175.11 miles from New York; Single ticket, $5.25; Special ticket, $4.70;
Excursion ticket, $7.25.

SUSQUEHANNA, NEAR SHICKSHINNY.

SHICKSHINNY. *Altitude, 521 ft.*
180.70 miles from New York; Single ticket, $5.25; Special ticket, $4.85;
Excursion ticket, $7.45.

This place is much better than its sing-song name would imply. It is situated in the midst of wild mountain scenery and is as romantic a spot as exists in the valley. Besides the grand scenery, the fishing in the Susquehanna here is good, and black bass is plentiful. Shickshinny is located at the extreme southern outcrop of the Wyoming coal basin.

HICK'S FERRY. *Altitude, 521 ft.*
186.21 miles from New York; Single ticket, $5.30; Special ticket, $5.00;
Excursion ticket, $7.65.

BEACH HAVEN. *Altitude, 530 ft.*
188.92 miles from New York; Single ticket, $5.30; Special ticket, $5.10;
Excursion ticket, $7.75.

BERWICK. *Altitude, 504 ft.*
191.65 miles from New York; Single ticket, $5.30; Special ticket, $5.15;
Excursion ticket, $7.85.

Berwick is quite a manufacturing town, and here the extensive plant of the Jackson and Woodin Car Works is located. The manufacture of iron piping is largely carried on in the town.

BRIAR CREEK. *Altitude, 502 ft.*
194.6 miles from New York ; Single ticket, $5.30 ; Special ticket, $5.25 ;
Excursion ticket, $8.00.

WILLOW GROVE. *Altitude, 516 ft.*
196.33 miles from New York ; Single ticket, $5.30 ; Special ticket, $5.25 ;
Excursion ticket, $8.10.

LIME RIDGE. *Altitude, 509 ft.*
198.28 miles from New York ; Single ticket, $5.30 ; Special ticket, $5.25 ;
Excursion ticket, $8.15.

ESPY. *Altitude, 490 ft.*
201.69 miles from New York ; Single ticket, $5.30 ; Special ticket, $5.25 ;
Excursion ticket, $8.30.

BLOOMSBURG. *Altitude, 489 ft.*
204.14 miles from New York ; Single ticket, $5.35 ; Special ticket, $5.25 ;
Excursion ticket, $8.35.

Bloomsburg is a prosperous place, and is the capital of Columbia County. The angler will find excellent fishing here.

SUSQUEHANNA AT SHICKSHINNY.

Bloomsburg, conceded to be the most progressive and prosperous town along the Susquehanna, is one of the prettiest in the State, and owing to the large number of manufactories established within a few years is rapidly increasing in importance. Beautiful scenery, good fishing and fine roads commend it to the attention of the tourist. The Bloomsburg and Sullivan R.R. here connects with the D., L. & W. and affords easy access to the famous fishing and hunting grounds of Sullivan County.

ALONG THE "LACKAWANNA."

"The Adirondacks of Pennsylvania." The educational advantages of Bloomsburg are of the best, and the buildings of one of the largest Normal schools in the country, situated on the hill above the town, attract the eye for a considerable distance. Tourists will find Bloomsburg a desirable place to visit.

RUPERT. *Altitude, 482 ft.*
205.91 miles from New York ; Single ticket, $5.35 ; Special ticket, $5.25 ;
Excursion ticket, $8.15.

At this point connection is made with the Philadelphia and Reading's Catawissa Division, and the road crosses Fishing Creek. The summer tourist and fisherman alike will find Rupert an excellent place to spend the outing season.

CATAWISSA. *Altitude, 473 ft.*
207.15 miles from New York ; Single ticket, $5.35 ; Special ticket, $5.25 ;
Excursion ticket, $8.50.

DANVILLE. *Altitude, 157 ft.*

215.86 miles from New York ; Single ticket, $5.65 ; Special ticket, $ .51 ;
Excursion ticket, $8.85.

This busy town of 10,000 inhabitants, the capital of Montour County, is over 100 years old, and is delightfully situated in a valley between two mountain ranges.

The immense amount of ore found in the hills surrounding Danville made the town famous for the extent of its iron industry. At the present day three large mills are kept in almost constant operation. The first T rail ever made was rolled in Danville on October 8, 1845. During the last few years a number of factories have been erected and successfully operated.

The State Hospital for the Insane, one of the best conducted institutions in the State is located here. It is beautifully situated on a slight eminence about half a mile out of town, and is surrounded by a magnificent lawn and a farm of 250 acres.

Danville has about 20 churches of all denominations, two large club houses, and one of the finest theatres in central Pennsylvania.

A number of well-patronized summer boarding-houses are located a short distance out of town.

The summer tourist in search of rest and recreation, will find both in this region.

CHULASKY. *Altitude, 155 ft.*

219.13 miles from New York ; Single ticket, $5.80 ; Special ticket, $5.60 ;
Excursion ticket, $9.00.

CAMERON. *Altitude, 458 ft.*

220.93 miles from New York ; Single ticket, $5.90 ; Special ticket, $5.65 ;
Excursion ticket, $9.10.

NORTHUMBERLAND. *Altitude, 152 ft.*

227.83 miles from New York ; Single ticket, $6.05 ; Special ticket, $5.71 ;
Excursion ticket, $9.12.

Northumberland is the terminus of the division. Connection is here made with the Northern Central road (Pennsylvania system).

CLARK'S SUMMIT. *Altitude, 1,242 ft.*

154.89 miles from New York ; Single ticket, $4.80 ; Special ticket, $4.60 ;
Excursion ticket, $6.30.

Clark's Summit is the highest point between Scranton and Great Bend, and the road here runs through a series of deep cuts and over heavy grades. The country is magnificent, and abounds in fine farms. The attractions are many and varied, and several beautiful lakes and streams repay with fine catches the sportsmen who visit them.

GLENBURN. *Altitude, 1,260 ft.*

158.14 miles from New York ; Single ticket, $4.90 ; Special ticket, $4.70 ;
Excursion ticket, $6.45.

DALTON. *Altitude 986 ft.*

159.14 miles from New York ; Single ticket, $4.95 ; Special ticket, $4.75 ;
Excursion ticket, $6.50.

Dalton is to Scranton what many of those beautiful country towns in New Jersey are to New York, that is to say the country residence of many of the most prominent

NEAR NANTICOKE.

business and professional men of that active and thriving city. The beautiful drives, the invigorating air and the many and varied changes of scenery render this and the other villages in close proximity to it the most popular places along the line of the road for obtaining rest and comfort during the heated season.

LA PLUME. *Altitude, 877 ft.*

161.14 miles from New York; Single ticket, $5.00; Special ticket, $4.80; Excursion ticket, $6.70.

FACTORYVILLE. *Altitude, 890 ft.*

163.39 miles from New York; Single ticket, $5.10; Special ticket, $4.90; Excursion ticket, $6.65.

This growing town is principally noted for its fine dairy produce and farms. The mountain attractions are numerous and the drives pretty. A short stay here will well repay.

LAKE WINOLA, four and a half miles from Factoryville, is one of the most beautiful and largest sheets of water in Northern Pennsylvania, fed entirely by springs, and clear as crystal. It is surrounded by beautiful groves, and noted for its fine summer cottages, boating, bathing and fishing. Here are superb black bass, and pickerel in abundance that attract the angler from near and far. The altitude is 1,100 feet. The air is cool and bracing—free from malaria. There are many beautiful drives in the neighborhood, and the scenery is unsurpassed. A more delightful place cannot be found in the State to spend the summer months.

A large hotel, that will accommodate 400 people, is situated on the bluff, 80 feet above the lake. From it a fine view of the surrounding country is obtainable. Commodious stages connect with all the important trains from Factoryville.

NICHOLSON. *Altitude 765 ft.*

169.39 miles from New York ; Single ticket, $5.30 ; Special ticket, $5.00 ;
Excursion ticket, $6.90.

After passing through a tunnel over 2,000 feet long this pretty little place is brought to view. Tunkhannock and Martin Creeks form a junction below the village, and furnish good water power for the several manufacturing industries. Nicholson became known through the tanning industry, and the depletion of the forest about here is due to the incessant destruction of trees for tan bark.

FOSTER. *Altitude, 893 ft.*

175.14 miles from New York ; Single ticket, $5.50 ; Special ticket, $5.00 ;
Excursion ticket, $7.15.

KINGSLEY'S. *Altitude, 981 ft.*

179.14 miles from New York ; Single ticket, $5.60 ; Special ticket, $5.00 ;
Excursion ticket, $7.30.

ALFORD. *Altitude, 1,053 ft.*

182.64 miles from New York ; Single ticket, $5.75 ; Special ticket, $5.00 ;
Excursion ticket, $7.45.

Lackawanna & Montrose R. R.

This little road, which connects with the main line at Alford, has but three stations. The country through which it runs is both healthful and picturesque, and is well adapted for summer homes. The stations are :

HART LAKE. *Altitude, 1,592 ft.*

188.05 miles from New York ; Single ticket, $5.95 ; Special ticket, $5.20 ;
Excursion ticket, $7.85.

TIFFANY'S. *Altitude, 1,619 ft.*

192.31 miles from New York ; Single ticket, $6.05 ; Special ticket, $5.30 ;
Excursion ticket, $8.05.

Population, 2,000. **MONTROSE.** *Altitude, 1,800 ft.*

193.32 miles from New York ; Single ticket, $6.15 ; Special ticket $5.40 ;
Excursion ticket, $8.20.

The terminal of the newly constructed and picturesque Montrose and Lackawanna R. R. is situated in the very centre and highest point of a moderately hilly and finely cultivated region, equal in area to forty square miles, and is surrounded on all sides by the hills of the tortuous Susquehanna River, and the mountain ranges of the Lackawanna. The outlook to these distant hills and mountains, and into seven or eight counties of Pennsylvania and New York, over the intervening region of forests, orchards, cultivated fields and pleasant agricultural homes, presents in every direction views of rural beauty and picturesque loveliness.

A natural lake of about fifty acres lies at the foot of these hills on one side, while gently sloping down the other lies the village with its imposing court house and fine school building, its seven churches, its attractive village hotels, stores, and its many pretty homes, some of which are thrown open for the accommodation of summer guests.

Charming drives lead in every direction to natural lakes and streams lying but a few miles distant, and these afford excellent fishing. The water is pure and the air is full of exhilirating life-giving ozone. Here there are no mosquitoes, no fogs, no malaria, no sleepless nights. Montrose is within one hour of Binghamton and Scranton, six hours from New York and seven from Philadelphia.

It is destined to become a famous and popular summer resort.

NEW MILFORD. *Altitude, 1,087 ft.*

189.39 miles from New York ; Single ticket, $5.95 ; Special ticket, $5.00 ;
Excursion ticket, $7.70.

New Milford is in the heart of the tannery region, and a beautiful country. The scenery is picturesque, and varies from the fertile valley to the high, tree-clad mountain. The great number of lakes and streams in the mountains make it a favorite resort of fishermen. The village is a thriving one and supports several industries.

GREAT BEND. *Altitude, 860 ft.*

195.89 miles from New York ; Single ticket, $6.05 ; Special ticket, $5.00 ;
Excursion ticket, $7.75.

The spot is beautifully situated on a level plain surrounded by a framework of mountains, and the Susquehanna River flows through it. A mineral spring, whose waters contain many virtues, is also one of the features of the place. The scenery about here, and the village itself, attract a great many visitors. The Company has established shops and a round-house here. Great Bend possesses numerous industries which give the place some commercial importance.

CONKLIN, N. Y. *Altitude, 852 ft.*

200.89 miles from New York ; Single ticket, $6.10 ; Special ticket, $5.00 ;
Excursion ticket, $7.85.

CONKLIN CENTER. *Altitude, 864 ft.*

203.89 miles from New York ; Single ticket, $6.15 ; Special ticket, $5.00 ;
Excursion ticket, $7.90.

DELAWARE, LACKAWANNA & WESTERN R. R. 79

"THE PARLOR CITY," BINGHAMTON, N. Y.

BINGHAMTON. *Altitude, 845 ft.*

209.80 miles from New York; Single ticket, $6.15; Special ticket, $5.00;
Excursion ticket, $5.00.

Binghamton, the "Parlor City," is too well known to require any detailed description. It will be sufficient to say that it enjoys the distinction of being as beautiful a city as the Empire State can boast. The city has good water and the great manufacturing industries that have sprung up are due as much to this as to anything else. These industries first brought the railroad here, and so many lines centre in the city that it is fast taking rank among the great railroad centres of this country. The Chenango and Susquehanna Rivers flow through the city and give it a pleasing picturesqueness. Elegant residences and fine streets attract visitors, and a tour of the different districts meets with appreciation and approval.

The grand castle-like building known as the Binghamton State Hospital stands on the summit of an eastern hill, commanding a fine view of the city and the picturesque Susquehanna Valley. The main and other buildings connected with it shelter 1,300 insane inmates and five hundred attendants. This is one of the model institutions of the State.

A tribute to Binghamton's many advantages is the National Commerial Travelers' Home, the corner stone of which was laid October 9, 1894, with impressive ceremonies by the Grand Master of Masons of the State of New York, in the presence of Gov. Flower, of New York, Gov. Pattison, of Pennsylvania, their staffs and many other distinguished persons. The Home stands upon a bluff commanding a view of the entire city, and will cost when completed over $125,000. Mayor Geo. E. Green, of Binghamton, is President of the Commercial Travelers' Home Association of America.

Other public institutions are the new Federal building, just completed at a cost of $150,000; two Orphans' Homes, two Homes for Aged Women; an immense State armory, and two delightful parks

On account of its beauty Binghamton has been justly called "The Parlor City."

At Binghamton the Utica, and Syracuse, Binghamton and New York Divisions branch to the north; the former terminating at Utica, with a branch running from Richfield Junction to Richfield Springs, and the latter running direct to Oswego on Lake Ontario.

The Utica Division.

CHENANGO BRIDGE

215.02 miles from New York; Single ticket, $6.25; Special ticket, $5.00; Excursion ticket, $8.25.

CHENANGO FORKS. *Altitude, 893 ft.*

221.16 miles from New York; Single ticket, $6.25; Special ticket, $5.00; Excursion ticket, $8.60.

The Syracuse, Binghamton and New York Division branches here from the Utica Division. The "Forks" is an agricultural district, with a great many dairies. Considerable cheese is manufactured there.

WILLARDS.

222.15 miles from New York; Single ticket, $6.25; Special ticket, $5.00; Excursion ticket, $8.65.

GREENE. *Altitude, 937 ft.*

229.26 miles from New York; Single ticket, $6.25; Special ticket, $5.00; Excursion ticket, $8.80.

The railroad now enters the enchanting valley of the Chenango. This thriving village is prettily situated at the base of high hills, and the surroundings are delightful. Many industries, as well as good schools, thrive, churches are numerous, and a weekly newspaper is issued.

BRISBIN.

234.98 miles from New York; Single ticket, $6.25; Special ticket, $5.00; Excursion ticket, $8.85.

COVENTRY.

238.26 miles from New York ; Single ticket, $6.25 ; Special ticket, $5.00 ;
Excursion ticket, $8.90.

Coventry is a small village, with all the characteristics of a good agricultural section.

OXFORD. *Altitude, 980 ft.*

242.94 miles from New York ; Single ticket, $6.25 ; Special ticket, $5.00 ;
Excursion ticket, $9.00.

Oxford is a fine old town that boasts of a century's growth.
There are many springs in the surrounding hills which, by log conduits, supply the town with an abundance of pure water. The Chenango River, affording some choice scenery, flows through the valley, and around the base of the mountains. Nearly all the farms make a specialty of dairy produce. The cheese factories consume a very large portion of the milk supply of the district. The factories here are numerous and successful. Oxford possesses churches of all denominations, one or two schools, and one academy.

NORWICH. *Altitude, 1,014 ft.*

251.05 miles from New York ; Single ticket, $6.50 ; Special ticket, $5.00 ;
Excursion ticket, $9.00.

This is one of the most flourishing towns in Southern New York, having the advantages of water power on the Chenango River, and of ready markets north and south. The industries are miscellaneous and abundant. The manufacturing of dairy products being by no means the most important of them. As a resort, Norwich has long been famous. Six miles from the town, and along a good road, is Chenango Lake, a romantic sheet of water, possessing charming scenery and plenty of game fish. The Chenango River also is inviting to anglers. All the desirable features of civilization and good society exist in the village, and to this condition its thrift and prosperity may be attributed.

NORTH NORWICH.

257.09 miles from New York ; Single ticket, $6.50 ; Special ticket, $5.00 ;
Excursion ticket, $9.35.

SHERBURNE. *Altitude, 1,040 ft.*

262.11 miles from New York ; Single ticket, $6.50 ; Special ticket, $5.00 ;
Excursion ticket, $9.70.

Nature here is in her element, and one fond of her must be constantly in motion to enjoy her to the full. Among the attractions are Madison Pond, eight miles distant, a magnificent and transparent sheet of water where fish abound, and Mad Brook, a resort full of romantic beauty, a mile away ; then too there is a waterfall of sixty feet into a chasm, the sides of which rise one hundred feet on either side, and at the foot of these falls is a sulphur spring. Unrivalled scenery awaits the tourist from Pratt's and Hunt's mountains. The town is full of commercial enterprises, schools, churches, lodges, etc., and is surrounded by a remarkably fine agricultural region.

EARLVILLE. *Altitude, 1,107 ft.*

267.29 miles from New York; Single ticket, $6.60; Special ticket, $5.00.

Situated on the east branch of the Chenango River, on the line of Chenango and Madison counties, this pretty village offers unusual inducements to the summer tourist. It is in the midst of picturesque surroundings, fertile farms and charming drives. The railroad station is one mile away. Hamilton, with its well-established Colgate University, is six miles distant.

POOLVILLE. *Altitude, 1,100 ft.*

269.75 miles from New York; Single ticket, $6.65; Special ticket, $5.00.

HUBBARDSVILLE. *Altitude, 1,211 ft.*

273.98 miles from New York; Single ticket, $6.75; Special ticket, $5.00.

Situated on the east branch of the Chenango River, Hubbardsville is noted for the cultivation of hops and for dairy produce, these being the most important of its industries. The village lies at the head of the Chenango Valley. This is also the station for East Hamilton, half a mile distant.

NORTH BROOKFIELD. *Altitude, 1,182 ft.*

277.81 miles from New York; Single ticket, $6.85; Special ticket, $5.00.

This town of less than a thousand inhabitants is as busy a one for its size as the State can boast. It possesses saw mills, flour mills, wagon and sleigh manufactories, and quantities of hay, hops, cereals, and dairy products are shipped from here daily. It is located on the east branch of the Chenango River.

SANGERFIELD CENTRE. *Altitude, 1,190 ft.*

282.18 miles from New York; Single ticket, $6.95; Special ticket, $5.00.

WATERVILLE. *Altitude, 1,246 ft.*

283.44 miles from New York; Single ticket, $7.00; Special ticket, $5.00.

The town is situated on Oriskany Creek, in Oneida County. It is famous for its beautiful location, its fine society, churches and schools, and the extent of its manufacturing and dairy interests.

MARSHALL.

286.72 miles from New York; Single ticket, $7.10; Special ticket, $5.00.

PARIS. *Altitude, 1,422 ft.*

287.47 miles from New York; Single ticket, $7.10; Special ticket, $5.00.

Along the Richfield Branch.

On reaching RICHFIELD JUNCTION, which is four miles west of Paris, the Richfield Branch begins. It is 22 miles long, and the traveler's happiest thought is to arrive at Richfield Springs, one of the famous and most delightful watering places. Along this line a number of pretty little towns may be found, and the general character of the country is charming and interesting. The first station is

BRIDGEWATER. *Altitude, 1,184 ft.*
256.10 miles from New York ; Single ticket, $7.35 ; Special ticket, $5.15

At this point connection is made for points on the line of the Unadilla Valley Railway—viz.: " River Forks,," which is the station for " Unadilla Forks," Leonardsville, West Edmeston, Sweets, South Edmeston, New Berlin and points further south in the Unadilla Valley, down to its junction with the Susquehanna River by means of the Ontario & Western Railroad (New Berlin Branch).

The Unadilla Valley is famed for the salubrity of its climate ; although the days are warm the nights are always cool, and the broad Valley dotted here and there with blooded cattle grazing peacefully presents a scene of extreme beauty. Drouth is never known here, and the grass and foliage always maintain a beautiful green during the Summer season.

The beautiful Unadilla River flows the entire length of the Valley, winding in and out among oziers and willows with peaceful current.

The whole Valley, about forty (40) miles in length, is an attractive place for Summer residences.

There are no mosquitoes or other insect pests, and the Unadilla Valley Railway Company purposes inaugurating an especially good service for Summer residents.

Butternut Falls, between Leonardsville and West Edmeston, is a beautiful place containing a magnificent cascade and fine picnic grounds.

All of the hamlets on this line are beautiful little spots, and New Berlin, in the middle of the Valley, is, on account of its accessibility to Cooperstown and other well-known resorts, an attractive and pleasant place with historic interests of its own for Summer tourists. The drives hereabouts are endless and beautiful.

UNADILLA FORKS. *Altitude, 1,191 ft.*
296.97 miles from New York ; Single ticket, $7.35 ; Special ticket, $5.15.

WEST WINFIELD. *Altitude, 1,185 ft.*
299.13 miles from New York ; Single ticket, $7.40 ; Special ticket, $5.25.

This is a prosperous village of about 700 inhabitants, pleasantly situated in a valley which is considerably above the Mohawk River. The place thrives on account of its large manufacturing interests, and the industry and high moral standing of the community at large. Its agricultural and dairy interests are of great importance. Several churches, schools, and one academy are maintained, and a weekly paper is published. A branch of the Unadilla River flows through the village and furnishes power for the factories.

EAST WINFIELD. *Altitude, 1,191 ft.*
301.08 miles from New York ; Single ticket, $7.45 ; Special ticket, $5.30.

CEDARVILLE.

303.14 miles from New York; Single ticket, $7.50; Special ticket, $5.35.

The town, like its neighbors, the Winfields, is situated in Herkimer County, and is about two miles from the railroad station. Its location, at the head of a creek that flows into the Mohawk, lends it a romantic appearance. The Unadilla River rises two miles east, and affords excellent sport for anglers. Cheese-making is the principal industry. Several natural caves and springs may be found at Litchfield Hill, two miles away.

MILLER'S MILLS. *Altitude, 1,353 ft.*

304.83 miles from New York; Single ticket, $7.55; Special ticket, $5.40.

SOUTH COLUMBIA. *Altitude, 1,451 ft.*

309.55 miles from New York; Single ticket, $7.70; Special ticket, $5.55.

RICHFIELD SPRINGS. *Altitude, 1,750 ft.*

313.19 miles from New York; Single ticket, $7.80; Special ticket, $5.65; Excursion ticket, $10.75.

By steady advancement Richfield Springs has come to rank as one of the first watering-places in the country. The village has been fitted by nature for an ideal summer resort. With its elevation of 1,750 feet above the sea, nestles among the mountains of Otsego County, near the centre of New York State, it has every natural advantage to make it a charming place in which to spend the summer.

The summer season railroad connections make this spot of easy access from New York, as Pullman parlor car trains run to and fro every night and morning. The trip by the Delaware, Lackawanna and Western Railroad is through picturesque scenery, making the day journey desirable. Connections are made from Washington and Philadelphia, so as to render this the most desirable route from the south and southwest to Richfield Springs. The Otsego Stage and Steamboat Company make direct connections with through trains on the Delaware, Lackawanna and Western Railroad for Cooperstown during the summer season.

The scenery in and about Richfield Springs is captivating. The wooded hills and cultivated plains spread a landscape which is truly inspiring to look upon, and wonderfully invigorating to pass through.

Not the least important feature at this place is the number of drives through a picturesque country, upon well-cared-for roads, which enhance the pleasure, and make this pastime very popular with the guests. Among others are the following: To Mount Otsego, Otsego Lake, Cooperstown, the Mohawk Valley and Richard Croker's beautiful Stock Farm, Henderson Home; the one most popular of all is around Canadarago Lake, a distance of twelve miles over a road as smooth as a floor. Canadarago Lake is a delightful place for boating and fishing. A pleasure steamer plies daily for public or private accommodation. The main dock is but one mile from the village.

The erection of one of the most complete bathing establishments in the world, a few years since, has made the place famous as a water cure and bathing resort. The celebrated White Sulphur Spring supplies the new bathing establishment with mineral water, which is used for baths as well as for beverages, with almost incredible results in healing and restoring the feeble and infirm. Several prominent medical societies have met here during the past few years, and their resolutions concerning the baths have always been commendatory.

The hotels and boarding houses are good and numerous, and several may be found along the shores of Canadarago Lake. Churches of various denominations flourish, and the Springs boast of a daily paper.

Returning again to the Utica Division, the first station beyond Richfield Junction is

CLAYVILLE.
Altitude, 1,129 ft.

293.71 miles from New York ; Single ticket, $7.25 ; Special ticket, $5.00.

SAUQUOIT.
295.72 miles from New York ; Single ticket, $7.30 ; Special ticket, $5.00.

The village is situated on Sauquoit Creek, or River, a swift stream of crystal water, which has been found to be well adapted for brewing and dyeing purposes, among other uses. There are cotton, paper, saw and flour mills here, and one or two cheese factories.

CHADWICKS.
Altitude, 756 ft.

297.17 miles from New York ; Single ticket, $7.35 ; Special ticket, $5.00.

WASHINGTON MILLS.
Altitude, 634 ft.

299.31 miles from New York ; Single ticket, $7.40 ; Special ticket, $5.00.

NEW HARTFORD.
Altitude, 563 ft.

300.91 miles from New York ; Single ticket, $7.45 ; Special ticket, $5.00.

UTICA.
Altitude 410 ft.

304.92 miles from New York ; Single ticket, $7.60 ; Special ticket, $5.00.

This substantially built city ranks among the largest and most prosperous in the Empire State. It is famous for the number of its cotton mills, some of which are the largest in the world. Various industries are carried on here on a large scale, Utica being among the greatest of our manufacturing cities.

MASONIC HOME, UTICA, N. Y.

MASONIC SCHOOL, UTICA, N. Y.

Every convenience and commercial interest to be found in any first class city exists here. It is particularly noted for the number of its fine churches, schools and public buildings, and possesses also many elegant residences and beautiful streets. A palatial Masonic Home has recently been erected here by the Masonic fraternity of the State of New York and a large school in connection with the Home, for the orphans and other children of the fraternity.

Syracuse, Binghamton and New York R. R. and Oswego and Syracuse Division.

BARKER. *Altitude, 953 ft.*
226.04 miles from New York ; Single ticket, $6.15 ; Special ticket, $5.15 ;
Excursion ticket, $8.95.

WHITNEY'S POINT. *Altitude, 953 ft.*
230.44 miles from New York ; Single ticket, $6.55 ; Special ticket, $5.25 ;
Excursion ticket, $9.15.

LISLE. *Altitude, 960 ft.*
232.88 miles from New York ; Single ticket, $6.60 ; Special ticket, $5.30 ;
Excursion ticket, $9.20.

KILLAWOG. *Altitude, 998 ft.*
236.23 miles from New York ; Single ticket, $6.70 ; Special ticket, $5.35 ;
Excursion ticket, $9.35.

MARATHON. *Altitude, 1,058 ft.*
239.13 miles from New York ; Single ticket, $6.80 ; Special ticket, $5.45 ;
Excursion ticket, $9.50.

This thriving incorporated town, with many advantages generally enjoyed only by larger places, is situated in Cortland County. Established in the midst of an agricultural region, it is blessed with an abundance of farm and fruit produce, besides which it possesses numerous factories, mills and tanneries. There are many good hotels, churches and schools.

MESSENGERVILLE.
243.03 miles from New York ; Single ticket, $6.90 ; Special ticket, $5.55 ;
Excursion ticket, $9.65.

BLODGETT'S MILLS. *Altitude, 1,079 ft.*
249.28 miles from New York ; Single ticket, $7.00 ; Special ticket, $5.70 ;
Excursion ticket, $9.90.

CORTLAND. *Altitude, 1,111 ft.*
252.82 miles from New York ; Single ticket, $7.05 ; Special ticket, $5.80 ;
Excursion ticket, $10.00.

Cortland is a busy town, located on a beautiful river with a troublesome name, the Tioughnioga, which furnishes water power to many of the mills. A number of factories and foundries are to be found here, with wagon-making for the chief industry. The production of butter and cheese is also extensively carried on. The town is liberally supplied with churches, public and private schools; not the least among the latter being the State Normal School. Several newspapers thrive, and the best hotels are open the year round.

HOMER. *Altitude, 1,136 ft.*
255.49 miles from New York ; Single ticket, $7.05 ; Special ticket, $5.85 ;
Excursion ticket, $10.00.

Situated 33 miles south of Syracuse and 253 miles from New York, is one of the earliest settled towns in Cortland County. Its population is about 4,000. Main, a long, broad street, is bordered upon each side with rows of beautiful shade trees, it has broad well-paved walks, is lighted by electricity, and has an electric street railway. Each side is well-built up, there being three hotels, two national banks, several large and handsome brick business blocks, four churches, and a large, fine new academy employing fourteen teachers. It has a gravelly soil, filled with the purest water, and has a pure, healthful and bracing air, a place free from malaria and mosquitoes. It has telephones, telegraph and express connections, many enterprising manufacturing establishments, several flour mills, extensive water works, and a well-equipped fire department. It has, in short, all that which goes to make up the requirements of a progressive, active, thriving village. It is healthful and pleasant for summer residents or for those seeking a permanent home, all the surroundings that go to make a home attractive and satisfactory being ever present and always gratifying.

LITTLE YORK. *Altitude, 1,159 ft.*
259.75 miles from New York ; Single ticket, $7.10 ; Special ticket, $5.95 ,
Excursion ticket, $10.00.

PREBLE. *Altitude, 1,193 ft.*
262.46 miles from New York ; Single ticket, $7.10 ; Special ticket, $6.05 ;
Excursion ticket, $10.00.

The place is named after Commodore Preble, of naval renown. It is noted for the number of its dairies, and the excellence of its butter and cheese. By it flows the Tioughnioga River. The neighborhood is celebrated for its noble mountains, some of which stand 1,700 feet above sea level, and for its numerous lakes that afford splendid fishing. They are Hoag, Crooked, Green, Goodell and Little York lakes, each a beautiful sheet of water, teeming with fish. The valley is two miles wide at Preble, and the drives through it are delightful.

TULLY. *Altitude, 1,248 ft.*
267.16 miles from New York ; Single ticket, $7.15 ; Special ticket, $6.06 ;
Excursion ticket, $10.00.

TULLY LAKE PARK.

This popular summer resort lies one and a half miles south of Tully, and borders on Big Lake, which is a mile long and a quarter that distance wide. This lake is one of a chain of seven whose picturesqueness and beauty rival those of Killarney. These lakes are stocked with pickerel, bass and perch, and the fishing is excellent throughout the entire summer.

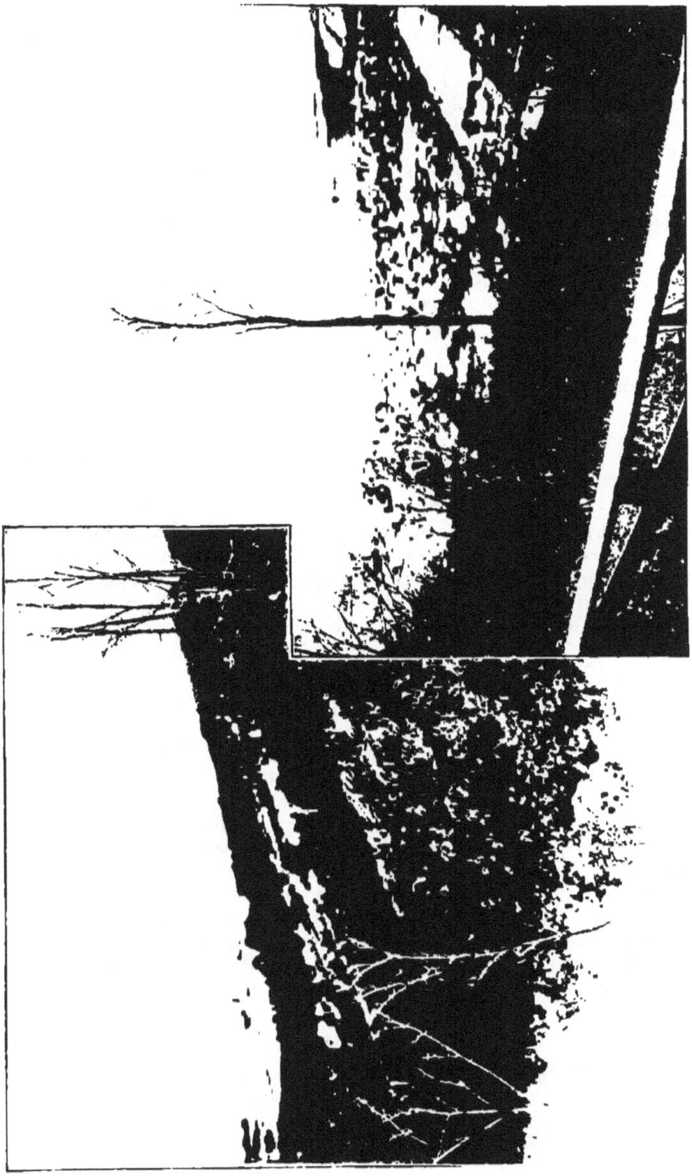

DELAWARE, LACKAWANNA & WESTERN R. R.

GENESEE VALLEY AT DANSVILLE, N. Y.

Tully Lake Park was organized and is managed upon the plan of the Thousand Island Park at Clayton. It has thirty cottages built and owned by residents of Syracuse and New York city. Besides this, there is a hotel large enough to accommodate one hundred guests.

During the months of July and August the Central New York Assembly holds its annual sessions on the shore of Big Lake, opposite the Park. The Assembly is patterned after the famous Chautauqua, and many speakers of national renown have been engaged for the coming season.

Tully Lake Park is famed for its high altitude, and is essentially a place where persons seeking rest and harmless recreation will find themselves thoroughly satisfied and at home.

APULIA. *Altitude, 1,240 ft.*

269.76 miles from New York ; Single ticket, $7.15 ; Special ticket, $6.06 ; Excursion ticket, $10.25.

ONATIVIA.

274.86 miles from New York ; Single ticket, $7.20 ; Special ticket, $6.06 ; Excursion ticket, $10.50.

JAMESVILLE. *Altitude, 585 ft.*

282.58 miles from New York ; Single ticket, $7.20 ; Special ticket, $6.06 ; Excursion ticket, $10.75.

The size of the four above-named towns is limited, each having the general characteristics of others in this section. They are centres of agricultural districts with a fertile soil, a healthy climate, scenery of more than ordinary attraction, and with an industrious and thriving population. The entire region is worthy of attention, and a trip through here will repay the tourist for his exertions.

SYRACUSE. *Altitude, 398 ft.*

289.22 miles from New York ; Single ticket, $7.25 Special ticket, $6.06 ; Excursion ticket, $11.00.

The capital of Onondaga County, Syracuse, is beautifully situated on Onondaga Lake, around which the great salt mines are centered. Syracuse is as famous as Droitwich for its salt, and its annual shipments are enormous. It is one of the chief cities on the Erie Canal, to which it furnishes a large amount of commerce. The iron, beer, pottery, brick, glass and cutlery industries also play an important part in the city's prosperity.

There are a great many hotels, churches and schools in the city. Here is also located the University of Syracuse. The Lackawanna Railroad finds Syracuse one of its largest distributing points for coal. The company here delivers upwards of half a million tons annually, part of which is shipped by canals and connecting railroads.

Taking it as city and business centre, Syracuse is among the most important in the United States.

LAKE SIDE. *Altitude, 398 ft.*

293.18 miles from New York ; Single ticket, $7.35 ; Special ticket, $6.15 ; Excursion ticket, $11.10.

PLEASANT BEACH. *Altitude, 372 ft.*

294.53 miles from New York.

F. BOOSS & BRO.

ESTABLISHED 1853.

IMPORTERS AND MAKERS OF

FINE FURS

Gold Medal,
Paris, 1878.

Highest Award,
Centennial, 1876.

45th SEASON.

SPECIALTIES IN

SEAL SKIN GARMENTS

And Newest Designs in Capes and Collarettes.

EVERYTHING IN FURS.

Furs taken on Storage during the Summer months. Repairs made during the Summer season at greatly reduced rates.

Beautiful Combinations in Fur Collarettes for Mountain and Seashore Wear.

F. BOOSS & BRO.,
449 BROADWAY, 26 MERCER ST., NEW YORK CITY.

Grand Street "L" Station.   TELEPHONE, 388 SPRING.

CATALOGUES MAILED ON APPLICATION.

Scranton Coal

Is mined and transported to market by the Delaware, Lackawanna & Western Railroad . . . . IT IS THE BEST

Holden & Sons

Agents

SYRACUSE, N. Y.
UTICA, N. Y.
OSWEGO, N. Y.

THE Lackawanna Nickel Plate Route

THROUGH BUFFET SLEEPING CARS

NEW YORK · TO · CHICAGO

WITHOUT CHANGE

SHORTEST ROUTE ∻ FASTEST TIME
LOWEST RATES ∻ ∻ ∻ ∻ ∻ ∻ ∻
URSURPASSED DINING CAR SERVICE

CALL ON AGENTS D., L. & W. R. R. FOR ALL INFORMATION, OR ADDRESS

F. J. MOORE, General Agent, Nickel Plate Road
23 Exchange St., Buffalo, N. Y.

A. W. JOHNSTON, General Superintendent   B. F. HORNER, General Passenger Agent
CLEVELAND, OHIO

MAPLE BAY.
295.76 miles from New York.

STILES. *Altitude, 380 ft.*
296.67 miles from New York; Single ticket, $7.45; Special ticket, $6.25;
Excursion ticket, $11.20.

BALDWINSVILLE. *Altitude, 389 ft.*
301.02 miles from New York; Single ticket, $7.50; Special ticket, $6.30;
Excursion ticket, $11.25.

This old town, originally called Columbia, and later Baldwin's Bridge, until the Post Office Department compromised on the present name, represents one of the most intelligent communities in Central New York. It possesses many churches and schools, and a good paper. Baldwinsville was settled in 1797 by Dr. James C. Baldwin, and it derives its name from him. It is one of the pleasantest spots in Onondaga County, and is located on the Seneca River, which furnishes several mills and factories with power. A fine grade of cheese is made here, and the neighborhood is justly celebrated for its good dairies and agricultural products. Fishing in Mass Lake is excellent.

LAMSONS. *Altitude, 394 ft.*
305.97 miles from New York; Single ticket, $7.60; Special ticket, $6.40;
Excursion ticket, $11.35.

Lamsons is given up to tanneries and a few other mills, and plays no very important part as a village. The village of Phenix, three and a half miles distant, is a very pretty place. It lies on the east bank of the Oswego River, and on the Oswego and Syracuse Canal. The population is over 2,000, and the village contains several churches, good schools and hotels.

SOUTH GRANBY. *Altitude, 370 ft.*
308.54 miles from New York; Single ticket, $7.65; Special ticket, $6.45;
Excursion ticket, $11.40.

FULTON. *Altitude, 386 ft.*
313.14 miles from New York; Single ticket, $7.75; Special ticket, $6.50;
Excursion ticket, $11.50.

An important town in Oswego County, with a population of over 10,000. It is situated on the Oswego River, twelve miles from its mouth, and has magnificent water power. Milling is the chief industry, and over 1,500 barrels of grain a day are milled. Next in importance come the cheese and dairy interests, which are also large. It is estimated that the annual shipment of the products of these industries is over 500 tons. Besides these, several tanneries, saw mills and foundries flourish here.

Fulton is an excellent place of residence, and possesses many churches of all denominations, public and private schools, and two or more weekly papers. Lake Neahtawanta is close to the railroad station, and the Oswego County fair grounds are near by.

NORTH FULTON. *Altitude, 379 ft.*
314.01 miles from New York; Single ticket, $7.75; Special ticket, $6.50;
Excursion ticket, $11.50.

MINETTO.   *Altitude, 327 ft.*

319.60 miles from New York; Single ticket, $7.90; Special ticket, $6.50; Excursion ticket, $12.00.

OSWEGO.   *Altitude, 297 ft.*

324.20 miles from New York; Single ticket, $7.95; Special ticket, $6.50; Excursion ticket, $12.00.

Oswego is the terminus of the division, and a pretty city it is. Situated on the shore of Lake Ontario, which appears like a mighty ocean, Oswego is the city of "Silver Gloss Starch," and as such it is known on account of the immense quantity of this commodity that it manufactures annually. The Oswego River divides the

BURTE POINT, OSWEGO, N. Y.

city and affords elegant residence sites on both shores. The lake front is also a popular place for private dwellings. Considering that the canal, lake and several lines of railroad furnish shipping facilities, it is not to be wondered at that Oswego is a prosperous and growing city. It has fine commercial institutions, banks, public buildings, and almost unlimited manufacturing industries. As a place of residence it has the appearance of an elegant and refined suburb, and the breezes from the lake render it delightfully cool and invigorating. In summer, the temperature, at the hottest, rarely exceeds 70°.

The celebrated Deep Rock Spring is situated here, and, for the accommodation of tourists and invalids, a fine hotel has been erected near it.

As far back as 1732 the Assembly at Albany appropriated moneys and appointed agents and interpreters to look after the sustaining of the trading post called Oswego. The French and English had severe engagements for its possession, as many as twenty thousand troops being massed here at one time. Some gallant attacks on the forts occurred, and many lives were sacrificed. In 1814 the British appeared off

Oswego, and, landing a land force, captured the city after a desperate struggle, taking some of its prominent citizens prisoners of war, the last of whom have but recently been laid to rest. Fort Ontario, now garrisoned by a company of the 9th Infantry, stands in a commanding position on a high bank on the east side of the river. The view of Lake Ontario from the ramparts is expansive and beautiful. The Life Saving Station nestles at the foot of the fort bank. An English lady writing to friends in the British Empire in 1848, thus describes the climate at Oswego : "When winter had once set in Oswego became a perfect Siberia. At length spring returned with its flowers, and converted our Siberia into an uncultivated Eden, rich in all the majestic charms of sublime scenery and primeval beauty and fertility. If ever the fond illusions of poets and philosophers, that Atlantis, that new Arcadia, that safe and serene Utopia, where ideal quiet and happiness have so often charmed theory, if ever this dream of social bliss, in some new planted region is to be realized, this unrivaled scene of grandeur and fertility bids fairest to be the place of its abode. Here the climate is serene and equal, the vigorous winters that brace the frame and call forth the power of mind and body to prepare for its approach are succeeded by a spring so rapid, the exuberance of vernal bloom bursts forth so suddenly after disappearance of those deep snows which cherish and fructify the earth, that the change seems like a magical delusion."

The plant of the Standard Oil Co.'s Shook factory, the Diamond Match Factory, the Oswego Starch Factory, and the Oswego Shade Cloth Company are among the largest institutions of their kind in the world. Malt, boilers and engines are manufactured in large quantities, and shipped to all parts of the globe. Millions of feet of Canadian lumber are received during the season of navigation. A new electric road has been constructed from the heart of the city to a beautiful summer retreat, three miles west, running on the lake side of the boulevard ; the view, as the summit of the boulevard hill is reached, and the descent begins, baffles description.

The Buffalo Division.

The tourist is now cordially invited to start afresh at Binghamton, where the Buffalo Division commences, and continue the journey westward. The first station is

LESTERSHIRE. *Altitude, 848 ft.*
212.55 miles from New York ; Single ticket, $6.20; Special ticket, $5 05 ; Excursion ticket. $8.10.

Of this place it may be said, that if humanity goes about barefoot, it is not because there is insufficient foot-wear in town. Here the manufacture of boots and shoes is more than equal to all the other industries combined.

WILLOW POINT. *Altitude, 848 ft.*
214.77 miles from New York ; Single ticket, $6.30 ; Special ticket, $5.15 ; Excursion ticket. $8.25.

VESTAL. *Altitude, 828 ft.*

217.90 miles from New York; Single ticket, $6.30; Special ticket, $5.25; Excursion ticket, $8.40.

APALACHIN. *Altitude, 819 ft.*

223.79 miles from New York; Single ticket, $6.50; Special ticket, $5.40; Excursion ticket, $8.60.

OWEGO. *Altitude, 819 ft.*

230.57 miles from New York; Single ticket, $6.60; Special ticket, $5.50; Excursion ticket, $8.85.

Owego is the capital of Tioga County. It is a pretty town with extensive agricultural interests, and many dairies and cheese factories. The Susquehanna River and several creeks flowing through the town furnish motive power for a number of manufactories and mills. It has churches of all denominations, many schools, and several bright newspapers. Owego was once the home of N. P. Willis, the poet, who for a quarter of a century, drew in from the romantic hills and valleys surrounding the town, much of the inspiration which made his verses famous the world over.

One mile from station is situated the well-known old private retreat for the insane and nervous, Glenmary, where so many of the afflicted have been restored to health and usefulness.

The Cayuga Division.

At Owego this division begins and runs northward to Ithaca, thirty-four miles. The first station is

CATTATONK. *Altitude, 859 ft.*

235.80 miles from New York; Single ticket, $6.75; Special ticket, $5.65; Excursion ticket, $9.15.

A small settlement on Cattatonk Creek, where agriculture takes precedence over everything else.

CANDOR. *Altitude, 900 ft.*

241.50 miles from New York; Single ticket, $6.90; Special ticket, $5.80; Excursion ticket, $9.45.

Candor is a flourishing little town of about 2,000 inhabitants, and is situated on Cattatonk Creek. It is famous for the number of its manufacturing industries. Churches of all denominations are here established, as well as a first-class newspaper. The town has grown rapidly, and shows a decided spirit of enterprise. This is the station for Spencer Springs.

WILLSEYVILLE.   *Altitude, 953 ft.*

245.55 miles from New York ; Single ticket, $7.05 ; Special ticket, $5.05 ;
Excursion ticket, $9.75.

CAROLINE.   *Altitude, 980 ft.*

252.42 miles from New York ; Single ticket, $7.30 ; Special ticket, $6.10 ;
Excursion ticket, $10.25.

ITHACA.   *Altitude, 307 ft.*

264.57 miles from New York ; Single ticket, $7.50 ; Special ticket, $6.10 ;
Excursion ticket, $10.50.

In all probability nature has been more lavish with her gifts in the vicinity of Ithaca than in any other one place in the Empire State. A great lake, a magnificent region where health and happiness abide, and where the eyes of mankind can feast until the soul is content and the mind is benumbed with bewilderment.

Ithaca has been called the "region of cascades," and the name is certainly appropriate to the surroundings. It would seem as though the hand of nature has busied itself to an unusual extent in carving out of the rocks the irregular crevices through which the silvery streams of crystal water plunge and turn until they reach their natural level. In addition may be found a great many ravines which have a peculiar interest attached to them. The delightful works of nature seem to partake of a form of phenomena, and are all the more interesting on that account. There are 96 falls by actual count which vary in height from 5 to 340 feet. One mile from the village is Ithaca Falls, 160 feet high, or 7 feet less than Niagara. The width of the fall is 150 feet. Nine miles from Ithaca are the world-famed Taughannock Falls, that glory in being 48 feet higher than Niagara.

All the falls are not directly within the town boundry, but there are fifteen close by, the height of each of which is over 100 feet. It is generally conceded that Cascadilla and Fall Creeks furnish the most enchanting of all the waterfall scenery. Taughannock Falls is the highest in the State, being 215 feet, while the rock rises 145 feet above it. The falls and surrounding scenery are almost unapproached for magnificence.

Ithaca is situated at the head of Cayuga Lake, and has a population of 12,000. It is principally famous as the seat of Cornell University, founded by Ezra Cornell, whose idea is best expressed by his own words : " I would found an institution where any person can find instruction in any study." The University has turned out many a learned scholar, and is too well known to require a detailed description.

Cayuga Lake is one of the finest inland lakes that makes Central New York so famous as a summer resort. It is forty miles long and lies between high hills that stretch along its entire length, and far beyond to the south. It is, also, one of the most magnificent lakes in this country, clear and of great depth, and surrounded with the most entrancing scenery. Lake fishing, which is always a delightful pastime, is here enjoyed every season by many enthusiastic fishermen who invariably catch sufficient lake trout, bass, etc., to convince them that old Cayuga Lake is the veritable Mecca of anglers.

The Buffalo Division.—Continued.

After passing Owego the next station is

LOUNSBURY. *Altitude, 807 ft.*
235.37 miles from New York; Single ticket, $6.70; Special ticket, $5.55;
Excursion ticket, $9.00.

This is a small town, pleasantly situated, and is desirable as a resort for city people who enjoy quiet and good air. The valley along this section is famous for the cultivation of tobacco, and it is a common sight to gaze upon plants growing upwards of six feet high. The industry of drying and curing the "weed" is both large and profitable.

NICHOLS. *Altitude, 789 ft.*
238.83 miles from New York; Single ticket, $6.75; Special ticket, $5.60;
Excursion ticket, $9.15.

A famous resort for fishermen. The Susquehanna River, at this point, furnishes its best fishing grounds.

LITCHFIELD. *Altitude, 797 ft.*
244.62 miles from New York; Single ticket, $6.85; Special ticket, $5.70;
Excursion ticket, $9.40.

WAVERLY. *Altitude, 833 ft.*
248.99 miles from New York; Single ticket, $6.95; Special ticket, $5.75;
Excursion ticket, $9.60.

This town has its principal importance in being at a junction of the Lehigh Valley and New York, Lake Erie and Western Railroads. At Athens, four miles distant, is located the immense plant of the Union Bridge Works.

WILLIWANNA. *Altitude, 801 ft.*
253.39 miles from New York; Single ticket, $7.00; Special ticket, $5.85;
Excursion ticket, $9.75.

LOWMANSVILLE. *Altitude, 828 ft.*
260.01 miles from New York; Single ticket, $7.15; Special ticket, $5.90;
Excursion ticket, $10.00.

Just back of this place, standing upon a towering hill, can be seen the monument erected in honor of Gen. Sullivan, who in the troublesome times of 1776 defeated the allied Indian forces near that spot.

ELMIRA. *Altitude, 857 ft.*
266.75 miles from New York; Single ticket, $7.25; Special ticket, $6.10;
Excursion ticket, $10.45.

Situated in the broad and fertile valley of the Chemung, surrounded by well-wooded hills rising from four to six hundred feet, this city presents many attractions to those seeking pleasure, health or even business.

Here are gathered about 42,500 people, among whom are many of State and national reputation. The streets are shaded by grand old trees; the homes are comfortable and attractive, and well-kept lawns on every side are evidences of thrift and culture.

Elmira is a city of churches; among the most notable of all the denominations is the Congregational Park Church, under the pastorship of the Rev. Thos. K. Beecher. The First Baptist Church is also new, and of modern architecture.

The New York State Reformatory, situated on a broad plateau at the foot of the western hills, is of much interest as illustrative of real reformation among the younger class of criminals. In itself, both in architecture and location, it is a striking building, and well repays one for a few hours' visit.

ELDRIDGE PARK, ELMIRA, N Y

Of parks there are four. The most important is "Eldridge Park," in the northern portion of the city. This contains about 40 acres, has a natural lake of crystal water, half a mile in circumference, and many miles of fine drives and walks. It also has pavilions, summer houses, a bear pit, and all the requisites of first-class pleasure grounds, which it is, not only for the people of Elmira, but also for those of many cities in the surrounding country. During the season of 1895 over 100,000 excursionists visited the various parks of Elmira.

Elmira Heights, a suberb of Elmira, is a bustling industrial town of 5,000 inhabitants engaged in the manufacture of window glass, bridges, bicycles, cotton goods and a dozen other things. All street car lines give transfers to Elmira Heights.

Here are about 20 miles of electric car roads running to and fro from all parts, as well as to the thriving village of Horseheads, six miles north.

In the northwestern part of the city is the Elmira College for Women. This educational institution is among the first in the land. Its location is high and healthy,

SCENE ON THE CHEMUNG, NEAR ELMIRA, N. Y.

and its grounds spacious. On East Hill, at an elevation of 200 feet, stands the Gleason Sanitarium, where invalids may find skilled medical care, or the pleasure seeker a quiet summer home.

The charming valley, at this point, is largely devoted to the culture of tobacco, and large crops are annually raised; as are also vegetables of the finest quality. The "hill country" is given up to dairies and the quality of their butter is gaining an enviable reputation.

ALONG THE CHEMUNG RIVER, ELMIRA, N. Y.

The Chemung, an Indian word which means "big horn," is a shallow stream, with a succession of rapids and long, still pools, known as "The Eddys." Above the city are some particularly fine bits of scenery, as the hills are very abrupt and wooded to the water's edge. Splendid camping grounds are to be found, near which run good springs of clear water, and much of this best of summer pastime is indulged in along the picturesque banks. Black bass fishing is also good. A fair number of manufactories are located here, and various industries are represented. Much material is shipped annually to all points of the surrounding country.

HORSEHEADS. *Altitude, 864 ft.*

271.11 miles from New York; Single ticket, $7.30; Special ticket, $6.10; Excursion ticket, $10.45.

BIG FLATS. *Altitude, 917 ft*

276.66 miles from New York ; Single ticket, $7.40 ; Special ticket, $6.15 ; Excursion ticket, $10.65.

This is the centre of the tobacco raising region.

CORNING. *Altitude, 931 ft.*

282.71 miles from New York ; Single ticket, $7.50 ; Special ticket, $6.25 ; Excursion ticket, $10.90.

This city has gained fame for the extent and excellence of its glass manufactories. It is the junction of the Fall Brook Railway.

PAINTED POST. *Altitude, 969 ft.*

286.08 miles from New York ; Single ticket, $7.55 ; Special ticket, $6.35.

Famous as historical grounds. A monument has just been dedicated in memory of the Indian Chief who made the term famous. It is well worth seeing.

COOPERS. *Altitude, 969 ft.*

288.80 miles from New York ; Single ticket, $7.55 ; Special ticket, $6.35.

CURTIS. *Altitude, 995 ft.*

291.55 miles from New York ; Single ticket, $7.55 ; Special ticket, $6.40.

CAMPBELLS. *Altitude, 1,014 ft.*

293.65 miles from New York ; Single ticket, $9.55 ; Special ticket, $6.45.

SAVONA. *Altitude, 1,059 ft.*

298.10 miles from New York ; Single ticket, $7.60 ; Special ticket, $6.55.

BATH. *Altitude, 1,102 ft.*

303.49 miles from New York ; Single ticket, $7.60 ; Special ticket, $6.60.

Bath is one of the loveliest cities of the plain in all New York. It has a population of 5,000 people, and as the country seat of Steuben, one of the largest counties in the State, it attracts hundreds of strangers every day, either on business or pleasure. The State Soldiers' Home at Bath is a model institution of which not only the State but the nation is justly proud. Here 1,500 old heroes are well cared for. The buildings and grounds are splendidly arrranged for the purpose and are beautiful in design and proportion. The Soldiers' Home band, the dress parade, and the veterans themselves are attractions that draw thousands of people to Bath.

No better fishing can be found in the State than in the surrounding little lakes and cold water streams. It is the center of a sportsman's paradise. At Bath all trains stop at the model dining rooms for lunch, and all passengers to Hammondsport and Lake Keuka make connection here with the B. & H. Railroad at Union Station.

Reports from the Fish Commissioners of the States of New York, Pennsylvania and New Jersey for 1894 and 1895 show that all streams bordering on the Lackawanna have been heavily stocked with all kinds of game and edible fish. No railroad in the world has so many trout streams along its course as the Lackawanna.

NEW YORK STATE SOLDIERS' HOME, BATH, N. Y.

KANONA. *Altitude, 1,145 ft.*
307.37 miles from New York ; Single ticket, $7.65 ; Special ticket, $6.70.

AVOCA. *Altitude, 1,194 ft.*
311.05 miles from New York ; Single ticket, $7.65 ; Special ticket, $6.75.

WALLACE. *Altitude, 1,233 ft.*
313.72 miles from New York ; Single ticket, $7.65 ; Special ticket, $6.80.

COHOCTON. *Altitude, 2,288 ft.*
318.84 miles from New York ; Single ticket, $7.65 ; Special ticket, $6.90.

ATLANTA. *Altitude, 1,319 ft.*
323.31 miles from New York ; Single ticket, $7.68 ; Special ticket, $6.95.

This village is also in the Cohocton Valley. Formerly called Bloods, it was thought that it might prove more prosperous if given a more pleasing name. Atlanta is a shipping point for an abundant supply of grapes which are grown around the village of Naples.

WAYLAND. *Altitude, 1,361 ft.*
329.10 miles from New York ; Single ticket, $7.95 ; Special ticket, $7.00.

We are now at the highest point of the Buffalo Division, and the magnificent view of the valley, with its rich and prosperous farms stretching for miles, invites the tourist to feast upon the grandeur of the landscape; if but for a moment. It is not only on account of the fact that Wayland offers this graceful picture in the large album of Nature that it ranks as a prosperous and interesting neighborhood, but also because husbandry flourishes and is necessarily foremost. Here vacationists will find pure air, plenty of milk, eggs and vegetable produce, together with clear wholesome water. Wayland excells in all these. The Portland Cement Company has a large factory here, which gives the town just enough life to make it agreeable. Passengers make direct connection here for Hornellsville, via Central New York and Western Railroad.

IN THE GENESEE VALLEY.

It is doubtful if the Empire State, famous for the number of its fertile valleys, can offer any other that presents so many charming characteristics of the Genesee. It is a series of magnificent farms, as fertile as any the world produces; it possesses winding rivers and rapid streams that dance in and out of patches of woodland, meeting each other in unexpected ways. The fruit alone that is grown annually in this valley is sufficient to supply almost all the markets of the State; and, as a grain-growing country, it produces more for its size than any other valley in the world. In the spring the air is heavy with the odor of blossoms, and in the fall the red and golden fruit hangs in clusters in the orchard.

PERKINSVILLE. *Altitude, 1,358 ft.*
351.11 miles from New York; Single ticket, $7.75; Special ticket, $7.00.

MILL CREEK BRIDGE, (118 FT.) DANSVILLE, N. Y.

DANSVILLE. *Altitude, 1,025 ft.*
336.38 miles from New York; Single ticket, $8.00; Special ticket, $7.00.
Excursion ticket $13.30.

The approach to Dansville, from either direction, is through a country abounding in picturesque scenery, which apparently culminates in the surroundings of this hill-encircled town. Lying 400 feet below the railroad, it is enclosed on three sides by an amphitheatre of hills which, on either hand, stretch far away and are lost on the dis-

THE SANATORIUM, DANSVILLE, N. Y.

GENESEE VALLEY FROM THE SANATORIUM, DANSVILLE, N. Y.

tant horizon. Like a vast living panorama, hundreds of square miles of valley and hill are spread out before the traveler, who is both surprised and delighted with the beauty of a picture of surpassing loveliness, rarely equalled in this or any foreign land. Nature is here more gently picturesque than rugged or grand. Although the hills rise upwards of a thousand feet, they are dotted almost to their summits with farms, vineyards and grain fields, which alternate with masses of evergreen and stretches of timber land.

On nearer acquaintance many hidden attractions are discovered by the artist and the lover of the beautiful—wild, rocky ravines, with precipitous sides and crystal cascades, deep gorges set with pine and hemlock, numerous mountain streams and tangled undergrowth, where the silence of the forest is broken only by the song of the bird or the whirr of the partridge. Stony Brook Glen, similar in its rocky formation and waterfalls to Watkins Glen, a favorite resort, is two miles from the town ; winding roads lead over the hills in every direction, and provide charming walks and drives without number. On the eastern slopes are vineyards, which though now covering hundreds of acres, are increasing yearly. This, in itself, speaks volumes for the healthfulness of the climate, for where grapes thrive miasmatic conditions are unknown. In the fertile garden valley a deep alluvial deposit furnishes rich soil for raising nursery stock—the chief industry of the town—in which many have invested capital ; and so favorable are conditions of growth that in two years trees attain a size and strength that require three years in other nursery centres. This is the home of the famous Genesee white winter wheat, so successfully raised here in large quantities, and the grain fields at every season form an attractive feature of the landscape.

The region within which Dansville is situated is salubrious. It is exempt from malaria, and the vital statistics justify its claim to favorable distinction in respect to diseases caused or prolonged by environment. This is probably due to its elevation above sea-level, swift running streams, dry, porous soil, evergreen forest growth, a climate equable and genial on account of its altitude, and more especially to the exceptional dryness and purity of the air. The Meterological Bureau Reports, and the weather maps of the Smithsonian Institute show that the narrow strip of Western New York State, forming the northerly divide of the Alleghaney chain draining into Lake Ontario, enjoying much less humidity than the surrounding country; indeed not until one approaches the pine forests of Northern Michigan, or the equally inhospitably dry plains west of the Mississippi River, can there be found any such low average. It is only this small section, within a region of twelve hundred miles of the Atlantic coast line, that this can be said. These combined influences make it a desirable place of residence or resort. And here on the eastern hill-slope, standing as a vision of hope and promise to thousands, is the Jackson Sanatorium, one of the largest and most complete health institution in the world. Many are attracted yearly to this favored spot, not less by nature's ample provision of pure air and beautiful scenery than by the opportunities afforded for recovery and recuperation under the care of skilled physicians.

The mountain spring which supplies the Jackson Sanatorium with water ranks as one of the most famous among home and foreign spas. Danville has a population of over 4,000; two railroads, gas and electric lighting, telegraph and telephone, eight mails daily, eight churches, a union school, an efficient fire department, good water power, chair, broom-handle, fruit-basket and reaper factories, extensive flour and health-food interests, planing and foundry plants, paper and pulp mills, three weekly newspapers and the monthly jou nals.

No change of cars is required between New York and Dansville, and the trip may be made in 9 hours. Time from Buffalo, two hours. Pullman cars are connected with all trains.

Those who have had the good opportunity to ride over the Lackawanna road by daylight, and are not prejudiced, agree that the view of the Genesee Valley; as seen from a car window, is not rivalled by any other landscape in this country. A glimpse of the valley is obtained at

GROVELAND. *Altitude, 418 ft.*

342.62 miles from New York; Single ticket, $8.10; Special ticket, $7.00.

MOUNT MORRIS. *Altitude, 585 ft.*

350.52 miles from New York; Single ticket, $8.18; Special ticket, $7.00.

This delightful village is situated on a tableland, and commands an uninterrupted view of the valley. To the west may be seen the High Banks, noted in history for the ravages of the red men whom General Sullivan was at one time commissioned to exterminate. The railroad crosses the Genesee River here. Mount Morris is a famous resort of the inhabitants of Buffalo, and in summer they collect here in great numbers. A huntsman's club has been formed, and is conducted with regulations similar to the Meadowbrook and other kindred clubs. The periodical "runs" are among the most exciting scenes that enter into the season's gayeties.

Bass fishing in the Genesee River is excellent, and attracts many. From Mount Morris to Geneseo, the capital of Livingston County, the drives over excellent roads are pleasing. This feature, above all the other worthy considerations, forms a decided attraction.

Extensive salt works are established here, and they form a principal feature of its commerce. At Mount Morris connection is made with Western New York and Pennsylvania.

LEICESTER. *Altitude, 660 ft.*

353.75 miles from New York; Single ticket, $8.25; Special ticket, $7.10.

GREIGSVILLE. *Altitude, 712 ft.*

357.07 miles from New York; Single ticket, $8.30; Special ticket, $7.20.

Greigsville is noted for its salt industry. One mine is 1,200 feet in depth, and the salt is taken out in enormous quantities. The amount of labor distributed can be imagined, when the figures relating to the out-put foot up to 800 tons per day. The village is surrounded by a magnificent farming country, and it is a pleasant region in which to spend a summer.

CRAIGS. *Altitude, 864 ft.*

360.40 miles from New York; Single ticket, $8.35; Special ticket, $7.30.

LINWOOD. *Altitude, 937*

363.18 miles from New York; Single ticket, $8.35; Special ticket, $7.40.

BUFFALO, ROCHESTER AND PITTSBURGH JUNCTION.

367.79 miles from New York ; Single ticket, $8.40 ; Special ticket, $7.55.

This, as the name implies, is a junction point with the Buffalo, Rochester & Pittsburgh Railroad. There are two salt shafts, 800 feet in depth, located here and getting ready to begin operations.

EAST BETHANY. *Altitude, 1,006 ft.*

371.82 miles from New York ; Single ticket, $8.45 ; Special ticket, $7.65.

EAST ALEXANDER. *Altitude, 941 ft.*

376.81 miles from New York ; Single ticket, $8.50 ; Special ticket, $7.70.

ALEXANDER. *Altitude, 933 ft.*

379.13 miles from New York ; Single ticket, $8.50 ; Special ticket, $7.75.

RAY *Altitude, 945 ft.*

381.80 miles from New York ; Single ticket, $8.60 ; Special ticket, $7.80.

DARIEN. *Altitude, 931 ft.*

384.79 miles from New York ; Single ticket, $8.65 ; Special ticket, $7.90.

FARGO. *Altitude, 836 ft.*

390.30 miles from New York ; Single ticket, $8.80 ; Special ticket, $8.00.

ALDEN. *Altitude, 858 ft.*

391.89 miles from New York ; Single ticket, $8.90 ; Special ticket, $8.00.

WEST ALDEN. *Altitude, 820 ft.*

393.53 miles from New York ; Single ticket, $8.95 ; Special ticket, $8.00.

LOONEYVILLE. *Altitude, 768 ft.*

396.22 miles from New York ; Single ticket, $9.00 ; Special ticket, $8.00.

EAST LANCASTER. *Altitude, 738 ft.*

398.47 miles from New York ; Single ticket, $9.05 ; Special ticket, $8.00.

LANCASTER. *Altitude, 699 ft.*

400.92 miles from New York ; Single ticket, $9.10 ; Special ticket, $8.00.

EAST BUFFALO. *Altitude, 622 ft.*

407.27 miles from New York; Single ticket, $9.25; Special ticket, $8.00.

At East Buffalo are located the extensive car shops of this railroad, where new cars are constructed and old cars rebuilt to be re-commissioned. The enormous coal chutes belonging to the Company are one mile long and have a storage capacity of 150,000 tons. A large yard and cattle pen are also among the Company's possessions at East Buffalo.

A busy little place called DEPEW, after Chauncey M. Depew, Esq., is close by, and promises to become famous as the greatest car manufacturing town in the United States.

BUFFALO. *Altitude, 582 ft.*

412.94 miles from New York; Single ticket, $9.25; Special ticket, $8.00.

This great city is the terminus of the road. It is the largest railroad centre in the State, and among the greatest of the entire nation. It has been said that a person can start at a given point in the large yards, and walk a hundred miles on the tops of freight cars. No exaggeration is indulged in, however, when the statement is made that cars from every railroad of any importance in the land are constantly represented on some one of the vast network of rails laid within the city limits.

Buffalo plays an active part as a distributing point for grain and lumber, the latter trade coming largely from Canada. The wharves along Lake Erie present a busy aspect at all times, and a day can be well spent among the shipping.

The wealth of the city is one of its most startling features, and millionaires are not by any means a rarity. The population aggregates about 265,000, which enables Buffalo to rank as the third city in the State.

With a water front of two and a half miles on Lake Erie, as well as on the Niagara River, and its location at the foot of the chain of great lakes, the reason why it plays such an active part in the commercial interests of the country is apparent.

The climate, on account of the influence of the lake winds, is naturally salubrious in summer. On the whole the streets are broad, well paved and well lighted, and the city enjoys a good sewerage system. Large and stately shade trees give Buffalo a pretty appearance, and specially delightful spots are the numerous parks and squares for which the city is noted. The public squares are named Franklin, Niagara, Prospect, Johnsons, Lafayette, and the Terrace. They were designed and laid out by Frederic Law Olmstead, who partly acquired his fame by the skill in forestry he displayed in Central Park, New York City.

The number of public buildings and charitable institutions, and the beauty and cost of their erection, is a source of pride with the Buffalonians. As to private residences, the city can boast of as many of great cost and beauty as any of its size in the United States, and as for hotels, there are many, "The Niagara" being one of the finest.

Passengers for Niagara Falls and points west change cars here. Connections are made with all other roads with little or no inconvience.

Florida East Coast Railway and Hotel System.

J. P. BECKWITH,
Traffic Manager.

J. D. RAHNER,
Assistant General Passenger Agent.

C. B. KNOTT,
General Superintendent Hotel System.

GENERAL OFFICES, ST. AUGUSTINE, FLORIDA.

Acadia and Thereabouts.

NOVA SCOTIA, CAPE BRETON AND PRINCE EDWARD ISLAND, REACHED BY THE CANADA, ATLANTIC AND PLANT STEAMSHIP LINE.

EACH successive summer, American summer resort tourists are discovering in quantities what hundreds of them have found out individually—the scenic beauties and the charming summer social life of Nova Scotia, Cape Breton and Prince Edward Island; the cooling breezes, the fine English roads, which delight the eye of the cyclist, the numerous streams teeming with fish, and woods and fields full of game, to the joy of the angler and hunter, and, in fact, every environment necessary to a perfect summer-resort region. Equally enjoyable is the sea trip by which these countries are reached. During the winter season the travel is naturally light, and only one sailing weekly is necessary; but when the summer sun bursts forth in all its warmth, the Canada, Atlantic and Plant Steamship Line increases the service to three ships weekly, and the fast steel passenger steamships of this line leave Boston crowded with tourists happy in the thought that, with only one night at sea, a foreign land is reached. The ships of this line were especially constructed for this service, being of modern design and built of steel, supplied with electricity throughout and with every convenience.

Two of the ships weekly ply between Boston and Halifax, while the third, after touching at Halifax, calls at Port Hawkesbury, Cape Breton, proceeding thence to Charlottetown, Prince Edward Island.

The shores of Nova Scotia, which are in view from the decks of the ships some time before Halifax is reached, are likened to those of Norway, being indented with

innumerable deep harbors, inlets and many rocky promontories and sea-swept ledges. Its summer climate is as soft as that of Southern Italy in May. Malaria is a stranger, and hay fever is unknown. Halifax may be justly termed the British stronghold of North America, as it is the headquarters of a large number of British troops and the Naval rendezvous of the British North Atlantic and West Indies squadrons. It is a busy, prosperous city, substantially built, and of characteristics decidedly foreign. The public gardens are said to be the finest in the world.

The visitor to the Provinces should not fail to spend a portion of his time on Cape Breton, making side trips to the Bras d'Or lakes and other points of interest on this fascinating island.

Charlottetown is the terminus of the Canada, Atlantic and Plant Line. Prince Edward Island is notable as a health spot, surrounded as it is by ocean and strait, whose waters have broken the shore line into numberless beautiful bays and estuaries. Its breezes are nothing but pure ones, bearing all the healthful tonic and ozone of old ocean itself, and its climate is delightful, free from penetrating fogs and excessive heat. It enjoys the distinction of being the most thoroughly cultivated territory on this side of the Atlantic, and is one great garden from end to end.

Bicycles are carried free by this line, and the sailing hour of one of these ships in the summer sees scores of devotees of the wheel, with more bicycles than other baggage. It is an inexpensive trip, the rates for passage and for meals being very low, while the service and cuisine, as on all Plant Steamships, are the best that could be desired.

Beautifully illustrated matter descriptive of the Maritime Provinces is issued by the Canada Atlantic and Plant Steamship Line. Four cents in stamps enclosed to J. J. Farnsworth, Eastern Passenger Agent, 261 Broadway, New York ; or Edward Sands, Asst. Gen. Passenger Agent, 290 Washington Street, Boston, will secure a copy of their book " Acadia and Thereabouts."

A vacation in Acadia will never be regretted.

The Kittatinny,

The Favorite Spring, Summer and Autumn Resort.

DELAWARE WATER GAP, MONROE CO., PENNA.

The "KITTATINNY," open from May 1st to November, hardly needs introduction to people familiar with the beautiful Delaware Valley.

It is the pioneer of the resort hotels of the State, and enjoys the present distinction of being one of the best known and most fortunate in beauty of location. From a quaint mountain inn of half a century ago, the Kittatinny has grown continuously and so added to its appointment with its ever-increasing popularity that to-day it is the largest and one of the best hotels on the Delaware, receiving 350 guests and possessing a fame as wide as that of the storied Water Gap itself.

The house stands on a smooth plateau two hundred feet above the river, with the perfect picture of the river and the towering mountains that form the "Gap" on the one hand, and a wealth of natural beauty the background on the other.

One hundred and fifty acres of private grounds form a park, with the lakes and mountain streams, rustic paths leading to every point of interest, and rustic structural to add to its effect.

Within the hotel the appointments are complete, and suggestive in many details of the delightful outing life of which this is the centre. The parlors, reception and reading rooms, office, corridors and bed-rooms are large, airy and tastefully furnished. A number of the bedrooms are en suite with bath and private balconies.

The dining-room, occupying the first floor of the main building, recently built, seats three hundred. The cuisine is in charge of an experienced chef. An unlimited supply of purest water from mountain springs is furnished in each, both hot and cold.

Other appointments include hydraulic elevator, gas, electric bells, billiard room, a well equipped livery, and an excellent orchestra.

The hotel is heated throughout by steam for the comfort of those desiring to come out in the early spring, or remaining through the fall.

Circulars and information as to how best to get here may be obtained at our New York Office, care The Recreation Department, *The Outlook*, 13 Astor Place, New York City, or by writing to the above address.

W. A. BRODHEAD & SONS,
Proprietors.

LOCAL AND LONG DISTANCE TELEPHONE.

GOLF GROUNDS NEAR HOTELS.

THE GLENWOOD.

DELAWARE WATER GAP, PA.
ELEVATION, 1,500 FT CAPACITY, 200.

Modern Brick House. High, cool and attractive. Fine Driving, Boating, Bathing and Fishing. Large well shaded lawns, pure spring water, electric bells, hot and cold baths, livery. Cuisine and service first-class. Convenient to all points of interest. Coach meets all trains. Local and Long Distance Telephone.

TERMS MODERATE, FOR CIRCULARS ADDRESS   P. R. JOHNSON.

Niagara River Line

THE SHORT AND PICTURESQUE ROUTE

....TO TORONTO....

Palace Steel Steamers

"CHICORA," "CHIPPEWA" and "CORMA"

Leave Lewiston and Niagara four times daily (except Sundays) for Toronto, Canada, on arrival of express trains from Falls and Buffalo, giving passengers a magnificient view of the scenery of Niagara River and Lake Ontario. Close connections made in Toronto with Steamers for Montreal, Thousand Islands and Lower St. Lawrence.

Tickets on sale at all offices of the Delaware, Lackawanna & Western, New York Central and West Shore Railways.

JOHN FOY, Manager, Toronto

Near-by Trout and Other Waters.

Along the route of the

DELAWARE, LACKAWANNA & WESTERN
RAILROAD

there are many very fine trout streams and black bass waters which are

OPEN TO THE PUBLIC,

and can be reached in a few hours from New York City. We name a few of them :

Alexander—Pickerel and black bass in waters near station.
Andover—The Pequest and tributaries, about one mile from station, afford fair trout fishing.
Apalachin—Trout are plentiful in lake Wyalusing, Cornalt Lake, and Lake of Meadows, all near station.
Atlanta—A few trout in adjacent creeks.
Augusta—Paulins Kill, one-eighth mile from station.
Baldwinsville Seneca River ; Pike, pickerel and some small muscalonge.
Bath—In Keuka Lake, excellent fishing ; salmon, trout, black bass, etc.
Beach Haven—Susquehanna River, near by, is well known for its black bass and wall-eyed pike fishing.
Berwick—Excellent black bass fishing in Susquehanna River, near station.
Bloomsburg—Trout in creek near by, and black bass and other fish in Susquehanna River, half mile from station.
Branchville—Paulins Kill, one-half mile from station.
Bridgewater—Some fishing as in Atlanta, which see.
Bridgeville—Pequest, one-half mile, and Beaver Brook, one mile from station ; both contain trout in fair numbers.
Budd's Lake—Black bass, etc.
Caroline—Six-Mile Brook, two miles from station, quite plentiful and getting better each year ; Boyer Creek, six miles from station ; Willow Creek, four miles from station.
Catawissa—Good black bass fishing.
Chatham—Canoe Brook, one mile east of station ; Spring Brook, three miles east of station ; Sandy Brook, three miles west of station ; trout are plentiful in all the above brooks, also in a number of nearby small streams ; two good hotels.
Chenango Forks—Chenango River at station ; black bass, perch and pickerel.
Chester—Two brooks contain trout, one two miles from station, the other two and one-half miles ; also South Branch, one and one-half miles from station.
Corning—Black bass and perch in Chemung River, one-quarter mile from station.
Cresco Station, Canadensis P. O., Pa.—Trout are very abundant in all the streams in this vicinity. Anglers who make this place their starting point will not have to go far to secure excellent trout fishing. We locate the following streams : Cranberry, one-quarter mile from station ; Devil's Hole, two miles west of station ; Brodhead Creek, east ; Mill Creek, one mile north ; Rattle Snake Creek, about one mile north ; Stony Run, three miles east ; Buck Hill, three miles north ; Middle Branch, three miles north ; Goose Pond Run, three miles northeast, and Spruce Cabin Run.
Cortland—Trout Brook, northeast of station ; Hoxeyville Brook, southeast of station.
Danville—See Berwick.
Delaware Water Gap, Pa.—Delaware River, near station, large but not very plentiful ; Marshall Creek, one-half mile from station, plenty ; Brodhead's Creek, one-quarter mile from station, plenty ; Caldeno Creek, half mile from station, plenty ; Cherry Creek, one-quarter mile from station, abundant but small ; Jersey Run, two miles from station, plentiful ; first-class hotels. Good black bass fishing in the Delaware near the Hulies.
Dover—Numerous lakes and ponds, within five to nine miles, that give good black bass, perch and pickerel fishing.
Elmhurst—Excellent trout fishing in brooks near by.
Espy Black bass in adjacent river, and trout in creeks.
Foster—The lakes close by give good black bass, pickerel and perch fishing, and trout are caught in brooks near station.
Franklin—Branch of Walkill River, near station ; black bass, pickerel, etc.
Fulton—Rock and black bass in waters near by.
Gouldsboro Same fishing as at Forks.
Henryville—At this station are the celebrated trout waters of the East and West branches of Brodhead's Creek.
Hick's Ferry Black bass and wall-eyed pike in river near by.
Homer—Lakes containing black bass, and numerous trout streams within a radius of ten miles.
Hopatcong—Lake Hopatcong ; black bass, rock bass, pike and pickerel are numerous.
Hunlocks—Same fishing as at Hick's Ferry.
Ithaca—In Cayuga Lake, one mile distant, black bass, rock bass, pike and pickerel are numerous.
Lyndhurst—Black and striped bass in the Passaic River about one-quarter mile from station.
Marathon—Black bass and pickerel near station.
Montrose—There are about thirty lakes in this vicinity that contain trout, black bass, pickerel and perch.
Morristown—Black bass, &c., in Lakes Pocahontas and Speedwell.
Moscow—Trout in brooks close to station.
Mount Pocono—Plenty of trout in adjacent streams.
Nanticoke—Good fishing for black bass, pickerel and wall-eyed pike.
North Brookfield—Trout are caught in Moscow Creek five miles from station.
Oxford—Black bass, pickerel and perch are plenty.
Pittston—Excellent black bass fishing.
Plymouth—See Pittston.
Pocono Summit—Good fishing for trout ; two streams.
Portland—Black bass in Delaware River near station.
Preble—Numerous lakes close to station contain black bass and pickerel in numbers.
Richfield Springs—Pickerel, black bass and perch are caught freely in Canadarago Lake, about one mile from station.
Shickshinny—Black bass and wall-eyed pike are plenty.
Spragueville—Brodhead's Creek near station is famous for its trout fishing.
Stanhope—Budd's Lake, one to three miles ; black bass, pickerel, etc.
Stroudsburg—Many good trout streams in this section.
Forest Park—"Bushkill," fifteen miles from Stroudsburg ; excellent fishing ; trout, black bass, perch, pickerel, etc.
Tobyhanna In creek of this name trout are numerous.
Tully—Tully and Big Lakes, one and a half miles. Stocked with bass, perch or pickerel.
Whitney's Point—Good black bass fishing ; also for pickerel, perch and sun-perch.
Willards—Same fishing as at Whitney's Point.
Willow Grove—Black bass in Susquehanna River, one-quarter mile distant.

GAME LAWS COMPILED BY
C. N. IRONSIDE,
OF LEEDS & IRONSIDE,
COUNSELORS AT LAW,
40 WALL ST., NEW YORK.

GAME LAWS

OF

New York, New Jersey and Pennsylvania.

●

NEW YORK.

Act of May 5th, 1892, as amended May, 1895, with further amendments to date.

Deer.—Wild deer shall not be caught, shot at, hunted or killed except from the 16th day of August to the 31st day of October, both inclusive. No person shall kill or take alive more than two deer in any season. In the counties of Ulster, Greene, Sullivan and Delaware no wild deer shall be killed at any ime within five years from the passage of this act. Deer shall not be hunted with dogs except from the 1st to the 15th day of October, both inclusive. Deer shall not be hunted with dogs in the counties of St Lawrence, Delaware, Greene, Washington, Ulster or Sullivan (except in towns of Highland, Cumberland, Tusten, Cochecton and Bethel in Sullivan County from October 1st to 15th) at any time. Dogs while chasing after deer in violation of the law may be killed by any person, and dogs of the breed used for hunting deer shall not be permitted to run at large in forests inhabited by deer, except between the days mentioned. Deer or venison killed in this State shall not be transported to any point within the State from or through any of the counties thereof, except that one carcass, or a part thereof, may be transported from the county where killed when accompanied by the owner. And no person shall so transport or accompany more than two deer in one year, but this does not apply to the head and feet or skin of deer severed from the body. No fawns shall be caught or killed at any time. No traps or any device whatever to catch or entice deer, including salt-licks, shall be used, nor shall deer be hunted, killed or captured by crusting, nor while they are yarded. No jack light or any other artificial light shall be used in hunting or killing deer except from Sept. 1st to 15th, both inclusive. The above prohibitions apply also to moose, caribon and antelope. The provision as to close season differs for Long Island.

Black and Gray Squirrels, Hares and Rabbits.—Black and gray squirrels, hares and rabbits shall not be hunted, shot at, killed or possessed except from October 15 to February 15 The use of ferrets in hunting rabbits is prohibited. The counties of Wayne, Onondaga and Oswego are exempt from the provisions of this section in so far as it relates to the killing or hunting with ferrets or hares, and rabbits. This section does not apply to Long Island.

Fur-bearing Animals.—Beavers shall not be caught or killed under penalty of $50 for each animal. In Cattaraugus, Oneida, Madison and Otsego counties no person shall catch or kill or attempt to do so, except upon his own premises, or within the limits of an incorporated village, nor have in his possession when killed, any mink, skunk, musk-rat or fox from May 1 to Nov. 16, except that foxes shall not be so killed or caught from May 1 to September 30.

Wild Fowl Web-footed wild fowl, except geese and brant, shall not be pursued, shot at, hunted, killed, possessed or sold between the last day of April and the 1st day of September, and shall not be pursued, shot at, hunted or killed, except during the hours in each day commencing one hour before sunrise and terminating one hour after sunset. On the Hudson River below the dam at Troy, boats propelled by hand may be used for shooting web-footed fowl. Such fowl shall not be pursued, shot at, hunted, killed or caught in any way, save with the gun resting at arm's length, and fired from the shoulder without any other rest, nor from any boat other than a boat propelled by hand or floating device ; nor from the use of any boughhouse at a greater distance than fifty feet from the shore or from a natural growth of grass or flags. This section does not apply to Long Island or Long Island Sound.

Quail—Quail shall not be pursued, shot at, hunted or killed except during the months of November and December ; they shall not be sold or possessed except during the months of November, December and January, but possession in January is forbidden unless it be proved by the possessor that said birds were killed within the lawful periods for killing the same or outside of the State, and they shall not be killed or possessed in the counties of Genesee, Wyoming, Orleans, Livingston, Monroe, Cayuga, Seneca, Wayne, Tompkins, Tioga, Odondaga, Ontario, Steuben, Cortland and Otsego, prior to the 1st day of November, 1898. Robbin's Island and Gardiner's Island are exempt from the provisions of this section.

Woodcock and Grouse.— Woodcock, ruffled grouse, commonly known as partridge, or any member of the grouse family, shall not be pursued, shot at, hunted or killed except from the 16th day of August to the 31st day of December, both inclusive. They shall not be sold or possessed except from the 16th day of August to the 31st day of January following ; possession or sale thereof during the month of January is forbidden unless it be proved by the possessor or seller that said birds were killed within the lawful period for killing the same or outside of the State. This section does not apply to Long Island. These birds or quail killed within the State shall not be transported to any point within or without the State from or through any of the counties thereof, or possessed for that purpose, except that they may be transported from the county where killed when accompanied by the owner.

Plover, Snipe and other Birds.—Wilson's, commonly known as English snipe, plover, rail, mud-hen, gallinule, grebe, bittern, surf-bird, curlew, water chicken, bay snipe or shore bird shall not be shot at, hunted, killed or possessed during the months of May, June, July and August, except in Long Island.

Wild Birds other than Game.—These shall not be killed or caught at any time or possessed after the same are dead. This provision does not affect any birds the killing of which is prohibited between certain dates, nor does it protect the English sparrow, crow, hawk, crane, raven, crow blackbird, common blackbird an 1 kingfisher.

Meadow Larks.—Meadow larks shall not be shot at, killed, possessed after they are dead at any time, except in Long Island.

Nests.—The nests of wild birds shall not be robbed or wilfully or needlessly destroyed, except when necessary to protect buildings or prevent their defacement. This section does not apply to the English sparrow, hawk, crane, crow, raven, blackbird, common blackbird and kingfisher.

Snaring.—English pheasants, ruffed grouse, commonly known as partridge, or any member of the grouse family, or quail, shall not be netted, trapped or snared, nor shall any person possess any of said birds so taken; nor shall any net, trap or snare of any kind be set for said birds. Such net, trap or snare may be summarily destroyed.

Mongolian Ring-Necked Pheasant.—No person shall kill, expose for sale or have in his or her possession after the same has been killed, any wild Mongolian ring-necked pheasant (*phasius torquatus*) prior to the year 1900. This section does not apply to the County of Suffolk.

Authority to Collect Birds for Scientific Purposes.—Certificates may be granted by any incorporated society of natural history in the State, or by the regents of the University of the State of New York, to any properly accredited person of the age of eighteen years or upwards, permitting the holder thereof to collect birds, their nests or eggs, for strictly scientific purposes only.

Fallow Fires.—Are unlawful between April 1st and June 10th and between September 1st and November 10th, but may be started on written permission of the fire warden and three days' notice between June 10th and September 1st.

Trout.—Trout shall not be fished for, caught, killed or possessed except from the 16th day of April to the 31st day of August, both inclusive, except in Long Island. They shall not be taken or possessed unless six inches in length, and if less than six inches in length and taken unintentionally shall be immediately replaced in the water from which taken without unnecessary injury.

Salmon Trout and Land-Locked Salmon.—Shall not be wilfully molested or disturbed while upon their spawning beds during close season, nor shall such fish nor any spawn or milt from any such fish be carried away while upon the spawning beds.

Salmon Trout.—Sometimes know as lake trout, and land-locked salmon, shall not be caught or killed in inland waters of this State, except from the 1st day of May to the 30th day of September, both inclusive. Possession of such fish during close season is prohibited unless it be proved that such fish were not caught in this State during such season. The provisions of this section do not apply to Long Island. These fish caught in any inland waters of the State shall not be transported to any point within or without the State from or through any of the counties thereof, or possessed for that purpose except when accompanied by the owner.

Black Bass and Oswego Bass. Black bass, Oswego bass, pickerel, pike or wall-eyed pike, shall not be fished for, caught or possessed, except from the 30th day of May to the 31st day of December, both inclusive, nor in Lake George or Schroon Lake, except from the 1st of August to the 31st of December, both inclusive, nor in Schoharie River or Foxe's Creek, except in August, till may 31, 1899. Otsego (?) bass may be taken from Otsego Lake by rod and reel or by hook and line held in the hand from January 1st to October 31st.

Pickerel, Pike and Wall-Eyed Pike.—Shall not be fished for, caught, killed or possessed, except from the 1st day of May to the 31st day of January, both inclusive; except that pickerel, bull-heads, cat-fish, eels, perch and sunfish may be fished for through the ice with hooks and lines or tip-ups in Lake Keuka or Crooked Lake or in any of the waters of the State not inhabited by trout, lake trout, salmon trout, black or Oswego bass or land-locked salmon or muskallonge, and by set lines in the Susquehanna River, and in the waters of Port Bay in the County of Wayne. Suckers, bull-heads, eels and dogfish may be caught at any time by hooking and spearing in Oneida Lake or river, or in any of the waters of the State not inhabited by trout, lake trout, land-locked salmon, muskallonge, black bass or Oswego bass, but pike, pickerel and wall-eyed pike may be taken with hook and line or spear, and muskallonge with hook and line in any of the inland waters of this State not inhabited by trout or salmon of any kind, during December, January and February, except in the waters of Cortland County. Suckers, bull-heads and eels may be caught in Seneca Lake with seines after permission first obtained from the Commissioners of Fisheries, Game and Forests. Pickerel may be taken through the ice from Otsego Lake by tip-ups or set lines and from said lake by rod and reel or hook and line held in the hand from January 1st to October 31st.

Bass.—Shall not be taken less than eight inches in length from any of the waters of this State, nor possessed; if such are caught they must be immediately replaced in the water whence taken, without injury.

Muskallonge shall not be fished for, caught or possessed, except from the 30th day of May to the last day of February, both inclusive.

Salmon shall not be fished for, caught, killed or possessed between the 15th day of August and the 1st day of March following. No salmon less than eighteen inches in length shall be intentionally taken alive from any of the waters of this State, nor possessed, and if taken shall be immediately returned to the waters from which it is taken without unnecessary injury.

Fishing within fifty rods of any fishway erected by the State, and any interference with the signboards there maintained, is forbidden.

Salt Water Striped Bass.—No salt water striped bass less than eight inches in length shall be intentionally taken from any of the waters of this State, nor possessed. If unintentionally taken shall be immediately replaced in the water from which it is taken without any unnecessary injury.

Pollution of Waters. No dyestuff, coal tar, refuse from gas houses, sawdust, shavings, tanbark, lime, or other deleterious, or poisonous, substances shall be allowed to run into any of the waters of this State, either private or public, in quantities destructive to the life of fish inhabiting the same. Nor shall fish be taken by shutting or drawing off any water for that purpose. The use of dynamite or any other explosives in any of the waters of this State is prohibited except for mining and mechanical purposes.

Stocking Waters from Streams.—No trout of any kind, salmon trout, or land-locked salmon, shall be taken from any of the waters of this State for the purpose of stocking a private pond or stream.

Fishing Through the Ice in any waters inhabited by trout, salmon trout, or land-locked salmon, during the closed season for any such fish, is prohibited.

Waters of the Adirondacks.—No fish, fish fry, spawn or milt, except speckled trout, brook, brown, salmon and rainbow, trout, Adirondack frost fish, or land-locked salmon, shall be placed in waters of the Adirondack regions except under the immediate supervision of the Commissioners of Fisheries.

Unlawful Devices.—Fishing by any device other than angling in the waters of the St. Lawrence or Niagara River nor in Lake Champlain, except during the months of March, April and May, and in the waters of Niagara County, except during the months of November, December, January, February and March, no fish may be taken except black bass and muskallonge, after permission being first obtained from the Commissioners of Fisheries, Game and Forests. The use of any device, except angling in the waters of Lake Erie within half a mile of the shore, or of any of the islands therein, nor in Cattaraugus Creek, or within five miles of the mouth thereof, or of any of the islands therein, nor within three miles of the mouth of the Niagara River. The waters of Lake Ontario, in the County of Jefferson, included between Blue Rock Point and the towns of Lyme and Cape Vincent, including Chaumont Bay, Griffin Bay and Three Mile Bay, in the County of Oswego, between the northerly line of the town of Mexico and Jefferson County line, are exempt from the provisions of this act. Taking fish by drawing off water in any pond or reservoir, is forbidden except in private ponds and under supervision of game wardens. Set lines are permitted in Canandaigua Lake.

Eel Weirs.—With laths not less than one inch apart may be maintained at any time in waters not inhabited by trout, lake trout, salmon trout or land-locked salmon, except in the Chemung River and its tributaries in the Counties of Steuben and Chemung, and in the Susquehanna River, provided there be a clear passage in the weir, at low water mark, of not less than ten feet.

Warren County.—Fishing is prohibited in East and West brooks, or tributaries, in the town of Caldwell; and in Harris, Edmund, Indian and Finkle brooks in the town of Bolton; at all times until April, 1899. The same applies to fishing for pike-perch, or great northern pike in Lake George or Glen Lake or any of their tributaries in Warren County between January 1st and June 15th; and to fishing for bullheads between January 1st and July 1st; and to fishing for black or Oswego bass in the town of Horicon between January 1st and July 10th. In Lake George, perch may be caught by angling at any time.

Salmon taken in nets from the Hudson River shall be immediately put back. Salmon, black bass, salmon trout and pike perch caught in nets in fishing for other fish in the Hudson River shall be thrown back into the water without unnecessary injury.

No device except angling shall be used for the capture of any fish except menhaden, in the waters of Raritan Bay or waters adjacent thereto in Richmond County, except that shad may be taken in shad nets between the 15th day of March and the 15th day of June, both inclusive.

Nets, set-nets, pounds or fykes, except those used for catching lobsters or crabs, shall not be used in the Harlem River, or the East River, or in the adjacent waters or confluent brooks.

NEW JERSEY.

BIRDS AND ANIMALS.	Open Season.
Ruffed Grouse	Oct. 31 to Dec. 16
Quail	Nov. 10 to Dec. 16
Woodcock	July and Sept. 30 to Dec. 16
Upland Plover	July 31 to Dec. 16
English Snipe	March, April and Aug. 26 to Dec. 16
Grouse and Pheasant	Oct. 31 to Dec. 16
Wild Turkey	Oct. 31 to Dec. 16
Web-Footed Wild Fowl	Aug. 31 to May 1

	Open Season.
Rabbit and Hare	Nov. 10 to Dec. 16
Deer	Nov. 25 to Dec. 15
FISH.	
Salmon Trout	March 1 to Oct. 1
Brook Trout	April 1 to July 15
Black and Owego Bass	May 30 to Dec. 1
Pickerel and Pike	April 1 to March 31

PENNSYLVANIA.

BIRDS AND ANIMALS.	Open Season.
Turkeys	Oct. 15 to Jan. 1
Ducks	Sept. 1 to May 1
Plover	July 15 to Jan. 1
Woodcock	July 4 to Jan. 1
Quail	Nov. 1 to Dec. 15
Ruffed Grouse or Pheasant	Oct. 1 to Jan. 1
Rail and Reed Bird	Sept. 1 to Dec. 1
Snipe and Wild Pigeons	Any time.
Elk and Deer	Oct. 1 to Dec. 15
Squirrels	Sept. 1 to Jan. 1
Hares and Rabbits	Nov. 1 to Jan. 1

	FISH.	Open Season.
Wall-Eyed Pike		June 1 to Feb. 1
Speckled Trout		April 15 to July 15
Salmon		May 30 to Jan. 1
Lake Trout		Jan. 1 to Sept. 30
Pickerel		June 1 to Jan. 1
Black and Rock Bass		May 30 to Jan. 1

Hunting and Fishing on Sunday unlawful.

In most of the States there is a penalty of from $5 to $50 for killing song-birds.

The Jackson Sanatorium DANSVILLE NEW YORK

Established 1858

CLEAR,
DRY ATMOSPHERE,
FREE FROM FOGS AND
MALARIA.

PURE SPRING WATER
FROM ROCKY HEIGHTS.

PERFECT DRAINAGE AND
SEWERAGE.

MAIN BUILDING ABSO-
LUTELY FIREPROOF.

A DELIGHTFUL home for those seeking health, rest or recreation. Under the personal care of regularly educated and experienced physicians Hillside location in Woodlawn Park, overlooking extended views of the famous Genesee Valley region, unsurpassed for healthfulness and beauty.

Elegant modern fire-proof main building and twelve cottages, complete in all appliances for health and comfort. Extensive apartments for treatment arranged for individual privacy. Skilled attendants. All forms of fresh and salt water baths: Electricity, Massage, Swedish Movements, etc. Vacuum treatments. Delsarte system of Physical Culture. Frequent lectures and lessons on Health Topics. Especial provision for quiet and rest; also for recreation, amusement and regular outdoor life. Delightful walks and drives.

Culinary Department under supervision of Mrs. Emma P. Ewing, Superintendent of Chautauqua Cooking School.

Steam heat, open fires, electric bells, safety elevator, telegraph, telephone, chapel, library, daily papers, and every provision for comfort, health and good cheer.

For illustrated pamphlet, testimonials, and other information, address

J. ARTHUR JACKSON, Secretary,

P. O. Box 1874.

H. GAZE & SONS
(LIMITED)

Tourist and Excursion Agents

ESTABLISHED 1844.

OFFICIAL TICKET AGENTS
For the Delaware, Lackawanna & Western Railroad, and all Principal Trunk Lines

ISSUES INDEPENDENT TRAVEL TICKETS
TO ALL PARTS OF

AMERICA
EUROPE, INDIA, AND AROUND THE WORLD

Passage Tickets by all Ocean Steamship Lines

ESCORTED PARTIES AT INCLUSIVE RATES AT FREQUENT INTERVALS
TO ALL PARTS OF

Great Britain, Norway, Sweden, Denmark
including North Cape, Russia, Turkey
Greece, France, Germany, Italy, Holy Land
The Nile, India, and Around the World

DESCRIPTIVE ILLUSTRATED PROGRAMMES FREE ON APPLICATION
Fullest information on all matters appertaining to travel
promptly furnished by mail

GAZE'S TOURIST GAZETTE
WITH MAPS

PUBLISHED MONTHLY   BY MAIL 10 CENTS

Chief American Office, 113 Broadway, New York, N. Y.

BOSTON, MASS. 201 Washington St.
CHICAGO, ILL., 220 S. Clark St.
PHILADELPHIA, PA., 14 So. Broad St.
PARIS, 2 Rue Scribe

London, 142 Strand (Chief Office)

BRANCH OFFICES AND AGENCIES THROUGHOUT THE WORLD

MOUNT POCONO
PENNSYLVANIA

THIS popular summer resort is situated on one of the spurs of the Pocono Mountains, Monroe County, Penna., one and one-fourth miles from Mount Pocono station.

The House commands a fine view of mountain, forest and valley, the picture framed by the Blue Ridge twenty miles distant, with Pocono Knob and Delaware Water Gap prominent features in the landscape.

The Extensive Grounds covering four hundred acres are well wooded, yellow pine predominating. The broad lawns afford ample facilities for out-door sports; the golf links are well located and convenient of access.

The Accommodations are limited to one hundred and fifty guests. The house is heated with steam and has ample parlors, a casino and commodious porches. The rooms, several of which are en suite with private bath, are large and well furnished. The sanitary arrangements are of the most approved system.

Wiscasset Spring Water is the only water used in the house. There are three miles of trout stream of which the Wiscasset's guests have the exclusive use.

The Elevation, delightful scenery, healthful and exhilarating climate and freedom from mosquitos render The Wiscasset particularly desirable for a spring, summer or autumn sojourn. Reference will be exchanged with strangers.

ELEVATION, ONE THOUSAND EIGHT HUNDRED FEET

I. D. IVISON
Manager

ROUTES AND RATES.

ALEXANDRIA BAY, N. Y.
THE THOUSAND ISLANDS.

JUST where the blue waters of Lake Ontario find their outlet between Cape Vincent, N. Y., and Kingston, Can., the Thousand Islands of the St. Lawrence have their beginning, extending some forty miles down the river in picturesque groups, and forming in their entirety one of the loveliest and most varied fishing regions in the world.

It is now hardly more than a dozen years since the Thousand Islands began to attract widespread attention, yet the visitor will find along the route of the steamer, which bears him down the crystal current, numbers of large hotels, and hundreds of costly and palatial summer homes, which increase in numbers annually.

The tourist portion of the Thousand Islands begins, practically speaking, at Clayton, the terminus of the Rome, Watertown & Ogdensburg Railroad. From this point steamers ply to Alexandria Bay, touching at intermediate points. The first landing is made at Round Island. This is a prominent cottage community. It is non-sectarian, and numbers among its permanent summer residents many prominent people from the large cities.

Thousand Island Park, a Methodistic community, is two miles below, and also has its hotel and numerous cottages, as well as a large "tabernacle."

Central Park is prettily located midway down the American channel.

About ten miles below Clayton, Alexandria Bay is located. In the immediate vicinity are many of the most costly and beautiful summer villas. The "Bay" is the focus of a large summer travel, steamers coming and going constantly.

Near Alexandria Bay, and like that village, also upon the mainland, is Edgewood Park, chiefly occupied by Cleveland families; and one mile distant is Westminster Park, which has a good hotel and Presbyterian tendencies.

The fishing at the Thousand Islands will always be its chief charm with the general visitor, and, thanks to the protection of recently enacted State laws and the activity of the Anglers' Association, the fishing is always improving. Boatmen, with safe and natty St. Lawrence skiffs, the most beautiful of all water craft, may be engaged at any of the hotels by the day or week.

Daily excursions are made among the islands from all the hotels, upon swift and roomy steamboats.

EXCURSION No. 9.—ALEXANDRIA BAY AND RETURN.

Delaware, Lack. & Western R. R..to Utica.
Rome, Watertown & Ogdbg R.R..to Clayton.
Thousand Island Steamboat Co...to Alexandria Bay.
Returning *via* same route.

THROUGH RATES.

New York	$16 00	Berwick	$14 80
Paterson	16 00	Bloomsburg	15 35
Newark	16 00	Danville	15 75
Morristown	16 00	Binghamton	10 55
Dover	16 00	Greene	9 80
Hackettstown	16 00	Oxford	9 25
Washington	16 00	Norwich	8 95
Water Gap	15 35	Sherburne	8 50
Stroudsburg	15 15	Waterville	7 65
Scranton	13 05	Richfield Springs	8 25
Pittston	13 45	Vestal	10 90
Kingston	13 75	Owego	11 40
Wilkesbarre	13 75	Waverly	12 15
Plymouth	13 90	Elmira	12 05
Nanticoke	14 00	Corning	13 35
Shickshinny	14 35	Bath	14 35

EXCURSION No. 7.—ALEXANDRIA BAY AND RETURN.

Delaware, Lack. & Western R. R..to Syracuse.
Rome, Watertown & Ogdbg. R. R..to Clayton.
Thousand Island Steamboat Co...to Alexandria Bay.
Returning *via* same route.

THROUGH RATES.

New York	$16 00	Wilkesbarre	$12 40
Paterson	16 00	Plymouth	12 55
Newark	16 00	Nanticoke	12 70
Morristown	16 00	Shickshinny	13 05
Dover	16 00	Berwick	13 50
Hackettstown	15 95	Bloomsburg	14 00
Washington	15 55	Danville	14 00
Water Gap	14 75	Binghamton	9 95
Stroudsburg	14 55	Cortland	8 25
Scranton	12 40	Vestal	10 30
Pittston	12 40	Owego	10 75
Kingston	12 40	Waverly	11 25
		Elmira	$11 25

EXCURSION No. 153.—ALEXANDRIA BAY AND RETURN.

Delaware, Lack. & Western R. R..to Oswego.
Rome, Watertown & Ogdbg. R. R..to Clayton.
Thousand Island Steamboat Co...to Alexandria Bay.
Returning *via* same route.

THROUGH RATES.

New York	$16 00	Wilkesbarre	$14 05
Paterson	16 00	Plymouth	14 15
Newark	16 00	Nanticoke	14 25
Morristown	16 00	Shickshinny	14 65
Dover	16 00	Berwick	15 05
Hackettstown	16 00	Bloomsburg	15 60
Washington	16 00	Danville	16 05
Water Gap	15 05	Binghamton	10 85
Stroudsburg	15 45	Cortland	9 15
Scranton	13 35	Syracuse	7 65
Pittston	13 70	Owego	11 65
Kingston	14 05	Waverly	12 15
		Elmira	$12 15

EXCURSION NO. 154.—ALEXANDRIA BAY AND RETURN.

Delaware, Lack. & Western R. R...to Oswego.
Rome, Watertown & Ogdbg. R.R...to Clayton.
Thousand Island Steamboat Co...to Alexandria Bay.
Thousand Island Steamboat Co...to Clayton.
Rome, Watertown & Ogdbg. R.R...to Utica.
Delaware, Lack. & Western R. R...to starting point.

EXCURSION NO. 155.—REVERSE OF THE PRECEDING.

THROUGH RATES.

New York..........	$19 75	Plymouth..........	$14 75
Paterson..........	19 15	Nanticoke..........	14 90
Newark............	19 75	Shickshinny.......	15 25
Morristown........	18 70	Berwick...........	15 70
Dover.............	18 20	Bloomsburg........	16 20
Hackettstown......	17 45	Danville..........	16 65
Washington........	17 10	Binghamton........	11 25
Water Gap.........	16 25	Greene............	11 05
Stroudsburg.......	16 05	Oxford............	11 05
Scranton..........	13 95	Norwich...........	11 05
Pittston..........	14 35	Cortland..........	11 05
Kingston..........	14 65	Owego.............	12 30
Wilkesbarre.......	14 65	Waverly...........	13 05
	Elmira...........	$13 75	

EXCURSION ST 16.—UTICA TO ALEXANDRIA BAY AND RETURN.

Rome, Watertown & Ogdbg. R. R...to Clayton.
Thousand Island Steamboat Co...to Alexandria Bay.
Returning via same route.
Sold only in connection with Summer Excursion Ticket passing through Utica.
Rate,.............$6 75

ASHEVILLE, N. C.

In the centre of a region poetically designated as "The Land of the Sky," is Asheville, N. C.

In Western North Carolina, between the Blue Ridge on the east and the Alleghanies on the west, lies this beautiful valley. It is a land of bright skies, incomparable climate, and picturesque scenery, whose praises have been sung by poets and whose beauties of stream, valley and mountain height have furnished subject and inspiration to the sketcher's hand. The city is situated in the heart of the mountains, 2,300 feet above the level of the tide. Romantic scenery surrounds the town on every side, and the approach to it from either direction leads through a panorama of enchanting views. On the one hand there rises the beautiful Blue Ridge; on the other, the picturesque Alleghanies; at their feet flow the clear waters of the French Broad.

There is scarcely a more beautiful valley than this, and certainly none more rich in all that would attract health-seeker, lounger, invalid or dreamer. The climate is superb.

EXCURSION NO. 314 Y.—ASHEVILLE, N. C. AND RETURN.

*Limit from Buffalo, six months from date of sale.
Limited to three (3) months from date of sale.

Good for use south bound only within fifteen (15) days from date of issue as stamped on back of ticket; and must be presented to the ticket agency of the initial line at the destination point for identification and validation before they can be used for the return trip, and are then good returning only within fifteen (15) days from such validation as stamped on the back of ticket; in all cases, however, tickets must be used within the extreme limit.

Del., Lack. & Western R. R......to Manunka Chunk.
Pennsylvania Railroad............to Washington.
Southern Railway................to Asheville.
Returning via same route.

THROUGH RATES.

Stroudsburg........	$31 05	Cortland..........	$36 60
Scranton..........	31 05	Syracuse..........	37 65
Pittston..........	31 05	Fulton............	38 65
Kingston..........	31 05	Oswego............	39 05
Wilkesbarre.......	31 05	Owego.............	34 85
Montrose..........	33 35	Ithaca............	35 60
Binghamton........	34 85	Waverly...........	34 85
Greene............	36 05	Elmira............	34 85
Oxford............	36 90	Corning...........	35 60
Norwich...........	37 40	Bath..............	35 60
Sherburne.........	38 05	Atlanta...........	35 60
Waterville........	39 30	Wayland...........	35 60
Richfield Springs..	41 10	Dansville.........	35 60
Utica.............	40 55	Mt. Morris........	35 60
	*Buffalo,........	$35 60	

EXCURSION NO. 333 Y.—ASHEVILLE, N. C. AND RETURN.

Limited to three (3) months from date of sale.
Delaware, Lack. & Western R. R....to New York.
Pennsylvania Railroad.............to Washington.
Southern Railway..................to Asheville.
Returning via same route.

THROUGH RATES.

Summit............	$30 80	Oxford............	$39 00
Morristown........	31 25	Norwich...........	39 00
Dover.............	31 75	Sherburne.........	39 25
Hackettstown......	32 45	Waterville........	39 25
Washington........	32 85	Richfield Springs.	40 75
Stroudsburg.......	33 85	Utica.............	39 25
Scranton..........	36 00	Cortland..........	40 00
Pittston..........	36 55	Syracuse..........	40 00
Kingston..........	36 80	Fulton............	40 00
Wilkesbarre.......	36 85	Oswego............	40 00
Montrose..........	38 20	Owego.............	38 85
Binghamton........	38 00	Ithaca............	40 50
Greene............	38 80	Waverly...........	39 60
	Elmira...........	$39 45	

ATLANTIC CITY, N. J.

Atlantic City claims for itself to be the most popular resort in this country—an all-year-round health-restoring and pleasure-giving place, unsurpassed in the plenitude of its accommodations

Although immediately on the beach (many houses being but a few feet from the surf), it is a city of ten thousand inhabitants, which, at the height of the summer season, is increased to a hundred thousand.

In summer, bathing, fishing, driving, boating, and like sea-shore divertisements are its offerings to the well who go there for a rest and change from the monotony of every-day affairs.

For the invalid there is ozone-freighted air breezes, tempered by journeys over thousands of miles of ocean, cool, comfortable nights for repose, and all the facilities enjoyed in cities of the larger size.

Fine avenues, beautiful cottages, magnificently appointed hotels, street cars, electric lights, a perfect sewerage, and first-class drinking water, brought from the mainland.

Prominent as it is, as a summer resort, it is hardly less so as a winter sanitarium—many of its hotels being filled to their utmost.

It lays claim to being only sixty miles from the gulf stream, the influence of which is directly attested by its temperature, being several degrees higher in winter than cities sixty miles inland.

EXCURSION NO. 65 Y.—ATLANTIC CITY AND RETURN.

Limited to six (6) months from date of sale.
Del., Lack. & Western R. R.....to Manunka Chunk.
Pennsylvania Railroad...........to Atlantic City.
Returning *via* same route.
(Good for passage *via* either Philadelphia (Broad St. Station) or Amboy Division to Camden.)

THROUGH RATES.

Stroudsburg	$ 6 10	Cortland	$13 10
Scranton	8 50	Syracuse	14 25
Pittston	8 50	Fulton	15 25
Kingston	8 50	Oswego	15 65
Wilkesbarre	8 50	Owego	11 50
Montrose	10 80	Ithaca	12 55
Binghamton	11 50	Waverly	11 50
Greene	12 30	Elmira	11 50
Oxford	12 80	Corning	12 45
Norwich	13 15	Bath	13 70
Sherburne	13 60	Atlanta	14 80
Waterville	14 25	Wayland	15 00
Richfield Springs	15 60	Dansville	15 30
Utica	14 25	Mt. Morris	16 20
		Buffalo	$18 10

EXCURSION NO. 66 Y.—ATLANTIC CITY AND RETURN.

Limited to six (6) months from date of sale.
Delaware, Lack. & Western R. R....to New York.
Pennsylvania Railroad.............to Atlantic City.
Returning *via* same route.
(Good for passage *via* either Philadelphia (Broad St. Station) or Amboy Division to Camden.)

EXCURSION NO. 152 Y.—ATLANTIC CITY AND RETURN.

Limited to six (6) months from date of sale.
Delaware, Lack. & Western R. R....to New York,
Central Railroad of New Jersey....to Bound Brook,
Philadelphia & Reading Railroad..to Atlantic City,
Returning *via* same route.

EXCURSION NO. 151 Y.—ATLANTIC CITY AND RETURN.

Limited to six (6) months from date of sale.
Delaware, Lack. & West. R. R....to New York,
C. R. R. of N. J. *via* Perth Amboy..to Winslow June'n,
Philadelphia & Reading R. R.....to Atlantic City.
Returning *via* same route.

THROUGH RATES FOR EITHER EXCURSION.

Summit	$ 5 80	Richfield Springs	$15 75
Morristown	6 25	Utica	14 25
Dover	6 75	Cortland	15 00
Hackettstown	7 45	Syracuse	16 00
Washington	7 85	Fulton	16 50
Stroudsburg	8 85	Oswego	17 00
Scranton	11 00	Owego	13 85
Pittston	11 40	Ithaca	15 50
Kingston	11 80	Waverly	14 60
Wilkesbarre	11 85	Elmira	15 45
Montrose	13 20	Corning	15 90
Binghamton	13 50	Bath	16 75
Greene	13 80	Atlanta	17 90
Oxford	14 00	Wayland	18 20
Norwich	14 00	Dansville	18 70
Sherburne	14 25	Mount Morris	18 70
Waterville	14 25	Buffalo	21 00

EXCURSION NO. 67 Y.—ATLANTIC CITY AND RETURN.

Limited to six (6) months from date of sale.
Del., Lack. & Western R. R.....to Manunka Chunk.
Pennsylvania Railroad.............to Atlantic City.
Pennsylvania Railroad...........to New York.
Del., Lack. & Western R. R......to starting point.

EXCURSION NO. 68.—REVERSE OF THE PRECEDING.

(Good for passage *via* either Philadelphia (Broad St. Station) or Amboy Division to Camden.)

THROUGH RATES.

Stroudsburg	$ 8 80	Cortland	$15 00
Scranton	10 00	Syracuse	16 00
Pittston	10 45	Fulton	17 00
Kingston	10 80	Oswego	17 50
Wilkesbarre	10 80	Owego	13 75
Montrose	12 30	Ithaca	15 15
Binghamton	12 50	Waverly	14 90
Greene	13 30	Elmira	15 90
Oxford	13 80	Corning	16 85
Norwich	14 15	Bath	18 10
Sherburne	14 30	Atlanta	19 25
Waterville	14 30	Wayland	19 60
Richfield Springs	15 65	Dansville	20 00
Utica	14 30	Mount Morris	21 75
		Buffalo	$21 75

BAR HARBOR, ME. (MT. DESERT.)

This Island (named by Champlain in 1604, L'isle des Monts Desert) is about one hundred miles (water route) east of Portland, Maine. Bar Harbor is the principal village, containing numerous residences and hotels. The Island, which is about fourteen miles by eight, contains a wonderful variety of nature's beauties in the same line. Mountains, the highest on the Atlantic coast, beautiful valleys, lakes of great depth and peculiar surroundings, roaring streams and great brooks. It is very popular from the fact that the varied character of its charms attracts alike the mountaineer, the hunter, the yachtsman, artist, naturalist, and the poet.

EXCURSION S T 7.—BOSTON TO BAR HARBOR AND RETURN.

Boston & Maine Railroad.............to Portland.
Maine Central Railroad..............to Bath.
Knox & Lincoln Railroad............to Rockland.
Boston & Bangor Steamship Co....to Bar Harbor.
Returning *via* same route.
Rate.........................$10 00

*EXCURSION S T 8.—BOSTON TO BAR HARBOR AND RETURN.

Boston & Maine Railroad.............to Portland.
Maine Central Railroad..............to Bath.
Knox & Lincoln Railroad............to Rockland.
Portland, Bangor, Mt. Desert and
  Machias Steamboat Co...........to Bar Harbor.
Returning *via* same route.
Rate.........................$10 00

*EXCURSION S. T. 11.—BOSTON TO BAR HARBOR AND RETURN.

Boston & Maine Railroad............to Portland.
Maine Central Railroad.............to Bar Harbor.
Returning *via* same route.
Limited to continuous passage between Portland and Bar Harbor.
Rate.........................$11 50

*EXCURSION S T 10.—BOSTON TO BAR HARBOR AND RETURN.

Boston & Bangor Steamship Co.'s Steamer ...... { to Bar Harbor and return.
Rate.... .... $7 50

* Sold only in connection with Summer Excursion Ticket to, or passing through Boston.

†EXCURSION S T 28.—PORTLAND TO BAR HARBOR AND RETURN.

Maine Central Railroad............ { to Bar Harbor and return.
Limited to continuous passage in both directions.
Rate............................$8 50

†EXCURSION S T 29.—PORTLAND TO BAR HARBOR AND RETURN.

Maine Central Railroad .... to Bath.
Knox & Lincoln Railroad............to Rockland.
Boston & Bangor Steamship Co.......to Bar Harbor.
Returning via same route.
Rate...........................$7 00

†EXCURSION S T 30.—PORTLAND TO BAR HARBOR AND RETURN.

Maine Central Railroad........... to Bath.
Knox & Lincoln Railroad............to Rockland.
Portland, Bangor, Mt. Desert and
 Machias Steamboat Co ....to Bar Harbor.
Returning via same route.
Rate $7 00

† Sold only in connection with Summer Excursion Ticket to, or passing through, Portland.

BARNEGAT CITY, N. J.

Barnegat is one of the oldest and most celebrated settlements on the Jersey coast, and many are the traditions that cluster about its shores, so full of peril to sailors. The very name means "dangerous breakers," and many an old sailor would testify to the fitness of the appellation.

The town, located near the shores of Barnegat Bay, is the Metropolis of the fishing-grounds of New Jersey. The bay and inlet are the favorite haunts of bluefish, as well as the home of every other species native to the waters of that section.

In addition to its fishing resources, oysters are plentiful, and wild fowl are found in great abundance.

Yachts, tackle and sportsmen's supplies may be obtained from the seafaring people, of which the population is largely composed.

EXCURSION NO. 275.—BARNEGAT CITY AND RETURN.

Del., Lack. & Western R. R.....to Manunka Chunk.
Pennsylvania R. R. via Trenton.to Whiting's.
Tuckerton Railroad ....to Manahawken.
Pennsylvania Railroad..........to Barnegat City.
Returning via same route.

THROUGH RATES.

Water Gap	$6 00	Ithaca	$12 65
Stroudsburg.......	6 30	Waverly..........	12 05
Scranton..........	8 65	Elmira	12 75
Pittston...........	8 65	Corning	13 00
Kingston..........	8 65	Oxford............	11 80
Wilkesbarre......	8 65	Norwich..........	12 10
Binghamton......	10 45	Sherburne........	12 55
Greene....	11 25	Waterville........	13 45
Oswego...........	15 05	Richfield Springs...	14 60
Owego............	11 30	Utica	14 25

Cortland...........	$12 20	Wayland..........	$15 55
Syracuse......	13 65	Dansville.	15 55
Bath	14 25	Mount Morris.....	16 10
Atlanta............	15 25	Buffalo	16 10

EXCURSION No. 276.—BARNEGAT CITY AND RETURN.

Del., Lack. & Western R. R.........to New York.
Pennsylvania R. R. via Trenton....to Whiting's.
Tuckerton Railroad ....to Manahawken.
Pennsylvania Railroad ....to Barnegat City.
Returning via same route.

THROUGH RATES.

Morristown.........$	5 75	Richfield Springs ..$	15 25
Dover.....	6 25	Cortland	14 50
Hackettstown......	6 95	Syracuse	15 50
Washington.......	7 35	Fulton	16 00
Water Gap.........	8 20	Oswego...	16 50
Stroudsburg........	8 35	Owego.	13 40
Scranton	10 50	Ithaca............	15 00
Pittston...........	10 90	Waverly..........	14 10
Kingston..........	11 30	Elmira	14 95
Wilkesbarre.......	11 35	Corning	15 40
Binghamton.......	12 50	Bath.....	16 25
Greene............	13 30	Atlanta...........	17 40
Oxford............	13 50	Wayland	17 70
Norwich..........	13 50	Dansville.........	18 20
Sherburne........	13 75	Mount Morris......	18 20
Waterville........	13 75	Buffalo	20 50
Utica	13 75		

BEACH HAVEN, N. J.

EXCURSION NO. 277.—BEACH HAVEN AND RETURN.

Del., Lack. & Western R. R.....to Manunka Chunk.
Pennsylvania R. R. via Trenton.to Whiting's.
Tuckerton Railroad............to Manahawken.
Pennsylvania Railroad.........to Beach Haven.
Returning via same route.

THROUGH RATES.

Water Gap.........$	6 00	Cortland...........$	12 20
Stroudsburg........	6 30	Syracuse	13 65
Scranton	8 65	Oswego	15 05
Pittston	8 65	Owego...........	11 30
Kingston.........	8 65	Ithaca	12 65
Wilkesbarre.......	8 65	Waverly.........	12 05
Binghamton.......	10 45	Elmira...........	12 75
Greene...	11 25	Corning	13 70
Oxford...........	11 80	Bath.............	14 95
Norwich..........	12 10	Atlanta...........	16 10
Sherburne	12 55	Wayland..	16 45
Waterville........	13 45	Dansville.........	16 85
Richfield Springs...	14 60	Mount Morris.....	17 55
Utica	14 25	Buffalo	19 35

EXCURSION NO. 278.—BEACH HAVEN AND RETURN.

Del., Lack. & Western R. R.........to New York.
Pennsylvania R. R. via Trenton... to Whiting's.
Tuckerton Railroad....... ....to Manahawken.
Pennsylvania Railroad............to Beach Haven.
Returning via same route,

THROUGH RATES.

Morristown ....$	5 75	Utica............$	13 75
Dover	6 25	Cortland..........	14 50
Hackettstown.....	6 95	Syracuse	15 50
Washington.	7 35	Fulton	16 00
Water Gap........	8 20	Oswego	16 50
Stroudsburg.......	8 35	Owego............	13 40
Scranton	10 50	Ithaca............	15 00
Pittston..........	10 90	Waverly..........	14 10
Kingston.........	11 30	Elmira	14 95
Wilkesbarre.......	11 35	Corning	15 40
Binghamton......	12 50	Bath	16 25
Greene...........	13 50	Atlanta...........	17 40
Oxford...........	13 50	Wayland	17 70
Norwich..........	13 50	Dansville.........	18 20
Sherburne........	13 75	Mount Morris.....	18 20
Waterville........	13 75	Buffalo	20 50
Richfield Springs...	15 25		

BETHLEHEM, N. H.
(WHITE MOUNTAINS.)

This village is said to be the highest of any east of the Rocky Mountains—*i. e.*, 1,500 feet above the level of the ocean. It is quite famous as a resort for persons afflicted with hay-fever, who find here a relief. The Hay-Fever Club assembles at Bethlehem annually. Pure air, convenience to the many attractive resorts in the Presidential range in the White Mountains and the facilities offered by a good sized village, are only a few of the claims of this pretty region.

Exc. S T 37.—BOSTON TO BETHLEHEM AND RETURN.

Bos. & Maine R. R (Lowell Sys.).to Nashua.
Boston & Maine R. R ....to Concord.
Boston & Maine R. R.......... ...to Bethlehem June.
Profile & Franconia Notch R. R..to Bethlehem.
Returning *via* same route.
Sold only in connection with Summer Excursion Ticket to, or passing through, Boston.
Rate......................$10 00

Exc. S T 46.—BOSTON TO BETHLEHEM AND RETURN.

Boston & Maine Railroad..........to North Conway.
Me. C. R. R. (White Moun. Line).to Crawford House.
Me. C. R. R. (White Moun. Line) to Fabyan's.
Boston & Maine Railroad........ to Bethlehem Junc.
Profile & Franconia Notch R. R..to Bethlehem.
Returning *via* same route.
Sold only in connection with Summer Excursion Ticket to, or passing through, Boston.
Rate......................$10 00

Exc. S T 38.—BETHLEHEM JUNCTION TO BETHLEHEM AND RETURN.

Profile & Fran. Notch R. R. to Bethlehem and return.
Sold only in connection with Summer Excursion Ticket passing through Bethlehem Junction.
Rate......................$1 00

BLOCK ISLAND, R. I.

To be at once far out at sea and yet on terra firma—is what Block Island offers to the dwellers of the city and country. A change of air is certainly to be obtained here if anywhere, for it is a sea island—south from Point Judith about ten miles.

It is reached by steamer from New London.

EXCURSION No. 35.—BLOCK ISLAND AND RETURN.

Delaware, Lack. & Western R. R....to New York.
Norwich Line Steamers..............to New London.
Steamer Block Island ....to Block Island.
Returning *via* same route.

THROUGH RATES.

Morristown	$5 55	Waterville	$14 30
Dover	6 05	Cortland	14 30
Hackettstown	6 75	Syracuse	15 30
Washington	7 15	Oswego	16 30
Water Gap	8 00	Owego	13 15
Stroudsburg	8 15	Ithaca	14 80
Scranton	10 30	Waverly	13 00
Pittston	10 70	Elmira	14 75
Kingston	11 10	Corning	15 20
Wilkesbarre	11 15	Bath	16 05
Binghamton	12 30	Atlanta	17 20
Greene	13 10	Wayland	17 50
Oxford	13 30	Dansville	17 75
Norwich	13 30	Mount Morris	17 75
Sherburne	14 00	Buffalo	20 30

EXCURSION No. 176.—BLOCK ISLAND AND RETURN.

Delaware, Lack. & Western R. R....to New York.
Fall River Line Steamers..........to Newport.
Steamer......................to Block Island.
Returning *via* same route.

THROUGH RATES.

Morristown	$8 25	Utica	$16 25
Dover	8 75	Cortland	17 00
Hackettstown	9 45	Syracuse	18 00
Washington	9 85	Oswego	19 00
Water Gap	10 70	Owego	15 85
Stroudsburg	10 85	Ithaca	17 50
Scranton	13 00	Waverly	16 60
Pittston	13 40	Elmira	17 45
Kingston	13 80	Corning	17 80
Wilkesbarre	13 85	Bath	18 75
Binghamton	15 00	Atlanta	19 80
Greene	15 80	Wayland	20 20
Oxford	16 00	Dansville	20 60
Norwich	16 00	Mount Morris	20 60
Sherburne	16 25	Buffalo	23 00
Waterville	16 25		

BOSTON, MASS.

These Excursion tickets to Boston have been prepared for use in connection with extension tickets of D., L. & W. R, R, issue, from Boston and returning to Boston, thus making complete round-trip tickets from point of sale. *These forms are not for sale except in connection with the extension tickets.*

EXCURSION No. 125.—BOSTON AND RETURN.

Delaware, Lack. & Western R. R......to New York.
Fall River Line Steamers. ....to Fall River.
N. Y., New Haven & Hartford R. R....to Boston.
Returning *via* same route.

THROUGH RATES.

Morristown	$9 25	Utica	$17 25
Dover	9 75	Cortland	18 00
Hackettstown	10 45	Syracuse	19 00
Washington	10 85	Oswego	20 00
Water Gap	11 70	Owego	16 85
Stroudsburg	11 85	Ithaca	18 50
Scranton	14 00	Waverly	17 60
Pittston	14 40	Elmira	18 45
Kingston	14 80	Corning	18 90
Wilkesbarre	14 85	Bath	19 75
Binghamton	16 00	Atlanta	20 90
Greene	16 80	Wayland	21 20
Oxford	17 00	Dansville	21 70
Norwich	17 00	Mount Morris	21 70
Sherburne	17 25	Buffalo	24 00
Waterville	17 25		

EXCURSION No. 126.—BOSTON AND RETURN.

Delaware, Lack. & Western R. R...to New York.
Fall River Line Steamers............to Fall River.
N. Y., New Haven & Hartford R.R to Boston.
Fitchburg Railroad................to Saratoga.
Delaware & Hudson Canal Co. (*via* Howe's Cave)................to Binghamton.
Delaware, Lack. & Western R. R...to starting point.

EXCURSION No. 127.—REVERSE OF THE PRECEDING.

THROUGH RATES.

Scranton	$17 00	Ithaca	$19 25
Pittston	17 35	Waverly	18 60
Kingston	17 65	Elmira	19 30
Wilkesbarre	17 65	Corning	19 85
Binghamton	16 95	Bath	20 60
Greene	17 75	Atlanta	21 35
Oxford	18 30	Wayland	21 70
Norwich	18 65	Dansville	22 05
Cortland	18 70	Mount Morris	22 60
Owego	17 85	Buffalo	24 90

EXCURSION NO. 129.—BOSTON AND RETURN.

Delaware, Lack. & Western R. R...to New York.
Fall River Line Steamer............to Fall River.
N. Y., New Haven & Hartford R. R. to Boston.
Fitchburg Railroad .... to Mechanicsville.
Delaware & Hudson Canal Co. (*via*
— Howe's Cave)..................to Binghamton.
Delaware, Lack. & Western R. R...to starting point.

EXCURSION NO. 130.—REVERSE OF THE PRECEDING.

THROUGH RATES.

Scranton	$15 50	Ithaca	$17 80
Pittston	15 85	Waverly	17 50
Kingston	16 15	Elmira	17 85
Wilkesbarre	16 15	Corning	18 40
Binghamton	15 50	Bath	19 15
Greene	16 30	Atlanta	19 90
Oxford	16 85	Wayland	20 25
Norwich	17 20	Dansville	20 60
Cortland	17 25	Mount Morris	21 15
Owego	16 40	Buffalo	22 50

EXCURSION NO. 128.—BOSTON AND RETURN.

Delaware, Lack. & Western R. R..to Binghamton.
Delaware & Hudson Canal Co., (*via*
Howe's Cave)..................to Mechanicsville.
Fitchburg Railroad.... ....to Boston.
Returning *via* same route.

THROUGH RATES.

Scranton	$16 20	Elmira	$16 05
Greene	14 50	Corning	16 60
Oxford	15 05	Bath	17 35
Norwich	15 40	Atlanta	18 10
Cortland	15 45	Wayland	18 45
Owego	14 60	Dansville	18 80
Ithaca	16 00	Mount Morris	19 35
Waverly	15 35	Buffalo	19 50

EXCURSION NO. 131.—BOSTON AND RETURN.

Delaware, Lack. & Western R. R..to Binghamton.
Del. & Hud. C. C. *via* Howe's Cave..to Saratoga.
Fitchburg Railroad...............to Boston.
Fitchburg Railroad................to Mechanicsville.
Delaware & Hudson Canal Co....to Binghamton.
Delaware, Lack. & Western R. R..to starting point.

EXCURSION NO. 132.—REVERSE OF THE PRECEDING.

THROUGH RATES.

Scranton	$18 65	Elmira	$18 50
Greene	16 95	Corning	19 05
Oxford	17 50	Bath	19 80
Norwich	17 85	Atlanta	20 55
Cortland	17 90	Wayland	20 90
Owego	17 05	Dansville	21 25
Ithaca	17 15	Mount Morris	21 80
Waverly	17 80	Buffalo	22 20

CALDWELL, N. Y. (Lake George.)

EXC. S T 18.—SARATOGA TO CALDWELL AND RETURN.

Delaware & Hud. Canal Co..to Caldwell and return.
Sold only in connection with Summer Excursion.
Ticket to or passing through Saratoga.
Rate.... .. ..$2 88.

CAPE MAY, N. J.

The distinctive characteristics of Cape May are its delightful temperature, magnificent beach and surf, grand ocean view, and the charm of its refined society. The beach is probably the finest for surf bathing in the world.

EXCURSION NO. 60 Y.—CAPE MAY AND RETURN.

Limited to six (6) months from date of sale.
Del., Lack. & Western R. R... to Manunka Chunk.
Pennsylvania Railroad..........to Cape May.
Returning *via* same route.
(Good for passage *via* either Philadelphia (Broad Street Station) or Amboy Division *via* Camden.)

THROUGH RATES.

Stroudsburg	$ 6 60	Cortland	$13 20
Scranton	9 00	Syracuse	14 65
Pittston	9 00	Fulton	15 65
Kingston	9 00	Oswego	16 05
Wilkesbarre	9 00	Owego	12 00
Montrose	11 30	Ithaca	13 05
Binghamton	11 50	Waverly	12 00
Greene	12 30	Elmira	12 00
Oxford	12 80	Corning	12 95
Norwich	13 15	Bath	14 20
Sherburne	13 60	Atlanta	15 30
Waterville	14 45	Wayland	15 70
Richfield Springs	15 60	Dansville	16 10
Utica	14 75	Mount Morris	16 80
		Buffalo	$18 60

EXCURSION NO. 61 Y.—CAPE MAY AND RETURN.

Limited to six (6) months from date of sale.
Delaware, Lack. & Western R. R .....to New York.
Pennsylvania Railroad............. to Cape May.
Returning *via* same route.
(Good for passage *via* either Philadelphia (Broad Street Station) or Amboy Division *via* Camden.)

THROUGH RATES.

Summit	$ 6 30	Richfield Springs	$16 25
Morristown	6 75	Utica	14 75
Dover	7 25	Cortland	15 50
Hackettstown	7 95	Syracuse	16 50
Washington	8 35	Fulton	17 00
Stroudsburg	8 55	Oswego	17 50
Scranton	11 50	Owego	14 35
Pittston	11 90	Ithaca	15 75
Kingston	12 30	Waverly	15 10
Wilkesbarre	12 35	Elmira	15 95
Montrose	13 70	Corning	16 40
Binghamton	13 50	Bath	17 25
Greene	14 30	Atlanta	18 40
Oxford	14 50	Wayland	18 70
Norwich	14 50	Dansville	19 20
Sherburne	14 75	Mount Morris	19 50
Waterville	14 75	Buffalo	21 50

EXCURSION NO. 62 Y.—CAPE MAY AND RETURN.

Limited to six (6) months from date of sale.
Del., Lack. & Western R. R....to Manunka Chunk.
Pennsylvania Railroad..........to Cape May.
Pennsylvania Railroad..........to New York.
Del., Lack. & Western R.....to starting point.

EXCURSION NO. 63 Y.—REVERSE OF THE PRECEDING.

Limited to six (6) months from date of sale.
(Good for passage *via* either Philadelphia (Broad Street Station) or Amboy Division *via* Camden.)

THROUGH RATES.

Stroudsburg	$ 9 30	Cortland	$15 50
Scranton	10 50	Syracuse	17 00
Pittston	10 95	Fulton	17 50
Kingston	11 30	Oswego	18 90
Wilkesbarre	11 30	Owego	15 35
Montrose	12 80	Ithaca	15 65
Binghamton	13 00	Waverly	15 40
Greene	13 80	Elmira	16 40
Oxford	14 70	Corning	17 35
Norwich	14 65	Bath	18 60
Sherburne	14 80	Atlanta	19 75
Waterville	14 80	Wayland	20 10
Richfield Springs	16 15	Dansville	20 50
Utica	14 80	Mount Morris	22 25
		Buffalo	$22 25

ALONG THE CHEMUNG, AT APALACHIN.

CAPE VINCENT, N. Y.

EXCURSION NO. 177.—CAPE VINCENT AND RETURN.

Delaware, Lack. & Western R. R. to Utica.
Rome, Watert'n & Ogdensb'g R. R. to Cape Vincent.
Returning *via* same route.

THROUGH RATES.

New York	$15 25	Berwick	$14 05
Paterson	15 25	Bloomsburg	14 60
Newark	15 25	Danville	15 00
Morristown	15 25	Binghamton	9 80
Dover	15 25	Greene	9 05
Hackettstown	15 25	Oxford	8 50
Washington	15 25	Norwich	8 20
Water Gap	14 60	Sherburne	7 75
Stroudsburg	14 40	Waterville	6 90
Scranton	12 30	Richfield Springs	7 50
Pittston	12 70	Vestal	10 15
Kingston	13 00	Owego	10 65
Wilkesbarre	13 60	Waverly	11 40
Plymouth	13 15	Elmira	12 10
Nanticoke	13 25	Corning	12 60
Shickshinny	13 60	Bath	13 60

EXCURSION NO. 178.—CAPE VINCENT AND RETURN.

Delaware, Lack. & Western R. R. to Syracuse.
Rome, Watert'n & Ogdensb'g R. R. to Cape Vincent,
Returning *via* same route.

THROUGH RATES.

New York	$15 25	Washington	$14 30
Paterson	15 25	Water Gap	13 50
Newark	15 25	Stroudsburg	13 30
Morristown	15 25	Scranton	11 20
Dover	15 25	Pittston	11 55
Hackettstown	14 70	Kingston	11 85

Wilkesbarre	$11 85	Danville	$13 90
Plymouth	12 00	Binghamton	8 70
Nanticoke	12 10	Cortland	7 00
Shickshinny	12 50	Vestal	9 05
Berwick	12 50	Owego	9 50
Bloomsburg	13 45	Waverly	10 00
		Elmira	$10 00

EXCURSION NO. 179.—CAPE VINCENT AND RETURN.

Delaware, Lack. & Western R. R. to Oswego,
Rome, Watert'n & Ogdensb'g R. R. to Cape Vincent.
Returning *via* same route.

THROUGH RATES.

New York	$15 25	Kingston	$12 80
Paterson	15 25	Wilkesbarre	12 80
Newark	15 25	Plymouth	12 90
Morristown	15 25	Nanticoke	13 00
Dover	15 25	Shickshinny	13 40
Hackettstown	15 25	Berwick	13 80
Washington	15 25	Bloomsburg	14 35
Water Gap	14 40	Danville	14 80
Stroudsburg	14 20	Binghamton	9 60
Scranton	12 10	Cortland	7 90
Pittston	12 45	Syracuse	6 40
		Vestal	$9 95

CHARLOTTETOWN, P. E. I.

(See Halifax, Nova Scotia.)

Page 137.

CHATHAM, MASS.
EXCURSION No. 280—CHATHAM AND RETURN.

Delaware, Lack. & Western R. R. ....to New York.
Fall River Line Steamers..............to Fall River.
Old Colony Railroad..................to Chatham.
Returning *via* same route.

THROUGH RATES.

Morristown	$10 25	Waterville	$19 00
Dover	10 75	Cortland	19 00
Hackettstown	11 45	Syracuse	20 00
Washington	11 85	Oswego	21 00
Water Gap	12 70	Owego	17 85
Stroudsburg	12 85	Ithaca	19 50
Scranton	15 00	Waverly	18 60
Pittston	15 40	Elmira	19 45
Kingston	15 80	Corning	19 90
Wilkesbarre	15 85	Bath	20 75
Binghamton	17 00	Atlanta	21 90
Greene	17 80	Wayland	22 25
Oxford	18 00	Dansville	22 70
Norwich	18 00	Mount Morris	22 70
Sherburne	18 70	Buffalo	25 00

CHAUTAUQUA LAKE, N. Y.

This magnificent sheet of water is situated on a table land 1,400 feet above the sea level, and enjoys the distinction of being the highest navigable inland sea on the continent. Situated in Western New York in the county of Chautauqua, it is eighteen miles long and ranges from one to five miles in width.

In many respects this lake is the most magnificent in this country. Aside from its altitude, the scenery along its shores is of such a beautiful character that artists find fresh snatches to paint each recurring season. The water is deep and transparent, and as pure as crystal. No wonder, then, that it should abound in fine game fish, and yearly attract anglers to its shore. The air is always cool and invigorating, and here malaria is absolutely unknown. The boating and bathing are superb, and the drives along the shores of the lake and back in the hills are unsurpassed, and scarcely to be equalled anywhere. These features have combined to draw admiring thousands of intellectual holiday-seekers here every summer, and to establish several large well-appointed hotels.

The class of people that patronize Chautauqua are lovers of the beautiful in nature, who appreciate all that the Creator has bestowed upon it, and know how to get pleasure out of every daylight moment, and invigorating and restful sleep out of the calm, cool nights.

A fleet of steamers ply on the lake daily, and carry excursionists all around it. The scene on the water in the daytime, and for

SNAP SHOT.—NO. 6 AT 70 MILES PER HOUR.

that matter after moondawn, is one of animation. Steam yachts, launches, row boats and shells are darting in all directions, and the "lone fisherman" sits in quiet contemplation, awaiting the "tug" of a bass or pickerel. In the fall the duck shooting about the coves and nooks is excellent, and gunners flock there with the same regularity as the wild fowl.

The *Chautauqua Assembly*, organized in 1874, holds its meetings every July and August. The purpose of the enterprise is to combine the recreations of a summer resort with intellectual culture and improvement. The Assembly is a great educational institution that attracts teachers of all grades here, both for information and to commune about their fraternal interests, and this has proved itself one of the most prominent features of attraction. The Assembly grounds are at Point Chautauqua. To lovers of gayety, Lakewood, a few miles distant, offers every opportunity. And among many of the most beautiful drives in this neighborhood, is from Jamestown to Mayville; and, as for aquatic attractions, a sail on the lake is a beautiful sight that awaits the person who will spend the time in steaming from Jamestown through the narrows.

EXCURSION NO. 4.—CHAUTAUQUA AND RETURN.

Delaware, Lack. & Western R. R....to Buffalo.
Western New York & Penn. R. R....to Mayville.
Chautauqua Lake Steamboat Co.....to Chautauqua.
Returning *via* same route.

EXCURSION NO. 345.—CHAUTAUQUA AND RETURN.

Delaware, Lack. & Western R. R....to Buffalo.
Western New York & Penn. R. R....to Mayville.
Chautauqua Lake Railway.....to Chautauqua.
Returning *via* same route.

THROUGH RATES FOR EITHER EXCURSION.

New York	$17 00	Greene	$11 70
Paterson	17 00	Oxford	12 55
Newark	17 00	Norwich	13 05
Morristown	17 00	Sherburne	13 70
Dover	17 00	Owego	9 50
Hackettstown	16 90	Ithaca	9 50
Washington	16 50	Waverly	8 75
Water Gap	15 70	Elmira	8 25
Stroudsburg	15 50	Corning	8 00
Scranton	12 65	Bath	6 95
Pittston	12 65	Atlanta	5 95
Kingston	12 65	Wayland	5 75
Wilkesbarre	12 65	Dansville	5 75
Binghamton	10 50	Mount Morris	5 30

CLAYTON, N. Y.

EXCURSION NO. 13.—CLAYTON AND RETURN.

Delaware, Lack. & Western R. R.........to Utica.
Rome, Watertown & Ogdensburg R. R....to Clayton.
Returning *via* same route.

THROUGH RATES.

New York	$15 25	Hackettstown	$15 25
Paterson	15 25	Washington	15 25
Newark	15 25	Water Gap	14 60
Morristown	15 25	Stroudsburg	14 40
Dover	15 25	Scranton	12 30

Pittston	$12 70	Oxford	$8 50
Kingston	13 00	Norwich	8 20
Wilkesbarre	13 00	Sherburne	7 75
Plymouth	13 15	Waterville	6 90
Nanticoke	13 25	Richfield Springs	7 50
Shickshinny	13 60	Vestal	10 15
Berwick	14 05	Owego	10 65
Bloomsburg	14 60	Waverly	11 40
Danville	15 00	Elmira	12 10
Binghamton	9 80	Corning	12 60
Greene	9 05	Bath	13 60

EXCURSION NO. 11.—CLAYTON AND RETURN.

Delaware, Lack. & Western R. R........to Syracuse.
Rome, Watertown & Ogdensburg R. R...to Clayton.
Returning *via* same route.

THROUGH RATES.

New York	$15 25	Wilkesbarre	$11 70
Paterson	15 25	Plymouth	11 85
Newark	15 25	Nanticoke	12 00
Morristown	15 25	Shickshinny	12 35
Dover	15 25	Berwick	12 80
Hackettstown	15 25	Bloomsburg	13 30
Washington	14 80	Danville	13 80
Water Gap	14 00	Binghamton	9 20
Stroudsburg	13 80	Cortland	7 50
Scranton	11 70	Vestal	9 55
Pittston	11 70	Owego	10 00
Kingston	11 70	Waverly	10 50
Elmira			$10 50

EXCURSION NO. 180.—CLAYTON AND RETURN.

Delaware, Lackawanna & Western R. R...to Oswego.
Rome, Watertown & Ogdensburg R. R....to Clayton.
Returning *via* same route.

THROUGH RATES.

New York	$15 25	Kingston	$13 30
Paterson	15 25	Wilkesbarre	13 30
Newark	15 25	Plymouth	13 40
Morristown	15 25	Nanticoke	13 50
Dover	15 25	Shickshinny	13 90
Hackettstown	15 25	Berwick	14 30
Washington	15 25	Bloomsburg	14 85
Water Gap	14 90	Danville	15 30
Stroudsburg	14 70	Binghamton	10 10
Scranton	12 60	Cortland	8 40
Pittston	12 95	Syracuse	6 90
Vestal			$10 45

COOPERSTOWN, N. Y.

EXCURSION NO. 14.—COOPERSTOWN AND RETURN.

Delaware, Lack. & Western R. R..to Richfield Sp'gs.
Otsego L. Steamboat Co. and stage to Cooperstown.
Returning *via* same route.

THROUGH RATES.

New York	$11 45	Greene	$5 40
Paterson	11 45	Oxford	4 85
Newark	11 45	Norwich	4 55
Morristown	11 45	Sherburne	4 05
Dover	11 45	Waterville	3 20
Hackettstown	11 45	Bridgewater	2 70
Washington	11 45	West Winfield	2 60
Water Gap	10 95	Clayville	3 00
Stroudsburg	10 80	Sauquoit	3 05
Scranton	8 65	Utica	3 50
Pittston	9 00	Owego	7 00
Kingston	9 35	Ithica	8 35
Wilkesbarre	9 35	Waverly	7 75
Plymouth	9 45	Elmira	8 45
Nanticoke	9 60	Corning	9 10
Shickshinny	10 00	Bath	9 90
Berwick	10 40	Atlanta	10 70
Bloomsburg	10 90	Wayland	10 95
Danville	11 40	Dansville	11 20
Binghamton	6 20	Mount Morris	11 80
Buffalo			$12 00

DELAWARE, LACKAWANNA & WESTERN R. R.

EXCURSION NO. 395.—COOPERSTOWN AND RETURN.

Del., Lack, & Western R. R..to Binghamton.
Delaware & Hud. Canal Co...to C. & C. V. R. R. Junc.
Cooperst'n & Char. Val'y R. R.to Cooperstown.
Returning *via* same route.

THROUGH RATES.

New York	$12 00	Shickshinny	$7 80
Paterson	11 50	Berwick	8 25
Newark	12 00	Bloomsburg	8 75
Morristown	11 20	Danville	9 20
Dover	10 75	Cortland	5 70
Hackettstown	10 00	Owego	4 90
Washington	9 00	Ithaca	6 25
Water Gap	8 75	Waverly	5 65
Stroudsburg	8 70	Elmira	6 35
Scranton	6 50	Corning	6 90
Pittston	6 85	Bath	7 65
Kingston	7 20	Atlanta	8 40
Wilkesbarre	7 20	Wayland	8 75
Plymouth	7 30	Mount Morris	9 10
Nanticoke	7 45		9 65
Buffalo	$11 50		

EXCURSION NO. 2.—COOPERSTOWN AND RETURN.

Del., Lack. & Western R. R..to Binghamton.
Delaware & Hud. Canal Co..to C. & C. V. R. R. Junc.
Cooperst'n & Char. Val'yR.R.to Cooperstown.
Otsego L. Stea'b'tCo. & Stage.to Richfield Springs.
Del., Lack. & Western R. R..to starting point.

EXCURSION NO. 3.—REVERSE OF THE PRECEDING.

THROUGH RATES.

New York	$11 65	Berwick	$9 70
Paterson	11 65	Bloomsburg	10 20
Newark	11 65	Dansville	10 70
Morristown	11 65	Binghamton	5 50
Dover	11 65	Cortland	6 75
Hackettstown	11 50	Owego	6 30
Washington	11 10	Ithaca	7 70
Water Gap	10 25	Waverly	7 05
Stroudsburg	10 10	Elmira	7 75
Scranton	8 00	Corning	8 40
Pittston	8 35	Bath	9 25
Kingston	8 05	Atlanta	9 85
Wilkesbarre	8 05	Wayland	10 05
Plymouth	8 80	Dansville	10 55
Nanticoke	8 90	Mount Morris	11 10
Shickshinny	9 30	Buffalo	12 50

Exc. S. T. 32.—C. & C. V. JUNCTION TO COOPERSTOWN AND RETURN.

C. & C. Valley Railroad..to Cooperstown and return.
Sold only in connection with summer Excursion Ticket to, or passing through Cooperstown & Charlotte Valley R. R. Junction.
Rate............$1 30

COTTAGE CITY (Martha's Vineyard), MASS.

Cottage City developed into a summer resort through the ministrations of the Methodists. Captivated by the beauty and healthfulness of the location, they built an enormous tabernacle for public worship and set up their tents around it. Presently the tents became cottages, and, as the population increased, a large summer town was built, which has attracted many visitors other than those who came to worship.

The shores of Martha's Vineyard, on which Cottage City is located, are exceedingly attractive, and their fascinations are greatly enhanced by the animation which always prevails upon the surrounding waters. All the marine travel between New York and Boston, and between Boston and the South passes through Holmes' Hole and Vineyard Sound, and these bits of ocean are always alive with shipping. Bluffs and cliffs overhang the shore in many places, and many beautiful islets are separated from the mother island by a narrow strip of water.

EXC. NO. 20.—COTTAGE CITY (MARTHA'S VINEYARD) AND RETURN.

Delaware, Lack. & Western R. R...to New York.
Fall River Line Steamers...........to Fall River.
Old Colony Railroad................to New Bedford.
New Bedford, Vineyard, Nantucket } to Cottage City.
 & Cape Cod S. B. Line............}
Returning *via* same route.

THROUGH RATES.

Morristown	$8 50	Waterville	$17 25
Dover	9 00	Cortland	17 25
Hackettstown	9 70	Syracuse	18 25
Washington	10 10	Oswego	19 25
Water Gap	10 95	Owego	16 10
Stroudsburg	11 10	Ithaca	17 75
Scranton	13 25	Waverly	16 85
Pittston	13 05	Elmira	17 70
Kingston	14 05	Corning	18 15
Wilkesbarre	14 10	Bath	19 00
Binghamton	15 25	Atlanta	20 15
Greene	16 05	Wayland	20 45
Oxford	16 25	Dansville	20 95
Norwich	16 25	Mount Morris	20 95
Sherburne	16 95	Buffalo	23 25

CRAWFORD HOUSE, N. H. (WHITE MOUNTAINS.)

The Crawford House is situated on a plateau 2,000 feet above the sea, and commands a magnificent view of Mt. Washington (6,293 feet), and Mt. Monroe (5,349 feet). The bridle path up Mt. Washington passes over Mounts Pleasant, Monroe, Franklin and Clinton, and is said to afford finer views than any other route.

Within easy reach of the Crawford House are, the Notch, a huge chasm in the mountains, which rises 2,000 feet on either side; Silver Cascade and Sylvan Glade Cataract, between which it is hard to award the palm; and Mount Willard, commanding a view down the Notch.

EXC. S. T. 39.—FABYAN'S TO CRAWFORD HOUSE AND RETURN.

Me. C. R. R. (White Moun. Line)..to Crawford House.
Sold only in connection with Summer Excursion Ticket to, or passing through Fabyan's.
Rate ....50 cents

EXC. S. T. 40.—BOSTON TO CRAWFORD HOUSE AND RETURN.

Boston and Maine Railroad......to North Conway.
Me. C. R. R. (White Moun. Line).to Crawford House.
Returning *via* same route.
Sold only in connection with Summer Excursion Ticket to, or passing through Boston.
Rate...............$9 25

CRESCO, PA.

LOCAL EXCURSION.
(Good for continuous passage only.)

THROUGH RATES.

*New York	$4 45	Nanticoke	$3 20
Passaic	4 05	Shickshinny	3 45
Paterson	3 90	Berwick	3 75
Boonton	3 35	Bloomsburg	4 05
*Newark	4 45	Danville	4 40
*Roseville	4 45	Great Bend	3 55
Orange	4 15	Binghamton	4 10
Mountain	4 05	Greene	4 90
South Orange	4 00	Oxford	5 40
Milburn	3 85	Norwich	5 75
Short Hills	3 85	Sherburne	6 20
Summit	3 80	Waterville	7 05
Chatham	3 60	Richfield Springs	8 20
Madison	3 50	Utica	7 90
Morristown	3 35	Cortland	5 80
Dover	2 85	Syracuse	7 25
Hopatcong Station	2 55	Oswego	8 65
Andover	2 55	Owego	4 95
Newton	2 85	Ithaca	6 30
Franklin	3 35	Waverly	5 65
Hackettstown	2 15	Elmira	6 40
Washington	1 75	Corning	7 00
Scranton	2 15	Bath	7 75
Pittston	2 55	Atlanta	8 65
Kingston	2 90	Wayland	8 90
Wilkesbarre	2 90	Dansville	9 20
Plymouth	3 05	Mount Morris	9 75
		Buffalo	$12 20

* Tickets good until used.

DANSVILLE, N. Y.

LOCAL EXCURSION.
(Good for continuous passage only.)

THROUGH RATES.

*New York	$13 30	Pittston	$8 00
Passaic	12 90	Kingston	8 45
Paterson	12 80	Wilkesbarre	8 45
Boonton	12 20	Plymouth	8 55
*Newark	13 30	Nanticoke	8 80
*Roseville Ave	13 30	Shickshinny	9 05
Orange	13 00	Berwick	9 05
Mountain	13 00	Bloomsburg	10 00
South Orange	12 95	Danville	10 50
Milburn	12 80	Great Bend	5 65
Short Hills	12 80	Binghamton	5 10
Summit	12 70	Greene	5 85
Chatham	12 55	Oxford	6 40
Madison	12 05	Norwich	6 75
Morristown	12 30	Sherburne	7 20
Dover	11 80	Waterville	8 05
Hopatcong Station	11 25	Richfield Springs	9 20
Andover	11 60	Utica	8 90
*Newton	11 80	Owego	4 25
Franklin	12 30	Ithaca	5 60
Hackettstown	11 10	Waverly	3 55
Washington	10 70	Elmira	2 80
Portland	10 05	Corning	2 20
Water Gap	9 85	Bath	1 35
Stroudsburg	9 70	Atlanta	60
Scranton	7 60	Buffalo	2 70

* Good for stop-over.

DELAWARE WATER GAP, PA.

LOCAL EXCURSION.
(Good for continuous passage only.)

THROUGH RATES.

‡New York	$3 70	Mountain	$3 25
‡Passaic	3 25	South Orange	3 20
Paterson	3 10	Milburn	3 05
‡Newark	3 70	Short Hills	3 00
‡Roseville Ave	3 70	Summit	3 00
Orange	3 35	Chatham	2 80
		Madison	2 70

Morristown	$2 55	Greene	5 60
Dover	2 05	Oxford	6 15
Hopatcong Station	1 70	Norwich	6 45
Andover	1 85	Sherburne	6 90
Newton	2 05	Waterville	7 75
Franklin	2 55	Richfield Springs	8 95
Hackettstown	1 35	Utica	8 60
Washington	95	Cortland	6 55
Scranton	2 95	Syracuse	8 00
Pittston	3 35	Oswego	9 40
Kingston	3 70	Owego	5 60
Wilkesbarre	3 70	Ithaca	7 00
Plymouth	3 85	Waverly	6 40
Nanticoke	4 00	Elmira	7 10
Shickshinny	4 25	Corning	7 75
Berwick	4 55	Bath	8 55
Bloomsburg	4 85	Atlanta	9 35
Danville	5 20	Wayland	9 00
Great Bend	4 25	Dansville	9 90
Binghamton	4 80	Mount Morris	10 40
		Buffalo	$12 95

‡ Tickets good until used.

DENMARK LAKE, N. J.

EXCURSION NO. 291.—LAKE DENMARK AND RETURN.

Del., Lack. & Western R. R......to Chester Junction.
Morris County Railroad....... to Lake Denmark.
Returning via same route.

THROUGH RATES.

New York	$2 25	South Orange	$1 75
Paterson	1 55	Milburn	1 55
Boonton	90	Summit	1 40
Newark	2 00	Madison	1 20
Orange	1 80	Morristown	1 00

ELMHURST, PA.

LOCAL EXCURSION.
(Good for continuous passage only.)

THROUGH RATES.

‡New York	$5 60	Nanticoke	$1 55
Passaic	5 75	Shickshinny	1 80
Paterson	5 60	Berwick	2 10
Boonton	5 05	Bloomsburg	2 40
‡Newark	5 60	Danville	2 75
‡Roseville	5 60	Great Bend	2 35
Orange	5 90	Binghamton	2 90
Mountain	5 75	Greene	3 70
South Orange	5 70	Oxford	4 25
Milburn	5 55	Norwich	4 55
Short Hills	5 50	Sherburne	5 00
Summit	5 50	Waterville	5 85
Chatham	5 30	Richfield Springs	7 05
Madison	5 20	Utica	6 70
Morristown	5 05	Cortland	4 65
Dover	4 55	Syracuse	6 05
Hopatcong Station	4 25	Oswego	7 45
Andover	4 35	Owego	3 75
Newton	4 55	Ithaca	5 10
Franklin	5 05	Waverly	4 45
Hackettstown	3 85	Elmira	5 20
Washington	3 45	Corning	5 85
Scranton	50	Bath	6 65
Pittston	90	Atlanta	7 45
Kingston	1 25	Wayland	7 65
Wilkesbarre	1 25	Dansville	8 00
Plymouth	1 40	Mount Morris	8 55
		Buffalo	$11 00

‡ Tickets good until used.

FABYAN'S, N. H. (WHITE MOUNTAINS.)

Possessing, as it does, a most central location in the famous White Mountain region, Fabyan's presents to the summer tourist not only the attractions usual to mountain resorts, but the unceasing novelty which is invariably part of a thoroughfare of travel. It is the starting point for the ascent by rail of Mt. Washington. The hotel is as popular as any in the White Mountains, possesses all the modern conveniences, and from its porches and windows a very extended view of the entire White Mountain region is to be had.

EXCURSION S. T. 41.—BOSTON TO FABYAN'S AND RETURN.

Boston & Maine Railroad..........to North Conway.
Me. C. R. R. (White Moun. Line)..to Fabyan's.
Returning *via* same route.
Sold only in connection with Summer Excursion Ticket to, or passing through, Boston.
Rate..............$9 45

MOUNT PLEASANT, N. H.

At Mount Pleasant Station (½ mile E. of Fabyan's) is the Mount Pleasant House, most charmingly situated directly in front of the Presidential range, with Mt. Washington looming up in the foreground. From

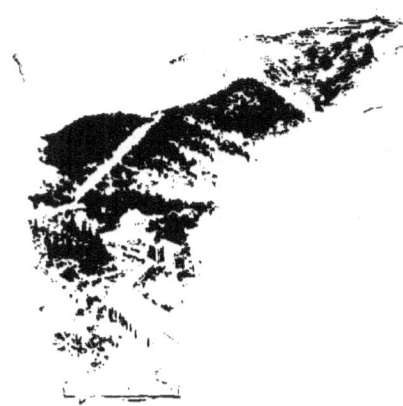

THE ASCENT TO SUMMIT OF MT. WASHINGTON AS SEEN FROM MT. PLEASANT HOUSE.

no other house in the White Mountains can such a perfect and magnificient view of Mt. Washington and its sentinel companions be obtained. From its spacious piazzas one can watch the upward climbing of the cog-wheel trains, almost to the very summit, 6,293 feet into the sky.

Trains for the summit are taken a few steps from the hotel, and trains of the Maine Central and of the Boston and Maine roads stop at the door.

FALMOUTH, MASS.

EXCURSION No. 281.—FALMOUTH AND RETURN.

Delaware, Lack. & Western R. R ...to New York.
Fall River Line Steamers..............to Fall River.
Old Colony Railroad............. ...to Falmouth.
Returning *via* same route.

THROUGH RATES.

Morristown........	$ 8 75	Greene.............	$16 30
Dover.............	9 25	Oxford.............	16 50
Hackettstown.....	9 95	Norwich...........	16 50
Washington.......	10 35	Sherburne.........	17 20
Water Gap........	11 20	Waterville........	17 50
Stroudsburg......	11 35	Cortland..........	17 50
Scranton.........	13 50	Syracuse..........	18 50
Pittston.........	13 90	Oswego............	19 50
Kingston.........	14 30	Owego.............	16 35
Wilkesbarre......	14 35	Ithaca............	18 00
Binghamton......	15 50	Waverly...........	17 10
Elmira...........	17 95	Wayland...........	20 75
Corning..........	18 40	Dansville.........	21 20
Bath.............	19 25	Mount Morris.....	21 20
Atlanta..........	20 40	Buffalo...........	23 50

FORT TICONDEROGA, N. Y. (LAKES GEORGE and CHAMPLAIN.)

*EXCURSION S. T. 19—SARATOGA TO LAKE CHAMPLAIN AND RETURN (*via* LAKE GEORGE.)

Delaware & Hudson Canal Co....to Ft. Ticonderoga.
Delaware & Hudson Canal Co....to Baldwin.
Lake George Steamer........ ...to Caldwell.
Delaware & Hudson Canal Co... to Saratoga.
Rate..............$6 00

EXCURSION S. T. 20.—SARATOGA TO LAKE CHAMPLAIN AND RETURN (*via* LAKE GEORGE).

Delaware & Hudson Canal Co....to Caldwell.
Lake George Steamer.. ....to Baldwin.
Delaware & Hudson Canal Co...to Ft. Ticonderoga.
Delaware & Hudson Canal Co....to Saratoga.
Rate..............$6 00

* Sold only in connection with Summer Excursion Ticket to, or passing through, Saratoga.

GENEVA, N. Y. (SENECA LAKE.)

The pretty town of Geneva, with a population of 9,000, is pleasantly situated on the shores of Seneca Lake. It is celebrated as well for its schools and churches, as for the fertility and beauty of the surrounding country. It was the principal seat of the Senecas, and there still remains in the vicinity an ancient fortification erected by the "mound builders," as well as an old Indian cemetery, which has not as yet been desecrated by the plow. The climate of this section is fine, and the means of living abundant. The mineral springs near by are highly esteemed for their health restoring properties.

Seneca Lake (thirty-six miles by two) is one of the largest and most beautiful in New York State.

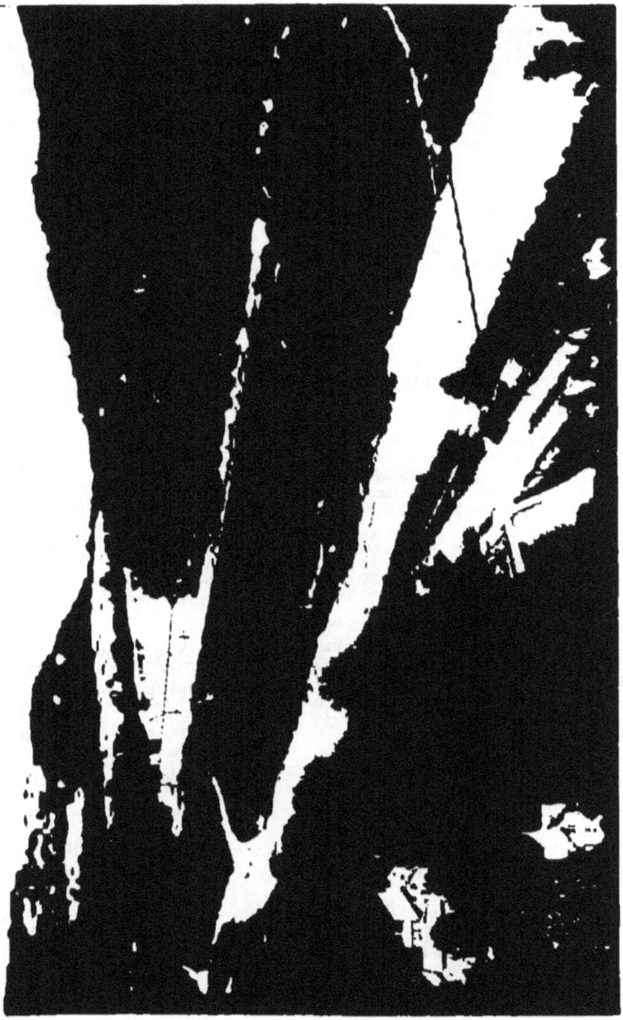

DELAWARE WATER GAP, LOOKING NORTH.

EXCURSION No. 165.—GENEVA (SENECA LAKE) AND RETURN.

Delaware, Lack. & Western R. R. .....to Elmira.
Pennsylvania R. R. (via Havana Glen) to Watkins.
Seneca Lake Steamer.......... ......to Geneva.
Returning via same route.

THROUGH RATES.

New York..........	$12 05	Danville.............	$9 10
Paterson	12 05	Binghamton........	4 90
Newark..........	12 05	Greene....	5 25
Morristown	11 65	Oxford.............	5 75
Dover.............	11 15	Norwich	6 10
Hackettstown	10 45	Sherburne.........	6 55
Washington........	10 05	Waterville.........	7 40
Water Gap	9 25	Richfield Springs ..	8 60
Stroudsburg........	9 05	Utica..............	8 25
Scranton	7 00	Owego..	4 00
Pittston............	7 00	Waverly..........	3 00
Kingston	7 00	Corning	3 00
Wilkesbarre.......	7 00	Bath.....	3 95
Plymouth	7 15	Atlanta..........	4 75
Nanticoke.........	7 30	Wayland	5 00
Shickshinny	7 65	Dansville.........	5 95
Berwick	8 10	Mount Morris ...	5 55
Bloomsburg........	8 60	Buffalo	7 30

EXURSION S. T. 21.—ELMIRA TO GENEVA (SENECA LAKE) AND RETURN.

Pennsylvania Railroad. ....to Watkins.
Seneca Lake Steamer............... ... to Geneva.
Returning via same route.
Sold only in connection with Summer Excursion Ticket passing through Elmira.
Rate.............$2 15

EXCURSION S. T. 33.—CORNING TO GENEVA AND RETURN.

Fall Brook Railway..........to Geneva and Return..
Sold only in connection with Summer Excursion Ticket passing through Corning.
Rate..............$2.30

GETTYSBURG, PA.

This field of action of the battle that was the turning point of the late war becomes each year a greater attraction to the old soldier, the student and tourist in general. The most important locations of the forces when at rest and in action have been designated by monuments, tablets, or the like.

EXCURSION 335 Y.—GETTYSBURG, PA., AND RETURN.

Limited to six (6) months from date of sale.

Del., Lack. & Western R. R........to Northumberland.
Pennsylvania Railroad .. ..to Hanover.
Western Maryland Railroad....to Gettysburg.
Returning via same route.

THROUGH RATES

Paterson	$9 45	Bloomsburg.......	$5 15
Boonton	9 45	Danville...........	4 65
Morristown	9 45	Montrose..........	9 75
Dover.............	9 45	Binghamton.......	10 05
Hackettstown	9 45	Greene	10 85
Washington.	9 45	Oxford.............	11 40
Stroudsburg........	9 45	Norwich..........	11 75
Scranton	7 45	Sherburne.........	12 15
Pittston,..........	7 15	Waterville.........	13 00
Kingston	6 70	Richfield Springs...	14 20
Wilkesbarre.......	6 70	Utica	13 85
Plymouth	6 60	Cortland	10 00
Nanticoke........	6 45	Syracuse	13 25
Shickshinny	6 05	Fulton.............	14 25
Berwick	5 65	Oswego...........	14 25

EXCURSION 334 Y.—GETTYSBURG, PA., AND RETURN.

Limited to six (6) months from date of sale.

Delaware, Lack & Western R. R......to Easton.
Lehigh Valley Railroad.............to Allentown.
Philadelphia & Reading Railroad .. to Gettysburg.
Returning via same route.

THROUGH RATES.

New York..........	$9 65	Morristown	$9 65
Newark...........	9 65	Dover	8 85
Paterson	9 65	Hackettstown	7 95
Boonton	9 65	Washington........	7 35

EXCURSION 348 Y.—GETTYSBURG, PA., AND RETURN.

Limited to six (6) months from date of sale.

Delaware, Lack. & Western R. R ...to Elmira.
Pennsylvania Railroad............to Hanover.
Western Maryland Railroad .. ....to Gettysburg.
Returning via same route.

THROUGH RATES.

Binghamton.......	$10 05	Bath..............	$11 05
Owego.	9 75	Atlanta....... ...	12 15
Ithaca...........	10 70	Wayland	12 55
Waverly...........	8 85	Dansville..........	12 95
Corning	9 80	Mount Morris......	13 65
		Buffalo	$15 45

GLEN HOUSE, N. H.
(WHITE MOUNTAINS.)

This mountain house is located fourteen miles from Glen Station on the Portland and Ogdensburg Division of Main Central R. R. or it can be reached by regular carriage line from summit of Mt. Washington.

From this hotel there is an uninterrupted view of the Presidential Peaks: Mount Washington, 6,300 feet; Mount Clay, 5,400 feet; Mount Jefferson, 5,700 feet; Mount Adams, 5,800 feet; and Mount Madison, 5,400 feet.

EXCURSION S. T. 42.—BOSTON TO GLEN HOUSE AND RETURN.

Boston & Maine Railroad...... ..to North Conway.
Me. C. R. R. (White Moun. Line)..to Glen Station.
Milliken's Stage Line........ ......to Glen House.
Returning via same route.
Sold only in connection with Summer Excursion Tickets to, or passing through Boston.
Rate.............$11 00

GLEN ISLAND, N. Y.

EXCURSION No. 390.—GLEN ISLAND AND RETURN.

Delaware, Lack. & Western R. R.....to New York.
Starin's Glen Island Line, from Pier } to Glen Island.
18, North River..............
Returning via same route.

THROUGH RATES.

Grove Street....	$ 70	Short Hills,........	$1 20
East Orange.......	75	Summit............	1 20
Brick Church........	80	Chatham	1 40
Orange	80	Madison.....	1 50
Highland Avenue...	90	Morristown	1 65
Mountain...........	95	Morris Plains	1 75
South Orange	1 00	Rockaway..........	2 00
Maplewood.........	1 05	Dover..............	2 15
Milburn..........	1 15		

HA-HA BAY AND LAKE ST. JOHN, P. Q.

EXCURSION S. T. 25.—MONTREAL TO HA-HA BAY OR CHICOUTIMI AND RETURN.

Richelieu & Ontario Nav. Co.'s Strs. or Grand Trunk Ry... } Montreal to Quebec.
Richelieu & Ontario Nav. Co.'s Steamers, Canada or Union. } Quebec to Ha-Ha Bay or Chicoutimi and return............
Returning *via* same route.
Sold only in connection with Summer Excursion Ticket to, or passing through Montreal.
Rate.................$13 00

EXCURSION S. T. 22.—QUEBEC TO HA-HA BAY OR CHICOUTIMI AND RETURN.

Richelieu & Ontario Nav. Co.'s Steamers, Canada or Union. } to Ha-Ha Bay or Chicoutimi and return.
Sold only in connection with Summer Excursion Ticket to, or passing through Quebec.
Rate..................$8 00

EXCURSION S. T. 52.—QUEBEC TO ROBERVAL AND RETURN.

Quebec and Lake St. John Railway............... } to Roberval and Return.
Sold only in connection with Summer Excursion Ticket to or passing through Quebec.
Rate..................$7 50

EXCURSION S. T. 53.—QUEBEC TO CHICOUTIMI AND RETURN.

Quebec & Lake St. John Railway......to Roberval.
Quebec & Lake St. John Railway......to Chicoutimi.
Returning *via* same route.
Sold only in connection with Summer Excursion Ticket to, or passing through Quebec.
Rate.................$9 00

EXCURSION S. T. 54.—QUEBEC TO CHICOUTIMI AND RETURN.

Quebec & Lake St. John Railway......to Roberval.
Quebec & Lake St. John Railway......to Chicoutimi.
Richelieu & Ontario Nav. Co.'s Strs., Canada or Union. } to Quebec.
Sold only in connection with Summer Excursion Ticket to, or passing through Quebec.
Rate..................$10 00

HALIFAX, N. S.
SUMMER SEASON, 1897.

Bi-weekly service between Boston and Halifax, *via* Canada Atlantic and Plant Line. Leave Boston every Tuesday and Saturday at noon, arriving at Halifax next afternoon. Returning, leave Halifax every Wednesday at 8 A. M., arriving Boston 10 A. M., next day. Leave Halifax every Saturday 10 P. M., arrive Boston Monday 7 A. M.

Weekly service between Boston, Hawkesbury and Charlottetown, touching at Halifax. Leave Boston every Tuesday noon, arrive Halifax Wednesday afternoon; leave Halifax 9 P. M., Wednesday, arrive Hawkesbury Thursday 9 A. M.; leave 10 A. M., arrive Charlottetown 6 P. M. Returning, leave Charlottetown every Friday 1 P. M., arrive Hawkesbury 11 P. M.; leave 11.30 P. M., arrive Halifax Saturday 11 A. M.; leave Halifax 10 P. M., Saturday, arrive Boston Monday 7 A. M.

During July and August there will be three sailings each week between Boston and Halifax.

EXCURSION S. T. 55.—BOSTON TO HALIFAX, N. S.

Plant Steamship Company..........to Halifax, N. S.
Returning *via* same route.
Sold only in connection with Summer Excursion Ticket to, or passing through Boston.
Rate............ $12 00

HACKETTSTOWN, N. J.
STATION FOR SCHOOLEY'S MOUNTAIN.
LOCAL EXCURSION.
(Good for continuous passage only.)
THROUGH RATES.

*New York	$2 45	Morristown	$1 20
Passaic	1 90	Dover	75
Paterson	1 75	Hopatcong Station	50
Boonton	1 20	Andover	55
*Newark	2 25	Newton	75
*Roseville Ave	2 25	Franklin	1 25
Orange	2 00	Washington	40
Mountain	1 90	Phillipsburg	1 00
South Orange	1 90	Easton	1 10
Milburn	1 75	Portland	1 15
Short Hills	1 65	Water Gap	1 35
Summit	1 65	Stroudsburg	1 55
Chatham	1 45	Scranton	3 55
Madison	1 35		

*Ticket good until used.

HART LAKE, PA.

EXCURSION NO. 350 L.—HART LAKE AND RETURN.
(Good for continuous passage only.)
Delaware, Lack. & Western R. R......to Alford.
Lackawana & Montrose Railroad......to Hart Lake.
Returning *via* same route.
THROUGH RATES.

Water Gap	$4 65	Wilkesbarre	$2 90
Stroudsburg	4 45	Plymouth	2 90
Spragueville	4 25	Nanticoke	3 05
Henryville	4 05	Shickshinny	3 45
Cresco	3 85	Clark's Summit	1 65
Mount Pocono	3 70	Glenburn	1 50
Pocono Summit	3 45	Dalton	1 45
Tobyhanna	3 30	La Plume	1 35
Gouldsboro	3 00	Factoryville	1 25
Moscow	2 60	Nicholson	95
Elmhurst	2 50	Foster	70
Scranton	2 00	Kingsley	55
Pittston	1 40	New Milford	70
Wyoming	2 60	Great Bend	95
Kingston	2 80	Binghamton	1 55

HARWICH, MASS.

EXCURSION NO. 282.—HARWICH AND RETURN.

Delaware, Lack. & Western R. R......to New York.
Fall River Line Steamers......to Fall River.
Old Colony Railroad......to Harwich.
Returning *via* same route.

THROUGH RATES.

Morristown	$ 9 55	Waterville	$18 30
Dover	10 05	Cortland	18 30
Hackettstown	10 75	Syracuse	19 30
Washington	11 15	Oswego	20 30
Water Gap	12 00	Owego	17 15
Stroudsburg	12 15	Ithaca	18 80
Scranton	14 30	Waverly	17 90
Pittston	14 70	Elmira	18 75
Kingston	15 10	Corning	19 20
Wilkesbarre	15 15	Bath	20 05
Binghamton	16 30	Atlanta	21 20
Greene	17 10	Wayland	21 55
Oxford	17 30	Dansville	22 00
Norwich	17 30	Mount Morris	22 00
Sherburne	18 00	Buffalo	24 30

HENRYVILLE, PA.

LOCAL EXCURSION.

(Good for continuous passage only.)

THROUGH RATES.

*New York	$4 20	Shickshinny	$3 70
Passaic	3 80	Berwick	4 00
Paterson	3 65	Bloomsburg	4 30
Boonton	3 10	Danville	4 65
*Newark	4 20	Great Bend	3 80
*Roseville Ave	4 20	Binghamton	4 35
Orange	3 90	Greene	5 10
Mountain	3 80	Oxford	5 65
South Orange	3 75	Norwich	6 00
Milburn	3 60	Sherburne	6 40
Short Hills	3 55	Waterville	7 25
Summit	3 55	Richfield Sprigs	8 45
Chatham	3 35	Utica	8 15
Madison	3 25	Cortland	6 05
Morristown	3 10	Syracuse	7 50
Dover	2 60	Oswego	8 90
Hopatcong Station	2 30	Owego	5 15
Andover	2 40	Ithaca	6 50
Newton	2 60	Waverly	5 90
Franklin	3 10	Elmira	6 60
Hackettstown	1 90	Corning	7 70
Washington	1 50	Bath	8 05
Scranton	2 40	Atlanta	8 85
Pittston	2 80	Wayland	9 10
Kingston	3 15	Dansville	9 40
Wilkesbarre	3 15	Mount Morris	9 95
Plymouth	3 30	Buffalo	12 45
Nanticoke	3 45		

* Ticket good until used.

PASSENGER TRAIN, ON SHEPHERD'S CROOK, GRAVITY RAILWAY.

HONESDALE, PA.

EXCURSION No. 396.—HONESDALE, PA., AND RETURN.

Delaware, Lack. & Western R. R......to Scranton.
Delaware and Hudson Canal Co......to Honesdale.
Returning via same route.

THROUGH RATES.

New York	$8 20	Oxford	$5 75
Paterson	8 00	Norwich	6 10
Boonton	7 45	Sherburne	6 55
Newark	8 20	Waterville	7 40
Morristown	7 45	Richfield Springs	8 55
Dover	6 95	Utica	8 25
Hackettstown	6 70	Cortland	6 15
Washington	5 85	Syracuse	7 60
Water Gap	4 90	Oswego	9 00
Stroudsburg	4 70	Owego	5 30
Pittston	2 40	Ithaca	6 70
Kingston	2 75	Waverly	6 00
Wilkesbarre	2 80	Elmira	6 75
Plymouth	2 85	Corning	7 35
Nanticoke	3 00	Bath	8 20
Shickshinny	3 40	Atlanta	9 00
Berwick	3 85	Wayland	9 20
Bloomsburg	4 35	Dansville	9 55
Danville	4 85	Mount Morris	10 10
Binghamton	4 45	Buffalo	12 55
Greene	5 25		

CRYSTAL LAKE.

Crystal Lake, near Honesdale, Pa., is situated in the southeastern corner of Susquehanna County, Pa., nearly 2,000 feet above sea level, and is a beautiful crystal lake covering an area of 600 acres and famed as the clearest and prettiest sheet of water in Pennsylvania, as well as for its wealth of fine fish.

HOPATCONG STATION N. J.

LOCAL EXCURSION.

(Good for continuous passage only.)

THROUGH RATES.

*New York	$2 05	Dover	$ 35
Passaic	1 50	Andover	55
Paterson	1 35	Newton	75
Boonton	80	Franklin	1 25
*Newark	1 85	Hackettstown	50
*Roseville Ave	1 85	Washington	85
Orange	1 65	Phillipsburg	1 40
Mountain	1 55	Easton	1 50
South Orange	1 50	Oxford Furnace	1 10
Milburn	1 35	Bridgeville	1 30
Short Hills	1 25	Delaware	1 40
Summit	1 25	Portland	1 55
Chatham	1 05	Water Gap	1 70
Madison	95	Stroudsburg	1 95
Morristown	80	Scranton	4 00
Denville	75		

*Tickets good until used.

HOT SPRINGS, N. C.

EXCURSION 336 Y.—HOT SPRINGS, N. C., AND RETURN.

Limit from Buffalo, six months from date of sale.
Limited to three (3) months from date of sale.
Good for use south-bound only within fifteen (15) days from date of issue as stamped on back of ticket, and must be presented at the ticket agency of the initial line at the destination point for identification and validation before they can be used for the return trip, and are then good returning only within fifteen (15) days from such validation as stamped on back of ticket; in all cases, however, tickets must be used within the extreme limit.

Del., Lack & Western R. R......to Manunka Chunk.
Pennsylvania Railroad.........to Washington.
Southern Railway.........…to Hot Springs.
Returning *via* same route.

Stroudsburg	$32 55	Sherburne	$39 55
Scranton	32 55	Waterville	40 80
Pittston	32 55	Richfield Springs	43 60
Kingston	32 55	Utica	42 05
Wilkesbarre	32 55	Owego	36 35
Montrose	34 85	Ithaca	37 10
Binghamton	36 35	Waverly	36 35
Cortland	38 10	Elmira	36 35
Syracuse	39 15	Corning	37 10
Fulton	40 15	Bath	37 10
Oswego	40 55	Dansville	37 10
Greene	37 55	Mount Morris	37 10
Oxford	38 40	Buffalo	37 10
Norwich	38 90		

EXCURSION 337 Y.—HOT SPRINGS, N. C., AND RETURN.

Limited to three (3) months from date of sale.

Delaware, Lack. & Western R. R... to New York.
Pennsylvania Railroad.............to Washington.
Southern Railway..... ....to Hot Springs.
Returning *via* same route.

THROUGH RATES.

Summit	$30 80	Norwich	$39 25
Morristown	31 25	Sherburne	39 25
Dover	31 75	Waterville	39 25
Hackettstown	32 45	Richfield Springs	40 75
Washington	32 85	Utica	39 25
Stroudsburg	33 85	Cortland	40 00
Scranton	36 00	Syracuse	41 00
Pittston	36 40	Fulton	41 50
Kingston	36 80	Oswego	42 00
Wilkesbarre	36 85	Owego	38 85
Montrose	38 20	Ithaca	40 50
Binghamton	38 00	Waverly	39 60
Greene	39 00	Elmira	40 45
Oxford	39 00		

HYANNIS, MASS.

EXCURSION No. 283.—HYANNIS AND RETURN.

Delaware, Lack. & Western R. R......to New York.
Fall River Line Steamers............to Fall River.
Old Colony Railroad..................to Hyannis.
Returning *via* same route.

THROUGH RATES.

Morristown	$9 25	Waterville	$18 00
Dover	9 75	Cortland	18 00
Hackettstown	10 45	Syracuse	19 00
Washington	10 85	Oswego	20 00
Water Gap	11 70	Owego	16 85
Stroudsburg	11 85	Ithaca	18 80
Scranton	14 00	Waverley	17 60
Pittston	14 40	Elmira	18 45
Kingston	14 80	Corning	18 99
Wilkesbarre	14 85	Bath	19 75
Binghamton	16 00	Atlanta	20 90
Greene	16 80	Wayland	21 25
Oxford	17 00	Dansville	21 70
Norwich	17 00	Mount Morris	21 70
Sherburne	17 70	Buffalo	24 00

ITHACA, N. Y.

LOCAL EXCURSION.
(Good for continuous passage only.)

THROUGH RATES.

*New York	$10 50	Portland	$7 20
Passaic	9 95	Water Gap	7 00
Paterson	9 90	Stroudsburg	6 80
Boonton	9 30	Scranton	5 00
*Newark	10 50	Pittston	5 00
Roseville Ave	10 50	Kingston	5 00
Orange	10 30	Wilkesbarre	5 00
Mountain	10 20	Plymouth	5 15
South Orange	10 05	Nanticoke	5 30
Milburn	9 95	Shickshinny	5 65
Short Hills	9 80	Berwick	6 10
Summit	9 80	Bloomsburg	6 60
Chatham	9 70	Danville	7 10
Madison	9 60	Great Bend	2 80
Morristown	9 40	Binghamton	2 20
Dover	8 95	Greene	3 00
Hopatcong Station	8 45	Oxford	3 55
Andover	8 70	Norwich	3 85
Newton	8 90	Sherburne	4 30
Franklin	9 40	Waterville	5 20
Hackettstown	8 20	Richfield Springs	6 35
Washington	7 80	Utica	6 00

*Tickets good until used and for stop-over.

EXCURSION S. T. 2.—OWEGO TO ITHACA AND RETURN.

Delaware, Lack. & Western Railroad......to Ithaca.
Returning *via* same route.
Sold only in connection with Summer Excursion.
Ticket passing through Owego.
Rate..............$1 40

HAMMONDSPORT, N. Y.

LAKE KEUKA, STEUBEN COUNTY, N. Y.

The Delaware, Lackawanna & Western Railroad connects at Bath with the Bath & Hammondsport Railroad, and a ride through the far-famed Pleasant Valley brings the traveler to Hammondsport, N. Y., at the head of Lake Keuka.

Here nestled among the vine-clad hills of Yates and Steuben Counties, lies Lake Keuka, "The Queen of Lakes," the most beautiful of the smaller lakes in America. In a country whose picturesqueness is far-famed, in the midst of scenery for which western New York is noted, this gem of inland waters has rapidly increased in fame and popularity. The quiet beauty of its waters, the novelty of its scenery, the salubrity of its atmosphere have gradually extended its name until to-day Lake Keuka is recognized as one of the most famous resorts in New York State. It is the land of health and recreation. No swamp land or malaria is found, no mosquitos are bred in the dry healthy air, and hay-fever is unknown.

Sailing, rowing, fishing and bathing are pastimes with which one wiles away the summer hours. From all parts of the country enthusiastic fishermen come to lure from the depths the fish which everywhere abound. The following endorsement from

LAKE KEUKA.

Seth Green, the late veteran fisherman and United States Fish Commissioner, speaks for itself:

"I think Lake Keuka unsurpassed by any waters in America as a fishing resort. The purity of the water, the large amount of fish food contained in the Lake, tend to put the fish in the finest condition for the table, and render them very strong and gamey when on the hook and line. During one of my sojourns in August, I took by hook and line 19 salmon trout weighing 113 pounds, and one day in October, 33 black bass, weighing 106 pounds."

The Lake is 22 miles long, divided about midway by a long bold promontory extending southward into its waters and terminating in "Bluff Point," one of the notable landmarks of this section, from whose lofty summits seven counties can be seen. Lake Keuka is 780 feet above sea level (and over 270 feet above its larger neighbor "Seneca" Lake, at the head of which is the famous Watkins Glen), and its shores and lofty hills remind the traveler of the banks of the River Rhine, where the wooded hills are covered for miles with vineyards. The precipitous sides of the Lake for miles are covered with farm houses, woodland glens and vineyards, while its water's edge is dotted with hotels and cottages, affording a panorama of unceasing beauty and interest to the tourist when viewed from the deck of the passing steamer.

The hotels of Lake Keuka are "Grove Springs," "Keuka," "Gibson's," and while at the head of the Lake is the "Fairchild House." All the hotels have spacious, cool rooms, broad verandas, and handsome surroundings of groves and grassy lawns, and connected with each, besides the dancing pavilions, bath houses, etc., are many cottages which are rented to families and parties.

Keuka Park, on the west shore of the Lake, four miles from Penn Yan, is a projecting circle of land rising gently from the water's edge, containing 160 acres, 40 acres of grove and 170 rods water frontage. Here are the large buildings of Keuka College, dozens of commodious cottages, and the College Boarding Hall, open to summer guests, the great ampitheatre and assembly pavilion, where thousands gather every summer to attend lectures, concerts and religious convocations, and delightful homes near where boarders are entertained. The streets are capital for wheelmen and ample facilities for boating and fishing supplied. Frequent mails, a money order P. O., steamers and stages, and an electric R. R. to Penn Yan, are among the conveniences of the Park.

Lake Keuka's grapes have a national reputation, while its champagnes are only rivalled by those of foreign vintages. Over 20,000 tons of grapes are annually grown, and

TRY → **GRAND IMPERIAL SEC** CHAMPAGNE

GERMANIA WINE CELLARS
HAMMONDSPORT AND RHEIMS
NEW YORK

many million gallons of still wines and bottles of champagne are produced. The wine cellars are well worth coming miles to see, and "the hospitality extended to the visitor is as broad as the sky."

The Germania Wine Cellars are situated in the beautiful and far-famed Pleasant Valley, between Hammondsport and Rheims. The cellars are prominently situated on the side of the hill with beautiful and extensive vineyards surrounding them. There are from 10,000 to 15,000 acres of fine vineyards in this great belt, from which the Germania cellars select the best and finest quality of grapes suitable for making their different wines. The grapes are picked and selected with great care, and every rotten and imperfect grape is carefully removed before going to the press to be made into wine.

The grapes picked from this vineyard received the highest award at the late World's Columbian Exposition, as being the finest table and wine grapes produced in America. The award received by this cellar for champagne has been claimed by many competing wine houses.

Their Imperial Sec. Champagne is well known, and can be found in all the leading wine houses in all the large cities of the United States. When asking your dealer for their champagne see that the name Germania Wine Cellars is on the label as it is a guarantee that the champagne is a pure wine, unadulterated, fermented by natural French process in the bottle. It takes from three to four years to perfect the wine. The Germania cellars save no expense or trouble in keeping up their goods to the standard and quality. This has been the secret of their great success in business ever since their modest beginning in the business, in the early history of wine culture in America. See Illustration on page 141.

The steamboat service upon the Lake is unexcelled. The Lake Keuka Navigation Company recently added to its fleet the steamer "Mary Bell," 150 feet long, built of steel, and designed through her light draft and powerful machinery to make the distance of 22 miles between Hammondsport and Penn Yan in about one hour. She has triple expansion engines, two boilers and twin screws, and capacity of accommodating 1,000 passengers. In addition to the "Mary Bell," the steamers of The Lake Keuka Navigation Company are the "Halsey," "Urbana," "Holmes," "West Branch," and "Lulu," and hardly an hour passes but that the summer sojourner upon the lake can, if he will, take a boat to some point of interest or "make train connections." Round trip from Hammondsport to Penn Yan, fifty cents.

Lake Keuka is nicely located for little excursion trips during one's outing. Niagara Falls is but three hours ride via the Delaware, Lackawanna & Western Railroad, while Watkin's Glen is but twenty miles distant. The New York State Soldiers' and Sailors' Home at Bath is reached in thirty minutes, and the beautiful drives along Lake Keuka's shores touch picturesque little hamlets, while the Lake and surrounding country, as viewed by a drive along the brow of its hills present a panorama unrivalled.

Those wishing a more detailed description of Lake Keuka and its environments should address The Lake Keuka Navigation Company, Hammondsport, N. Y., for their illustrated book, which will be mailed free.

EXCURSION NO. 6.—HAMMONDSPORT AND RETURN (LAKE KEUKA).

Delaware, Lack. & Western R. R...to Bath.
Bath and Hammondsport R. R...to Hammondsport.
Returning *via* same route.

THROUGH RATES.

New York	$12 50	Sherburne	$6 35
Paterson	12 00	Waterville	7 25
Newark	12 50	Richfield Springs	8 40
Morristown	11 50	Utica	8 50
Dover	11 00	Owego	3 50
Hackettstown	10 30	Ithaca	3 50
Washington	9 90	Binghamton	4 40
Water Gap	9 05	Waverly	2 70
Stroudsburg	8 90	Elmira	1 90
Scranton	6 55	Corning	1 30
Pittston	6 55	Atlanta	1 30
Kingston	6 55	Wayland	1 55
Wilkesbarre	6 55	Dansville	1 85
Greene	5 05	Mount Morris	2 85
Oxford	5 60	Buffalo	4 50
Norwich	5 90		

EXCURSION S. T. 5.—BATH TO HAMMONDSPORT (LAKE KEUKA).

Bath & Hammondsport R. R.... } to Hammondsport and return.
Sold only in connection with Summer Excursion Ticket passing through Bath.
Rate..........50 cents.

HAWKESBURY, CAPE BRETON.
[SEE HALIFAX, NOVA SCOTIA, PAGE 137.]

EXCURSION NO. 34.—GROVE SPRING, GIBSON'S OR KEUKA AND RETURN.

Del., Lack. & Western R. R.....to Bath.
Bath and Hammondsport R. R...to Hammondsport.
Lake Keuka Navigation Co.'s { to Grove Spring, Gibson's or Keuka.
Steamers..................}
Returning *via* same route.

THROUGH RATES.

New York	$12 80	Norwich	$6 20
Paterson	12 30	Sherburne	6 65
Newark	12 80	Waterville	7 55
Morristown	11 80	Richfield Springs	7 55
Dover	11 30	Buffalo	5 20
Hackettstown	11 60	Utica	8 40
Washington	10 20	Owego	3 75
Water Gap	9 35	Ithaca	4 25
Stroudsburg	9 20	Waverly	3 00
Scranton	6 85	Elmira	2 20
Pittston	6 85	Corning	1 60
Kingston	7 05	Atlanta	1 60
Wilkesbarre	7 05	Wayland	1 85
Binghamton	4 60	Dansville	2 15
Greene	5 35	Mount Morris	2 75
Oxford	5 90		

DELAWARE, LACKAWANNA & WESTERN R. R.

EXCURSION NO. 389.—OGAYAGO, UNIVERSITY OR PENN YAN AND RETURN.

Del., Lack. & Western R. R. . . to Bath.
Bath & Hammondsport R. R. . . to Hammondsport.
Lake Keuka Navigation Co.'s to Ogayago, University
Steamers . . . . or Penn Yan.
Returning *via* same route.

THROUGH RATES.

New York	$12 65	Norwich	$6 35
Paterson	12 45	Sherburne	6 80
Newark	12 65	Waterville	7 65
Morristown	11 90	Richfield Springs	8 80
Dover	11 40	Utica	8 50
Hackettstown	10 70	Owego	3 95
Washington	10 40	Ithaca	4 40
Water Gap	9 45	Waverly	3 20
Stroudsburg	9 30	Elmira	2 40
Scranton	7 15	Corning	1 75
Pittston	7 15	Atlanta	1 80
Kingston	7 25	Wayland	2 c5
Wilkesbarre	7 25	Dansville	2 35
Binghamton	4 75	Mount Morris	2 95
Greene	5 50	Buffalo	4 95
Oxford	6 00		

EXCURSION NO. 72.—PENN YAN AND RETURN.

Del., Lack. & Western R. R . . . . . to Corning.
Fall Brook Ry. (*via* W'k's Glen). to Penn Yan.
Lake Keuka Nav. Co.'s Steamers. to Hammondsport.
Bath & Hammondsport R. R. . . . . to Bath.
Del., Lack. & Western R. R. . . . . to starting point.

EXCURSION NO. 73.—REVERSE OF THE PRECEDING.

THROUGH RATES.

New York	$13 00	Norwich	$6 65
Paterson	12 70	Sherburne	7 10
Newark	13 co	Waterville	7 95
Morristown	12 20	Richfield Springs	9 15
Dover	11 75	Utica	8 80
Hackettstown	11 00	Owego	4 20
Washington	10 60	Waverly	3 45
Water Gap	9 75	Elmira	2 55
Stroudsburg	9 60	Corning	2 05
Scranton	7 50	Bath	2 05
Pittston	7 85	Atlanta	2 90
Kingston	8 15	Wayland	3 10
Wilkesbarre	8 15	Dansville	3 40
Binghamton	5 05	Mount Morris	3 95
Greene	5 80	Buffalo	6 50
Oxford	6 35		

EXCURSION NO. 424.—PENN YAN AND RETURN.

Del., Lack. & Western R. R. . . . . to Corning.
Fall Brook Ry. . . . . to Penn Yan.

THROUGH RATES.

New York	$12 65	Oxford	$6 0c
Paterson	12 35	Norwich	6 35
Newark	12 65	Sherburne	6 75
Morristown	11 90	Waterville	7 65
Dover	11 40	Richfield Springs	8 85
Hackettstown	10 70	Utica	8 50
Washington	10 30	Owego	3 90
Water Gap	9 45	Waverly	3 15
Stroudsburg	9 30	Elmira	2 4c
Scranton	7 15	Bath	2 60
Pittston	7 55	Atlanta	3 4c
Kingston	7 85	Wayland	3 6s
Wilkesbarre	7 85	Dansville	3 95
Binghamton	4 70	Mount Morris	4 50
Greene	5 50	Buffalo	7 00

LAKEWOOD, N. J.

EXCURSION 340 Y.—LAKEWOOD, N. J., AND RETURN.

Limited to six (6) months from date of sale.
Delaware, Lack. & Western R. R. . . . . . to New York.
Central R. R. of N. J. (*via* Red Bank). . to Lakewood.
Returning *via* same route.

THROUGH RATES.

Summit	$3 15	Richfield Springs	$13 10
Morristown	3 60	Utica	11 60
Dover	4 10	Cortland	12 35
Hackettstown	4 80	Syracuse	13 35
Washington	5 2c	Fulton	13 85
Stroudsburg	6 20	Oswego	14 35
Scranton	8 35	Owego	11 20
Pittston	8 75	Ithaca	12 85
Kingston	9 15	Waverly	11 95
Wilkesbarre	9 20	Elmira	12 80
Montrose	10 55	Corning	13 25
Binghamton	10 35	Bath	14 10
Greene	11 15	Atlanta	15 30
Oxford	11 35	Wayland	15 55
Norwich	11 35	Dansville	16 05
Sherburne	11 60	Mount Morris	16 05
Waterville	11 60	Buffalo	18 35

LONG BRANCH, N. J.

*EXCURSION NO. 173.—LONG BRANCH AND RETURN.

Delaware, Lack. & Western R. R. . . . to New York.
Pennsylvania Railroad . . . . to Long Branch.
Returning *via* same route.

*EXCURSION NO. 18.—LONG BRANCH AND RETURN.

Del., Lack. & Western R. R. . . to New York.
Central R.R. of N. J. Steamers. to Sandy Hook.
Central Railroad of N. J. . . . . to East Long Branch.
Returning *via* same route.

EXCURSION NO. 19.—LONG BRANCH AND RETURN.

Delaware, Lack. & Western R. R. . . to New York.
Central Railroad of N. J . . . . to Perth Amboy.
N. Y. & Long Branch R. R. . . . . to Long Branch.
Returning *via* same route.

THROUGH RATES FOR EITHER EXCURSION.

Morristown	$2 75	Oxford	$10 50
Dover	3 25	Norwich	10 50
Hackettstown	3 95	Sherburne	11 20
Washington	4 35	Waterville	11 50
Water Gap	5 20	Cortland	11 50
Stroudsburg	5 35	Syracuse	12 50
Scranton	7 50	Oswego	13 50
Pittston	7 90	Owego	10 35
Kingston	8 30	Ithaca	12 00
Wilkesbarre	8 35	Waverly	11 10
Plymouth	8 55	Elmira	11 95
Nanticoke	8 70	Corning	12 40
Shickshinny	9 10	Bath	13 25
Berwick	9 50	Atlanta	14 40
Bloomsburg	10 00	Wayland	14 70
Danville	10 20	Dansville	15 20
Binghamton	9 50	Mount Morris	15 20
Greene	10 30	Buffalo	17 50

*Good for passage between New York and Long Branch either *via* the boat and trains of the Sandy Hook route, or the trains of either the Central Railroad of New Jersey or the Pennsylvania Railroad.

EXCURSION NO. 17.—LONG BRANCH AND RETURN.

Delaware, Lack. & Western R. R.. to New Hampton.
Central Railroad of New Jersey . . . . to Perth Amboy.
New York & Long Branch R. R. . . to Long Branch.
Returning *via* same route.

THROUGH RATES.

Water Gap	$ 4 35	Sherburne	$11 20
Stroudsburg	4 50	Waterville	11 50
Scranton	6 65	Cortland	10 85
Pittston	7 00	Syracuse	11 50
Kingston	7 30	Oswego	11 50
Wilkesbarre	7 30	Owego	11 10
Plymouth	7 45	Ithaca	12 00
Nanticoke	7 60	Waverly	11 10
Shickshinny	7 95	Elmira	11 75
Berwick	8 40	Corning	12 40
Bloomsburg	8 90	Bath	13 25
Danville	9 35	Atlanta	14 40
Binghamton	9 50	Wayland	14 70
Greene	9 90	Dansville	15 20
Oxford	10 45	Mount Morris	15 70
Norwich	10 50	Buffalo	17 50

LURAY CAVERNS, VA.

Those who have visited these wonderful and recently discovered subterranean caverns testify that they form wonderful examples of nature's handiwork. Words cannot adequately describe them; they must be studied to be thoroughly realized. The vestibule of this subterranean mansion is attained by descending the stone steps of the cave, and once there the first sensation experienced by the visitor is one of awe, at the fearful stillness that reigns supreme, and this is in no way enlivened by the grotesque forms surrounding. Once mastered, however, these emotions turn to wonder. From an entrance hall, elaborate with stalacite decoration, numerous avenues lead into unknown depths. One of the corridors leads to the Fish Market, or rather to a cave which, to all appearances, is hung with row upon row of fish, so natural is the form of the pendants from above. The crystal lake with its unruffled ice-cold surface; the vegetable garden with ever erratic, but none the less vegetable like hangings. Numerous chambers, every one known from a striking resemblance to too easily recognized objects, and each filled with the quaint subterranean creations are connected one to the other by lanes, which appear as though covered by some giant hand; grottoes elaborated with the richest ornamentation; sparkling waterfalls, and figures and forms of indefinite shape inspire emotions of wonder, which grow with each new revelation. Here we find a Cathedral, with its ever noiseless organ; a hall of giants relieved by fluted columns and arches innumerable. A plateau-like spot, commonly known as the Elfin Ramble, together with Hades, Horey's Hall and Pluto's Chasm, and a variety of other equally fine attractions form but a limit to the marvelous sights these caverns contain. Here, nature has fashioned itself in its own erratic style. Nothing in the way of artificial adornment has been done here by man. These caves may be examined without much difficulty, as the obstructions are few, and may be easily surmounted by the anxious and ever-daring explorer.

EXCURSION 338 Y.—LURAY, VA., AND RETURN.

Limited to (6) months from date of sale.
Del., Lack. & Western R. R.....to Northumberland.
Pennsylvania Railroad ....to Harrisburg.
Cumberland Valley Railroad....to Hagerstown.
Norfolk & Western Railroad ..to Luray.
Returning *via* same route.

THROUGH RATES.

Paterson	$15 10	Bloomsburg	$10 60
Boonton	15 10	Danville	10 10
Morristown	15 10	Montrose	15 35
Dover	15 10	Binghamton	15 50
Hackettstown	15 10	Greene	16 30
Washington	15 10	Oxford	16 90
Stroudsburg	15 10	Norwich	17 25
Scranton	13 05	Sherburne	17 65
Pittston	12 55	Waterville	18 50
Kingston	12 20	Richfield Springs	19 70
Wilkesbarre	12 20	Utica	19 35
Plymouth	12 05	Cortland	16 40
Nanticoke	11 90	Syracuse	18 70
Shickshinny	11 50	Fulton	19 70
Berwick	11 10	Oswego	19 75

EXCURSION 339 Y.—LURAY, VA., AND RETURN.

Limited to six (6) months from date of sale.
Delaware, Lack. & Western R. R.... to Easton.
Lehigh Valley Railroad............to Allentown.
Philadelphia & Reading Railroad... to Harrisburg.
Cumberland Valley Railroad ....to Hagerstown.
Norfolk & Western Railroad ....to Luray.
Returning *via* same route.

THROUGH RATES.

New York	$15 35	Morristown	$15 10
Newark	15 10	Dover	14 30
Paterson	15 10	Hackettstown	13 40
Boonton	15 10	Washington	12 80

EXCURSION 349 Y.—LURAY, VA., AND RETURN.

Limited to six (6) months from date of sale.
Delaware, Lack. & Western R. R.....to Scranton.
Pennsylvania Railroad...............to Harrisburg.
Cumberland Valley Railroad ....to Hagerstown.
Norfolk & Western Railroad.........to Luray.
Returning *via* same route.

THROUGH RATES.

Binghamton	$15 50	Atlanta	$17 65
Owego	15 50	Wayland	18 15
Ithaca	16 20	Dansville	18 45
Waverly	14 35	Mount Morris	18 75
Corning	15 30	Buffalo	21 00
Bath	16 55		

MARION, MASS.

EXCURSION No. 284.—MARION AND RETURN.

Delaware, Lack. & Western R. R.. .. to New York.
Fall River Line Steamers,...............to Fall River.
Old Colony Railroad....................to Marion.
Returning *via* same route.

THROUGH RATES.

Morristown	$ 8 25	Waterville	$17 00
Dover	8 75	Cortland	17 00
Hackettstown	9 45	Syracuse	18 00
Washington	9 85	Oswego	19 00
Water Gap	10 70	Owego	15 85
Stroudsburg	10 85	Ithaca	17 50
Scranton	13 00	Waverly	16 60
Pittston	13 40	Elmira	17 45
Kingston	13 80	Corning	17 90
Wilkesbarre	13 85	Bath	18 75
Binghamton	15 00	Atlanta	19 90
Greene	15 80	Wayland	20 25
Oxford	16 00	Dansville	20 70
Norwich	16 00	Mount Morris	20 70
Sherburne	16 70	Buffalo	23 00

MATTAPOISETT, MASS.
EXCURSION NO. 285.—MATTAPOISETT AND RETURN.

Delaware, Lack. & Western R. R....to New York.
Fall River Line Steamers............to Fall River.
Old Colony Railroad ....to Mattapoisett.
Returning *via* same route.

THROUGH RATES.

Morristown.........	$ 8 50	Waterville.........	$17 25
Dover.	9 00	Cortland........ ..	17 25
Hackettstown......	9 70	Syracuse	18 25
Washington........	10 10	Oswego.............	19 25
Water Gap	10 95	Owego	16 10
Stroudsburg........	11 10	Ithaca..............	17 75
Scranton	13 25	Waverly...........	16 85
Pittston	13 65	Elmira.............	17 70
Kingston...........	14 05	Corning	18 15
Wilkesbarre........	14 10	Bath	19 00
Binghamton........	15 25	Atlanta.	20 15
Greene....	16 05	Wayland...........	20 50
Oxford..............	16 25	Dansville...........	20 95
Norwich...........	16 25	Mount Morris.. ..	20 95
Sherburne.........	16 95	Buffalo	23 25

MAUCH CHUNK, PA.

Mauch Chunk is situated in the picturesque gorge or cañon formed by the hand of nature for the passage of the Lehigh River through the mountains.

Besides being unique in its site, it possesses a wealth of beauty in its surroundings that has given it a prominent place among the mountain cities of the world. The scenery in every direction is superb. Every prospect is replete with wild beauty; every emotion excited by the outlook is one of admiration. Leading up from the city to the top of Mt. Pisgah is the celebrated Switchback Railroad, which lifts the passengers to an elevation of eighteen hundred feet above the waters of the river. The ascent, though absolutely safe, is exciting, and the view, both from the car and from the mountain's top, is magnificent. Within a few minutes' ride up the Lehigh is the beautiful Glen Onoko.

EXCURSION NO. 138.—MAUCH CHUNK AND RETURN.

Del., Lack. & Western Railroad....to Pittston.
Lehigh Valley Railroad...........to Mauch Chunk.
Returning *via* same route.

THROUGH RATES.

Water Gap.....	$5 30	Sherburne..........	$7 60
Stroudsburg... ...	5 10	Waterville.........	8 40
Scranton...........	3 60	Richfield Springs...	9 60
Binghamton........	5 50	Utica................	9 30
Greene.....	6 25	Syracuse	8 65
Oxford......	6 80	Oswego.	10 05
Norwich............	7 15		

EXCURSION NO. 139.—MAUCH CHUNK AND RETURN.

Del., Lack. & Western Railroad....to Kingston.
Wilkesbarre & Kingston St. Rail'y.to Wilkesbarre.
Lehigh Valley Railroad... ....to Mauch Chunk.
Returning *via* same route.

THROUGH RATES.

Water Gap..........	$5 35	Sherburne..........	$ 7 65
Stroudsburg.........	5 15	Waterville.........	8 45
Scranton...........	3 65	Richfield Springs...	9 65
Binghamton........	5 55	Utica	9 35
Greene..............	6 30	Syracuse	8 70
Oxford..............	6 85	Oswego.............	10 10
Norwich............	7 20		

EXCURSION NO. 140.—MAUCH CHUNK AND RETURN.

Delaware, Lack. & Western R. R..to Pittston.
Lehigh Valley Railroad ....to Mauch Chunk.
Lehigh Valley Railroad ....to Wilkesbarre.
Wilkesbarre & Kingston St, Rail'y.to Kingston.
Delaware, Lack. & Western R. R..to starting point.

EXCURSION NO. 141.—REVERSE OF THE PRECEDING.

THROUGH RATES.

Water Gap..........	$5 35	Sherburne..........	$ 7 65
Stroudsburg.........	5 15	Waterville.........	8 45
Scranton...........	3 65	Richfield Springs ..	9 65
Binghamton.......	5 55	Utica	9 35
Greene..............	6 30	Syracuse...........	8 70
Oxford	6 85	Oswego.............	10 10
Norwich............	7 20		

*EXCURSION NO. 142.—MAUCH CHUNK AND RETURN.

Delaware, Lack. & Western R. R..to Pittston.
Lehigh Valley Railroad... ....to Mauch Chunk.
Lehigh Valley Railroad............to New York.
From New York.........$6 80

*EXCURSION NO. 143.—MAUCH CHUNK AND RETURN.

Delaware, Lack. & Western R. R..to Kingston.
Wilkesbarre & Kingston Railway..to Wilkesbarre.
Lehigh Valley Railroad.............to Mauch Chunk.
Lehigh Valley Railroad .... to New York.
From New York.. .....$6 85

*NOTE.—Excursions Nos. 142 and 143 may be sold from any Line Station between New York and Scranton (inclusive) at the same rates as from New York. To make up the round trip from such Line Stations, agents will issue in connection with these tickets Form "C E" reading from "New York to Station Stamped on Back." Agents north of Scranton may issue these forms (142 and 143) in the same manner as stations south of that point, but will charge, in addition to the rate from New York, as follows:

Binghamton........	$2 50	Cortland.	$4 20
Greene..............	3 30	Syracuse	5 70
Oxford.............	3 80	Oswego.	7 10
Norwich.	4 20	Owego.............	3 35
Sherburne..........	4 60	Ithaca	4 70
Waterville..........	5 45	Waverly...........	4 10
Richfield Springs ...	6 65	Elmira	4 80
Utica	6 30		

EXCURSION NO. 166.—MAUCH CHUNK AND RETURN.

Delaware, Lack. & Western R. R..to Phillipsburg.
Lehigh Valley Railroad ... .to Mauch Chunk.
Returning *via* same route.

EXCURSION NO. 167.—MAUCH CHUNK AND RETURN.

Delaware, Lack. & Western R. R..to Easton.
Central Railroad of N. J........ to Mauch Chunk.
Returning *via* same route.

THROUGH RATES FOR EITHER EXCURSION.

New York...........	$5 55	Dover...............	$4 00
Paterson,............	4 95	Hackettstown.......	3 25
Newark.............	5 30	Washington.....	. 2 90
Morristown	4 45		

MAUCH CHUNK SWITCHBACK, PA.

EXCURSION S. T. 26.—UPPER MAUCH CHUNK TO SUMMIT HILL AND RETURN.

Mauch Chunk & Summit Hill) to Summit Hill and Railroad ..   ..(return.
Sold only in connection with Summer Excursion Ticket to, or passing through Mauch Chunk.
Rate..........75 cents.

MONTREAL. P. Q.

Is situated upon the southeast side of a triangular island formed by the mouths of the Ottawa, where, after a course of 600 miles, it flows into the St. Lawrence. Population, 200,000.

Back of the city, but within its limits, rises Mount Royal (700 feet), on the summit of which is a fine park. The city is on about the same spot where the Indian village Hockelaga existed when Cartier visited this neighborhood early in the sixteenth century.

It has been under English rule since 1761—prior to which it was in possession of the French.

EXCURSION NO. 91 A.—TO MONTREAL.

Delaware, Lack. & Western R. R....to Buffalo.
N. Y. Central & Hudson R. R. R....to Niagara Falls.
N. Y. Central & Hudson R. R. R....to Lewiston.
Niagara Navigation Co.'s Steamer..to Toronto.
Canadian Pacific Railway ....to Ottawa.
Canadian Pacific Railway, or Ottawa River Navi. Co.'s Steamer.... } to Montreal.

EXCURSION NO. 431 A.—TO MONTREAL.

Delaware, Lack. & Western R. R....to Buffalo.
N. Y. Central & Hudson R. R. R....to Niagara Falls.
N. Y. Central & Hudson R. R. R....to Lewiston.
Niagara Navigation Co.'s Steamer..to Toronto.
Canadian Pacific R'y, or Richelieu & Ontario Nav. Co.'s Steamer..... } to Montreal.

EXCURSION NO. 93 A.—TO MONTREAL.

Delaware, Lack. & Western R. R....to Buffalo.
N. Y. Central & Hudson R. R....to Niagara Falls.
N. Y. Central & Hudson R. R. R....to Lewiston.
Niagara Navigation Co.'s Steamer..to Toronto.
Grand Trunk R'lway, or Richelieu & Ontario Nav. Co.'s Steamer .... } to Kingston.
Grand Trunk R'lway, or Richelieu & Ontario Nav. Co.'s Steamer .... } to Prescott.
Grand Trunk R'lway, or Richelieu & Ontario Nav. Co.'s Steamer .... } to Montreal.

EXCURSION NO. 250 A.—TO MONTREAL.

Del., Lack. & Western R. R....to Buffalo.
Erie Railroad..............to Suspension Bridge.
Grand Trunk Railway.........to Port Dalhousie.
Steamer "Empress of India"..to Toronto.
Canadian Pacific Railway....to Ottawa.
Can. Pac. Railway, or Ottawa River Nav. Co.'s Steamer .. } to Montreal.

EXCURSION NO. 252 A.—TO MONTREAL.

Del., Lack. & Western R. R....to Buffalo.
Erie Railroad..............to Suspension Bridge.
Grand Trunk Railway.........to Port Dalhousie.
Steamer "Empress of India"..to Toronto.
Grand Trunk Railway, or Richelieu & Ontario Navigation Co.'s Steamer ...... } to Kingston.
Grand Trunk Railway, or Richelieu & Ontario Navigation Co.'s Steamer...... } to Prescott.
Grand Trunk Railway, or Richelieu & Ontario Navigation Co.'s Steamer ...... } to Montreal.

EXCURSION NO. 94 A.—TO MONTREAL.

Delaware, Lack. & Western R. R...to Buffalo.
N. Y. Central & Hudson R. R. R .. to Niagara Falls.
Grand Trunk Railway...........to Toronto.
Grand Trunk R'lway, or Richelieu & Ontario Nav. Co.'s Steamer.... } to Kingston.
Grand Trunk R'lway, or Richelieu & Ontario Nav. Co.'s Steamer.... } to Prescott.
Grand Trunk R'lway, or Richelieu & Ontario Nav. Co.'s Steamer... } to Montreal.

EXCURSION NO. 136 A.—TO MONTREAL.

Delaware, Lack. & Western R. R.to Buffalo.
N. Y. Central & Hudson R. R. R...to Niagara Falls.
N. Y. Central & Hudson R. R. R...to Lewiston.
Rome, Watertown & Ogdbg R. R.to Clayton.
Richelieu & Ont. Nav. Co.'s Str...to Alexandria Bay.
Richelieu & Ont. Nav. Co.'s Str...to Montreal.
(Good until October 1st.)

THROUGH RATES FOR EXCURSIONS 91A, 93A, 94A, 136A, 250A, 252A and 431A.

New York	$19 25	Bloomsburg	$18 50
Paterson	19 25	Danville	18 75
Newark	19 25	Binghamton	16 25
Morristown	19 25	Greene	16 55
Dover	19 25	Oxford	16 80
Hackettstown	19 15	Norwich	16 95
Washington	18 95	Cortland	17 00
Water Gap	18 55	Owego	15 70
Stroudsburg	18 45	Ithaca	16 40
Scranton	17 35	Waverly	15 30
Pittston	17 55	Elmira	14 95
Kingston	17 70	Corning	14 90
Wilkesbarre	17 70	Bath	14 75
Plymouth	17 80	Atlanta	14 20
Nanticoke	17 85	Wayland	14 10
Shickshinny	18 05	Dansville	13 90
Berwick	18 25	Mount Morris	13 55

EXCURSION NO. 96 A.—TO MONTREAL.

Delaware, Lack. & Western R. R. to Utica.
Rome, Watertown & Ogdbg R. R.to Clayton.
Richelieu & Ont. Nav. Co.'s Str...to Alexandria Bay.
Richelieu & Ont. Nav. Co.'s Str ..to Montreal.
(Good until October 1st.)

THROUGH RATES.

New York	$13 50	Bloomsburg	$12 80
Paterson	13 50	Danville	13 00
Newark	13 50	Binghamton	10 40
Morristown	13 50	Greene	10 05
Dover	13 50	Oxford	9 75
Hackettstown	13 40	Norwich	9 60
Washington	13 25	Sherburne	9 40
Water Gap	12 80	Waterville	8 95
Stroudsburg	12 70	Richfield Springs	9 25
Scranton	11 65	Cortland	10 85
Pittston	11 85	Owego	10 85
Kingston	12 00	Ithaca	11 50
Wilkesbarre	12 00	Waverly	11 20
Plymouth	12 10	Elmira	11 55
Nanticoke	12 15	Corning	11 80
Shickshinny	12 30	Bath	12 30
Berwick	12 55		

EXCURSION NO. 97 A.—TO MONTREAL.

Del., Lack. & Western R. R.....to Richfield Springs.
Del., Lack. & Western R. R, ...to Utica.
Rome, W't'n & Ogdbg. R. R ....to Clayton.
R. & O. Nav. Co.'s Steamers....to Alexandria Bay.
R. & O. Nav. Co.'s Steamers....to Montreal.
(Good until October 1st.)

THROUGH RATES.

New York	$14 40	Berwick	$13 45
Paterson	14 40	Bloomsburg	13 70
Newark	14 40	Danville	13 90
Morristown	14 40	Binghamton	11 30
Dover	14 40	Greene	10 95
Hackettstown	14 30	Oxford	10 65
Washington	14 15	Norwich	10 50
Water Gap	13 70	Sherburne	10 30
Stroudsburg	13 60	Waterville	9 85
Scranton	12 55	Cortland	11 75
Pittston	12 75	Owego	11 75
Kingston	12 90	Ithaca	12 40
Wilkesbarre	12 90	Waverly	12 10
Plymouth	13 00	Elmira	12 45
Nanticoke	13 05	Corning	12 80
Shickshinny	13 20	Bath	13 20

EXCURSION NO. 183 A.—TO MONTREAL.

Delaware, Lack. & Western R. R. to Syracuse.
Rome, W't'n & Ogdbg. R. R......to Clayton.
R. & O. Nav. Co.'s Steamers.....to Alexandria Bay.
R. & O. Nav. Co.'s Steamers......to Montreal.
(Good until October 1st.)

THROUGH RATES.

New York	$14 40	Nanticoke	$11 95
Paterson	14 10	Shickshinny	12 15
Newark	14 40	Berwick	12 35
Morristown	13 80	Bloomsburg	12 65
Dover	13 65	Danville	12 25
Hackettstown	13 25	Binghamton	10 25
Washington	13 05	Greene	10 20
Water Gap	12 65	Oxford	10 45
Stroudsburg	12 55	Norwich	10 65
Scranton	11 50	Cortland	9 40
Pittston	11 70	Owego	10 65
Kingston	11 85	Waverly	10 60
Wilkesbarre	11 85	Elmira	10 80
Plymouth	11 90		

EXCURSION NO. 156 A.—TO MONTREAL.

Delaware, Lack. & Western R. R. to Oswego.
Rome, Watert'on & Ogdbg. R. R. to Clayton.
R. & O. Nav. Co.'s Steamers...... to Alexandria Bay.
R. & O. Nav. Co.'s Steamers.......to Montreal.
(Good until October 1st.)

THROUGH RATES.

New York	$14 70	Nanticoke	$12 25
Paterson	14 40	Shickshinny	12 45
Newark	14 70	Berwick	12 65
Morristown	14 15	Bloomsburg	12 95
Dover	13 95	Danville	13 15
Hackettstown	13 55	Binghamton	10 55
Washington	13 35	Greene	10 50
Water Gap	12 95	Oxford	10 75
Stroudsburg	12 85	Norwich	10 95
Scranton	11 80	Cortland	9 70
Pittston	12 00	Syracuse	8 95
Kingston	12 15	Owego	10 95
Wilkesbarre	12 15	Waverly	11 20
Plymouth	12 20	Elmira	11 20

EXCURSION S. T. 34.—ALEXANDRIA BAY TO MONTREAL AND RETURN.

Richelieu & Ontario Navigation { to Montreal and
Co.'s Steamers.................. { return.
(Good until October 1st.)

Sold only in connection with Summer Excursion ticket to or passing through Alexandria Bay.

Rate............$8 50

ROUTES RETURNING FROM MONTREAL.

(Issued only in connection with routes to Montreal.)

To make round trip rates from New York, add the fare from New York to Montreal to that from Montreal to New York, *via* the desired route.

The round trip rates from any Line Station on Morris & Essex Division, Main Line or Buffalo Division, for routes *via* Buffalo and Niagara Falls, will be the same as those made from New York. For example, the round trip rate to Montreal and return *via* route of Excursion No. 91 A to Montreal, and that of Excursion No. 109 X from Montreal, would be $29.25 ($19 25+10) from New York, and would be the same from Elmira for a ticket made up of the same forms, but starting from Elmira and returning *via* New York to Elmira.

Round trip rates from any Line Station on the Morris & Essex Division, Main Line, or Utica Division, for routes going *via* Utica, and from any Line Station on the Morris & Essex Division, Main Line, Syracuse, Binghamton, and New York Division, or Oswego and Syracuse Division, for routes going *via* Syracuse or Oswego can be made in the same manner as for routes going *via* Buffalo and Niagara Falls.

Round trip rates from other stations will be as follows:—For routes going *via* Buffalo and Niagara Falls: Pittston, 40c.; Kingston, 80c.; Wilkesbarre, 85c.; Plymouth, 90c.; Nanticoke, $1.05; Shickshinny, $1.45; Berwick, $1.85; Bloomsburg, $2.35; Danville, $2.85; Oxford, $1.35; Norwich, $1.65; Cortland, $1.70, and Ithaca, $1.40, more than the round trip rate from New York.

For routes going *via* Utica: Pittston, 40c.; Kingston, 80c.; Wilkesbarre, 85c.; Plymouth, 90c.; Nanticoke, $1.05; Shickshinny, $1.45; Berwick, $1.85; Bloomsburg, $2.35; Danville, $2.85; Cortland, $1.70; Oswego, 85c.; Ithaca, $2 20; Waverly, $1.70; Elmira, $2.25; Corning, $2.90, and Bath, $3.75, more than the round trip rate from New York.

For routes going *via* Syracuse: Pittston, 40c.; Kingston, 80c.; Wilkesbarre, 85c.; Plymouth, 90c.; Nanticoke, $1.05; Shickshinny, $1.45; Berwick, $1.85; Bloomsburg, $2.35; Danville, $2.85; Oswego, 85c.; Waverly, $1.60, and Elmira, $2.25. more than the round trip rate from New York.

For routes going *via* Oswego: Pittston, 40c.; Kingston, 80c.; Wilkesbarre, 85c.; Plymouth, 90c.; Nanticoke, $1.05; Shickshinny, $1.45; Berwick, $1.85; Bloomsburg, $2.35; Danville, $1.85; Greene, 40c.; Oxford, 90c.; Norwich, $1.20; Oswego, 85c.; Waverly, $1.60, and Elmira, $2.25 more than the round trip rate from New York.

To make up such round trip tickets through Montreal from Line Stations, agents will issue Form C. E., reading *via* Delaware, Lackawanna & Western Railroad, "New York to Station stamped on back," which, in connection with the form to Montreal and that from Montreal to New York, makes a complete round trip from starting point.

*EXCURSION NO. 109 X.—MONTREAL TO NEW YORK.

Grand Trunk Railway...... to Rouse's Point.
Del. & Hudson Canal Co.'s Lines..to Plattsburg.
Del. & Hudson Canal Co.'s Lines { to Ft. Ticonderoga.
 or Lake Champlain steamer. {
Del. & Hudson Canal Co.'s Lines..to Saratoga.
Del. & Hudson Canal Co.'s Lines..to Troy.
N. Y. Central & Hudson R. R. R. to New York.

Rate............$10 00

*EXCURSION NO. 110 X.—MONTREAL TO NEW YORK.

Via same route as 109 X to Saratoga, thence
Del. & Hudson Canal Co.'s Lines.......to Albany.
Day Line Hudson River Steamers......to New York.

Rate............$9 60

*EXCURSION NO. 111 X.—MONTREAL TO NEW YORK.

Via same route as 109 X to Saratoga, thence
Del. & Hudson Canal Co.'s Lines.......to Albany.
People's (Night) Line H. R. Steamers..to New York.

Rate............$9 10

*EXCURSION NO. 112 X.—MONTREAL TO NEW YORK.

Grand Trunk Railway........ to Rouse's Point.
Del. & Hudson Canal Co.'s Lines..to Plattsburg.
Del. & Hudson Canal Co.'s Lines { to Ft. Ticonderoga.
 or Lake Champlain steamer.. {
Del. & Hudson Canal Co.'s Lines..to Baldwin.
Lake George Steamer........to Caldwell.
Del. & Hudson Canal Co.'s Lines..to Saratoga.
Del. & Hudson Canal Co.'s Lines..to Troy.
N. Y. Central & Hudson R. R. R. to New York.

Rate............$11 50

*EXCURSION NO. 113 X.—MONTREAL TO NEW YORK.

Via same route as 112 X to Saratoga, thence
Del. & Hudson Canal Co.'s Lines.......to Albany.
Day Line Hudson River Steamers......to New York.

Rate............$11 10

*EXCURSION NO. 114 X.—MONTREAL TO NEW YORK.

Via same route as 112 X to Saratoga, thence
Del. & Hudson Canal Co.'s Lines.......to Albany.
People's (Night) Line H. R. Steamers..to New York.

Rate............$10 45

DELAWARE, LACKAWANNA & WESTERN R. R.

*EXCURSION NO. 298 X.—MONTREAL TO NEW YORK.

Grand Trunk Railway............to St. John's.
Central Vermont Railroad........to Burlington.
Lake Champlain Steamer.........to Ft. Ticonderoga.
Del. & Hudson Canal Co.'s Lines..to Baldwin.
Lake George Steamer............to Caldwell.
Del. & Hudson Canal Co.'s Lines..to Saratoga.
Del. & Hudson Canal Co.'s Lines..to Troy.
N. Y. Central & Hudson R. R, R...to New York.
Rate............$11 50

*EXCURSION NO. 299 X.—MONTREAL TO NEW YORK.

Via same route as 298 X to Saratoga, thence
Del. & Hudson Canal Co.'s Lines.......to Albany.
Day Line Hudson River Steamers......to New York.
Rate............$11 10

*EXCURSION NO. 300 X.—MONTREAL TO NEW YORK.

Via same route as 298 X to Saratoga, thence
Del. & Hudson Canal Co.'s Lines.......to Albany.
People's (Night) Line H. R. Steamers..to New York.
Rate............$10 45

EXCURSION NO. 386 X.—MONTREAL TO NEW YORK.

N. Y. Central & Hudson R. R. R ......to New York.
Rate.........$10 00

EXCURSION NO. 428 X.—MONTREAL TO NEW YORK.

New York Central & Hudson River R. R.................... } to Albany.
Hudson River Day Line Steamers......to New York.
Rate............$9 00

EXCURSION NO. 429 X.—MONTREAL TO NEW YORK.

New York Central & Hudson R. R. R...to Albany.
People's Line (Night) H. R. Steamers ..to New York.
Rate............$8 95

*EXCURSION NO. 115 X —MONTREAL TO NEW YORK.

Grand Trunk Railway......... .. to St. John's.
Central Vermont Railroad........to Windsor.
Boston & Maine R. R...............to Brattleboro.
Central Vermont Railroad........to South Vernon.
Boston & Maine R. R.............to Springfield.
N. Y., New Haven & H. R. R......to New York.
Rate............$10 00

*EXCURSION NO. 116 X.—MONTREAL TO NEW YORK.

Grand Trunk Railway............to St. John's.
Central Vermont Railroad.... ,to White River Jc.
Boston & Maine Railroad (Lowell System)................ } to Concord.
Boston & Maine R. R.............to Nashua.
Boston & Maine Railroad (Lowell System)................ } to Boston.
N. Y., N. H. & H. R. R.............to Fall River.
Fall River Line Steamers .. ..to New York.
Rate.... ....$13 50

†EXCURSION NO. 117 X.—MONTREAL TO NEW YORK.

Canadian Pacific Railway...... } to Newport, Vt., (Lake Memphremagog).
Boston & Maine Railroad (Passumpsic Division)............ } to Wells River.
Boston & Maine Railroad ....to Nashua.
Boston & Main Railroad (Lowell System) .... } to Boston.
N. Y., N. H. & H. R. K... ... ...to Fall River.
Fall River Line Steamers .....to New York.
Rate............$13 50

†EXCURSION NO. 119 X.—MONTREAL TO NEW YORK.

Canadian Pacific Railway...... } to Newport, Vt. (Lake Memphremagog.)
Boston & Maine Railroad (Passumpsic Division)............ } to St. Johnsbury.
St. Johnsbury & L. Cham. R. R...to Lunenburg.
Maine Central R. R...............to Fabyan's.
Boston & Maine R. R............to Concord.
Boston & Maine R. R............to Nashua.
Boston & Maine R. R. (Lowell System).................... } to Boston.
N. Y., N. H. & H. R. R...........to Fall River.
Fall River Line Steamers.........to New York.
Rate..... ....$13 50

*EXCURSION NO. 301 X —MONTREAL TO NEW YORK.

Grand Trunk Railway............to St. John's.
Central Vermont Railroad .... .. to Montpelier.
Montpelier & Wells River R. R....to Wells River.
Concord & Montreal Railroad .. to Fabyan's.
Concord & Montreal Railroad....to Concord.
Concord & Montreal Railroad....to Nashua.
Boston & Main Railroad (Lowell System) .... } to Boston.
Fall River Line Steamers.........to New York.
Rate..... ....$13 50

†EXCURSION NO. 120 X.—MONTREAL TO NEW YORK.

Canadian Pacific Railway ..... } to Newport, Vt. (Lake Memphremagog).
Boston & Maine Railroad (Passumpsic Division)............ } to St. Johnsbury.
St. Johnsbury & L. Cham. R. R...to Lunenburg.
Maine Central R. R...............to Fabyan's.
Maine Central Railroad (White Mountains Line) .... } to Crawford House.
Maine Central Railroad (White Mountains Line).............. } to North Conway.
Boston & Maine Railroad.........to Boston.
N. Y., N. H. & H. R. R..........to Fall River.
Fall River Line Steamers.........to New York.
Rate............$13 50

*EXCURSION NO. 302 X.—MONTREAL TO NEW YORK.

Grand Trunk Railway............to St. John's.
Central Vermont Railroad........to Montpelier.
Montpelier & Wells River R. R....to Wells River.
Concord and Montreal Railroad....to Fabyan's.
Maine Central Railroad (White Mountains Line) .... } to Crawford House.
Maine Central Railroad (White Mountains Line).............. } to North Conway.
Boston & Maine Railroad ....to Boston.
N. Y., N. H. & H. R. R..........to Fall River.
Fall River Line Steamers.........to New York.
Rate............$13 50
* Not to be sold in connection with tickets to Montreal *via* the Canadian Pacific Railway.
† Not to be sold in connection with tickets to Montreal *via* the Grand Trunk Railway.

†EXCURSION NO. 147 X.—MONTREAL TO NEW YORK.

Canadian Pacific Railway...... } to Newport, Vt. (Lake Memphremagog.)
Boston & Maine Railroad (Passumpsic Division .. .. } to St. Johnsbury.
St. Johnsbury & Lake Champlain R. R...................... } to Lunenburg.
Maine Central R. R..............to Fabyan's.
Maine Central Railroad (White Mountains Line)............. } to Portland.
Boston & Maine Railroad.........to Boston.
N. Y., N. H. & H. R. R..........to Fall River.
Fall River Line Steamers .. ..to New York.
Rate............$14 80

***Excursion No. 303 X.—Montreal to New York.**

Grand Trunk Railway	to St. John's.
Central Vermont Railroad	to Montpelier.
Montpelier & Wells River R. R.	to Wells River.
Concord & Montreal Railroad	to Fabyan's.
Maine Central Railroad (White Mountains Line)	to Portland.
Boston & Maine Railroad	to Boston.
Old Colony Railroad	to Fall River.
Fall River Line Steamers	to New York.

Rate............$14 80

†**Excursion No. 118 X.—Montreal to New York.**

Canadian Pacific Railway	to Newport, Vt. (Lake Memphremagog.)
Boston & Maine Railroad Passumpsic Division	to St. Johnsbury.
St. John's'y & Lake Cham. R. R.	to Lunenburg.
Maine Central R. R.	to Fabyan's.
Boston & Maine R. R.	to Base Mt. Wash'n
Mount Washington Railroad	to Summit.
Miliken's Stage Line	to Glen House.
Miliken's Stage Line	to Glen Station.
Maine Central Railroad (White Mountains Line)	to North Conway.
Boston & Maine Railroad	to Boston.
N. Y., N. H. & H. R. R.	to Fall River.
Fall River Line Steamers	to New York.

Rate............$23 90

* Not to be sold in connection with tickets to Montreal *via* the Canadian Pacific Railway.

† Not to be sold in connection with tickets to Montreal *via* the Grand Trunk Railway.

MONTROSE, PA.
LOCAL EXCURSION.
(Good for continuous passage only.)
THROUGH RATES.

‡New York	$8 20	Shickshinny	$3 70
Passaic	7 95	Berwick	4 10
Paterson	7 80	Bloomsburg	4 60
Boonton	7 25	Danville	5 10
‡Newark	8 20	Great Bend	1 10
‡Roseville Ave	8 20	Binghamton	1 65
Orange	8 10	Greene	2 45
Mountain	7 95	Oxford	3 00
South Orange	7 90	Norwich	3 30
Milburn	7 75	Sherburne	3 75
Short Hills	7 70	Waterville	4 60
Summit	7 70	Richfield Springs	5 80
Chatham	7 50	Utica	5 45
Madison	7 40	Cortland	3 40
Morristown	7 25	Syracuse	4 80
Dover	6 75	Oswego	6 20
Hopatcong Station	6 45	Owego	2 50
Andover	6 35	Ithaca	3 85
Newton	6 75	Waverly	3 20
Franklin	7 25	Elmira	3 95
Hackettstown	6 05	Corning	4 60
Washington	5 65	Bath	5 40
Scranton	2 30	Atlanta	6 20
Pittston	2 60	Wayland	6 40
Kingston	3 05	Dansville	6 75
Wilkesbarre	3 05	Mount Morris	7 30
Plymouth	3 20	Buffalo	9 75
Nanticoke	3 45		

‡Tickets good until used.

MT. POCONO, PA.
LOCAL EXCURSION.
(Good for continuous passage only.)
THROUGH RATES.

‡New York	$4 65	Shickshinny	$3 15
Passaic	4 35	Berwick	3 45
Paterson	4 20	Bloomsburg	3 75
Boonton	3 65	Danville	4 10
‡Newark	4 65	Great Bend	3 30
‡Roseville Ave	4 65	Binghamton	3 85
Orange	4 45	Greene	4 65
Mountain	4 35	Oxford	5 20
South Orange	4 30	Norwich	5 50
Milburn	4 15	Sherburne	5 95
Short Hills	4 10	Waterville	6 80
Summit	4 10	Richfield Springs	8 00
Chatham	3 90	Utica	7 65
Madison	3 80	Cortland	5 60
Morristown	3 65	Syracuse	7 00
Dover	3 15	Oswego	8 40
Hopatcong Station	2 85	Owego	4 70
Andover	2 95	Ithaca	6 05
Newton	3 65	Waverly	5 40
Franklin	3 65	Elmira	6 15
Hackettstown	2 45	Corning	6 80
Washington	2 05	Bath	7 60
Scranton	1 85	Atlanta	8 40
Pittston	2 25	Wayland	8 60
Kingston	2 60	Dansville	8 95
Wilkesbarre	2 60	Mount Morris	9 50
Plymouth	2 75	Buffalo	12 00
Nanticoke	2 90		

‡Tickets good until used.

MT. TABOR, N. J.
Special Excursion Tickets issued on account of the Mount Tabor Camp Meeting Association. On sale from June 1st until October 31st.

RATES.

*New York	$1 40	Chatham	$ 55
*Hoboken	1 40	Madison	45
Kingsland	1 15	Morristown	30
Passaic	1 00	Morris Plains	20
Clifton	90	Rockaway	15
Paterson	80	Dover	25
West Paterson	80	Pt. Oram	35
Little Falls	75	Succasunna	55
Mountain View	60	Ironia	60
Lincoln Park	50	Chester	75
Boonton	25	Mt. Arlington	50
Harrison	1 15	Hopatcong Station	60
Newark	1 15	Stanhope	65
Roseville Ave	1 10	Waterloo	75
Grove St	1 00	Andover	1 05
East Orange	1 00	Newton	1 25
Brick Church	1 00	Lafayette	1 40
Orange	90	Branchville	1 60
Highland Ave	90	Franklin	1 75
Mountain	90	Hackettstown	1 00
South Orange	90	Pt. Murray	1 25
Maplewood	85	Washington	1 40
Wyoming, N. J.	80	Broadway	1 60
Milburn	80	Stewartsville	1 75
Short Hills	75	Phillipsburg	1 90
Huntly	70	Easton	1 95
Summit	65	New Hampton	1 60
Murray Hill	85	Oxford Furnace	1 60
Stirling	1 55	Bridgeville	1 75
Basking Ridge	1 20	Delaware	1 90
Bernardsville	1 25	Portland	2 00
Far Hills	1 45	Water Gap	2 20
Gladstone	1 55	Stroudsburg	2 40

*Tickets good until used.

MT. WASHINGTON, N. H.
(White Mountains.)

The summit of this well known mountain is six thousand two hundred and ninety-three feet above the sea level, with a railroad running to the top, and also a carriage road from the Summit to the Glen. It is a most popular diversion for tourists who pass through, as well as for those who spend the summer, to make the ascent to witness the rugged surroundings, the beautiful cloud views and the unequalled pictures at sunrise and sunset.

EXCURSION S T 43 —FABYAN'S TO MOUNT WASHINGTON AND RETURN.

Boston & Maine R. R............to Base Station.
Mount Washington Railway.........to Summit.
Sold only in connection with Summer Excursion Ticket to, or passing through Fabyan's.
Rate..............$6 00

MOUNT PLEASANT, N. H.

At Mount Pleasant Station (1¼ mile E. of Fabyan's) is the Mount Pleasant House, most charmingly situated directly in front of the Presidential range, with Mt. Washington looming up in the foreground. From no

THE ASCENT TO SUMMIT OF MT. WASHINGTON, AS SEEN FROM MT. PLEASANT HOUSE.

other house in the White Mountains can such a perfect and magnificent view of Mt. Washington and its sentinel companions be obtained. From its spacious piazzas one can watch the upward climbing of the cog-wheel trains, almost to the very summit, 6,293 feet into the sky.

Trains for the summit are taken a few steps from the hotel, and trains of the Maine Central and of the Boston and Maine roads stop at the door.

MUSKOKA LAKES, ONT.

Gravenhurst—reached from Toronto via the Northern and Northwestern Division of the Grand Trunk Railway, is properly called the Gateway to Muskoka, which latter is located at the foot of Muskoka Lake.

Gravenhurst is quite a town, and of growing importance. The several lakes, such as Joseph, Rosseau, afford rare opportunities for the sportsman, as they abound in salmon, trout, black bass, perch and speckled trout.

EXCURSION S. T. 23.—NIAGARA FALLS TO GRAVENHURST, TOUR OF LAKES OF MUSKOKA AND RETURN.

N. Y. Central & Hudson River R. R..to Lewiston.
Niagara Navigation Co.'s Steamers..to Toronto.
Grand Trunk Railway...............to Gravenhurst.
Muskoka & Geo. Bay Navigation } through Lake
Company.......................) Muskoka.
Lake Rosseau & Lake Jos. & return..to Gravenhurst.
Returning via same route.
Sold only in connection with Summer Excursion ticket to, or passing through Niagara Falls.
Rate.............$9 30

EXCURSION S T 24.—TORONTO TO GRAVENHURST, TOUR OF LAKES OF MUSKOKA AND RETURN.

Grand Trunk Railway..............to Gravenhurst.
Muskoka and Geo. Bay Navigation } through Lake
Company.......................) Muskoka.
Lake Ros. & Lake Joseph & return. to Gravenhurst.
Returning via same route.
Sold only in connection with Summer Excursion Ticket to, or passing through Toronto.
Rate.............$7 50

NANTUCKET, MASS.

Is about twenty miles long and "away out at sea." Its quaint, old-fashioned character and its peculiar social and physical aspects, prove very interesting to the new comer, as well as charming to the frequent visitor.

The town is full of reminders of a prosperity of the past.

Fishing, sailing, and like aquatic sports are here to be enjoyed.

EXCURSION NO. 21.—NANTUCKET AND RETURN.

Delaware. Lack. & Western R. R....to New York.
Fall River Line Steamers............to Fall River.
Old Colony Railroad................to New Bedford.
New Bedford, Vineyard, Nantucket { to Nantucket.
& Cape Cod S. B. Line..........)
Returning via same route.

THROUGH RATES.

Morristown......	$ 9 50	Waterville........	$18 25
Dover............	10 00	Cortland.........	18 25
Hackettstown....	10 70	Syracuse.........	19 25
Washington......	11 10	Oswego..........	20 25
Water Gap.......	11 95	Owego...........	17 10
Stroudsburg.....	12 10	Ithaca...........	18 75
Scranton........	14 25	Waverly..........	17 85
Pittston.........	14 65	Elmira...........	18 70
Kingston........	15 05	Corning..........	19 15
Wilkesbarre.....	15 10	Bath.............	20 00
Binghamton.....	16 25	Atlanta...........	21 15
Greene..........	17 05	Wayland.........	21 45
Oxford..........	17 25	Dansville.........	21 95
Norwich.........	17 25	Mount Morris.....	21 95
Sherburne.......	17 95	Buffalo...........	24 25

NARRAGANSETT PIER, R. I.

The very best of bathing facilities are to be found at this fashionable ocean resort.

The extended reputation it now enjoys is of comparatively recent date, but the quality of its attractions had only to be demonstrated to move "The Pier" into the very first of leading sea-side places.

It is directly on the ocean, with a smooth beach about a mile in extent.

EXCURSION No. 69.—NARRAGANSETT PIER AND RETURN.

Del., Lack. & Western R. R....to New York.
Stonington Line Steamers.....to Stonington.
N.Y., Providence & Boston R.R.to Kingston.
Narragansett Pier Railroad....to Narragansett Pier.
Returning *via* same route.

THROUGH RATES.

Morristown	$ 6 25	Waterville	$15 00
Dover	6 75	Cortland	15 00
Hackettstown	7 45	Syracuse	16 00
Washington	7 85	Oswego	17 00
Water Gap	8 70	Owego	13 85
Stroudsburg	8 85	Ithaca	15 50
Scranton	11 00	Waverly	14 10
Pittston	12 45	Elmira	15 45
Kingston	11 80	Corning	15 90
Wilkesbarre	11 85	Bath	16 75
Binghamton	13 00	Atlanta	17 90
Greene	13 80	Wayland	18 20
Oxford	14 00	Dansville	18 70
Norwich	14 00	Mount Morris	18 70
Sherburne	14 70	Buffalo	21 00

NEW BEDFORD, MASS.

New Bedford glories in the possession of one of the finest, as well as the most picturesque, harbors of the Atlantic coast. The entrance to the harbor, lying between Clark's Neck and Sconticut Point, is strongly fortified, and the wharf frontage extends along the broad Acushnet for two miles. Fairhaven, on the opposite shore of the river, is connected with the city by a long bridge. The city rises gradually from the water's edge, and the streets are shaded and beautified by fine old elms. A public driveway extending along the coast for five miles presents excellent views of the ocean and the islands which dot its surface. The various industries of New Bedford attract people of all nationalities, and an idle hour may be well passed in studying the various types of its inhabitants.

New Bedford is the starting point for the steamer ride to Nantucket, Martha's Vineyard, and Cottage City.

It has pleasant neighbors in the pretty summer towns of Fairhaven, Mattapoisett, Marion and Nonquit.

EXCURSION No. 286.—NEW BEDFORD AND RETURN.

Delaware, Lack. & Western R. R....to New York.
Fall River Line Steamers..............to Fall River.
Old Colony Railroad................to New Bedford.
Returning *via* same route.

THROUGH RATES.

Morristown	$ 7 50	Waterville	$16 25
Dover	8 00	Cortland	16 25
Hackettstown	8 70	Syracuse	17 25
Washington	9 10	Oswego	18 25
Water Gap	9 95	Owego	15 10
Stroudsburg	12 10	Ithaca	16 75
Scranton	12 25	Waverly	15 85
Pittston	12 65	Elmira	16 70
Kingston	13 05	Corning	17 15
Wilkesbarre	13 10	Bath	18 00
Binghamton	14 25	Atlanta	19 15
Greene	15 05	Wayland	19 50
Oxford	15 25	Dansville	19 95
Norwich	15 25	Mount Morris	19 95
Sherburne	15 95	Buffalo	22 25

NEWPORT, R. I.

This fashionable watering place probably takes first place in that it out-ranks all other of our resorts in age and in the social scale.

"Nature has lavished her riches on the spot. There is rare beauty in the land, its grass and shrubs; there is a surpassing charm in air and sky, and a fascination in the sea and its blue waters with gem-like isles."

The city is of itself a beautiful place; its habitations costly and elaborate. Its drives are world famous, particularly the cliff road, which, and in season, presents a magnificent array of gorgeous equippages and richly dressed people.

EXCURSION No. 64.—NEWPORT, R. I., AND RETURN.

Delaware, Lack. & Western R. R.....to New York.
Fall River Line Steamers,...............to Newport.
Returning *via* same route.

THROUGH RATES.

Morristown	$ 7 25	Waterville	$16 00
Dover	7 75	Cortland	16 00
Hackettstown	8 45	Syracuse	17 00
Washington	8 85	Oswego	18 00
Water Gap	9 70	Owego	14 85
Stroudsburg	11 85	Ithaca	16 50
Scranton	12 00	Waverly	15 60
Pittston	12 40	Elmira	16 45
Kingston	12 80	Corning	16 90
Wilkesbarre	12 85	Bath	17 75
Binghamton	14 00	Atlanta	18 90
Greene	14 80	Wayland	19 20
Oxford	15 00	Dansville	19 70
Norwich	15 00	Mount Morris	19 70
Sherburne	15 70	Buffalo	22 00

NIAGARA-ON-THE-LAKE, ONT.

EXCURSION S T 51.—NIAGARA FALLS TO NIAGARA-ON-THE-LAKE AND RETURN.

N. Y. C. & Hud. River R. R.,to Lewiston.
Niagara Nav. Co.'s Strs.,.....to Niagara-on-the-Lake.
Returning *via* same route.
Sold only in connection with Summer Excursion Tickets to, or passing through Niagara Falls.
Rate...........50 cents.

NIAGARA FALLS, N. Y.

This magnificent cataract, the grandeur of which has been but inadequtely dwelt upon by many celebrated writers, calls for far more elaborate treatment than in our limited space, even if we had words at command to do this wonder of Nature justice, we can allot to it. We are only able to hint at few of its marvels and to dilate a little on the unrivalled beauty of the ceaseless roaring "Thunder of Waters."

To the aborigines, this wonderful cataract was called "Ouy-a-ka-ra" and "Og-na-ka-ra" "Thunder of Waters," and thus it will be seen that even they, in all their simplicity, realized what a mighty work Nature had here accomplished. Niagara Falls never becomes monotonous to the visitor. Any one gazing upon it realizes how hard it is to be able to describe it adequately, for any attempt at word-painting of this rolling flood would prove but a poor travesty of the work of Almighty God.

Three distinct falls comprise the whole. These are the "Horse Shoe" on the Canadian side, "American" on the Niagara or United States side, and "Central," which descends between Luna and Goat Islands. Three thousand feet is the entire breadth of the combined falls.

Niagara ranks as the foremost of the world's wonders, and is visited annually by hundreds of thousands from all parts. Indeed many a newly married couple will spend their honeymoon there.

It has been stated that the sound of the falling waters can be heard at a distance of 24 miles, and that from eighteen to twenty-one millions of cubic feet of water descend per minute from the river above. The lakes and streams that find an outlet in the Niagara River drain five hundred thousand or more square miles of land, and the lakes and tributaries themselves cover a surface of one hundred and fifty thousand square miles.

The river in its onward flow to Lake Ontario has a fall of 334 feet. It dashes heedlessly on over rocks and islets and is lashed into foam all the way to Lewiston. No craft yet built —yes, one, the *Maid of the Mist*, on June 15, 1861, was successfully taken from the foot of the falls, through the rapids and whirlpool, and finally delivered on Lake Ontario—even were the water of sufficient depth, could sail the rapids. Several daring adventurers have sacrificed their lives to win fame and money by braving the rapids, the foremost among these was Captain Webb.

The State of New York having secured the rights to the lands adjacent to the Falls, has incorporated them into Niagara Park, which embraces the greatest points of interest on the American side. The park is open to the public free of charge. Goat Island, connected with this park by a bridge, offers the best view of the falls, and from Prospect Park, on the mainland, the scenery is magnificient. The drive along the Canadian shore affords a splendid view of the gorge and rapids.

Connected with the falls are innumerable points of interest, principal among which are the Cave of the Winds, Three Sisters Island, Burning Spring, the Whirlpool Rapids, Suspension and Cantilever Bridges. A sensational trip is that made across the river below the falls in a little steamer, the modern *Maid of the Mist*.

The drives around Niagara are very interesting, and the village itself, with its pretty homes, fine streets and great numbers of large well-kept hotels, should be explored by visitors.

EXCURSION NO. 36.—NIAGARA FALLS AND RETURN.

Delaware, Lack. & Western R. R...to Buffalo.
N. Y. Cent. & Hudson River R. R .to Niagara Falls.
Returning *via* same route.

THROUGH RATES.

New York	$16 00	Danville	$13 50
Paterson	16 00	Binghamton	9 00
Newark	16 00	Greene	9 95
Morristown	16 00	Oxford	10 45
Dover	15 90	Norwich	10 80
Hackettstown	15 15	Sherburne	11 25
Washington	14 75	Waterville	12 10
Water Gap	13 95	Vestal	8 65
Stroudsburg	13 75	Owego	8 00
Scranton	11 20	Ithaca	8 55
Pittston	11 20	Waverly	7 25
Kingston	11 35	Elmira	6 50
Wilkesbarre	11 35	Corning	6 25
Plymouth	11 50	Bath	5 25
Nanticoke	11 75	Atlanta	4 60
Shickshinny	12 30	Wayland	4 25
Berwick	12 90	Dansville	4 00
Bloomsburg	13 50	Mount Morris	3 50

*EXCURSION NO. 37.—NIAGARA FALLS AND RETURN.

Delaware, Lack. & Western R. R...to Buffalo.
N. Y. Cent. & Hudson River R. R .to Niagara Falls.
N. Y. Cent. & Hudson River R. R. ..to New York.
From New York........$17 00

*EXCURSION NO. 46.—NIAGARA FALLS AND RETURN.

Delaware, Lack. & Western R. R...to Buffalo.
N. Y., Lake Erie & Western R. R..to Niagara Falls.
N. Y., Lake Erie & Western R. R...to New York.
From New York........$16 00

*EXCURSION NO. 315.—NIAGARA FALLS AND RETURN.

Delaware, Lack. & Western R. R...to Buffalo.
N. Y., Lake Erie & Western R. R..to Niagara Falls.
N. Y., Lake Erie & Western R. R .to New York.
From New York........$16 00

EXCURSION NO. 387.—NIAGARA FALLS AND RETURN.

Del., Lack. & Western R. R......to Corning.
Fall Brook Ry. Co. (*via* Watkins).to Penn Yan.
Lake Keuka Nav. Co.'s Steamers.to Hammondsport.
Bath & Hammondsport R. R....to Bath.
Del., Lack. & Western R. R......to Buffalo.
N. Y. Cent. & Hud. River R. R ...to Niagara Falls.
N. Y. Cent. & Hud. River R. R..to Buffalo.
Del., Lack. & Western R. R......to starting point.

DELAWARE, LACKAWANNA & WESTERN R. R.

EXCURSION NO. 388.—REVERSE OF THE PRECEDING.

THROUGH RATES.

New York	$17 00	Binghamton	$10 40
Paterson	17 00	Greene	11 20
Newark	17 00	Oxford	11 75
Morristown	17 00	Norwich	12 05
Dover	17 00	Sherburne	12 30
Hackettstown	16 40	Waterville	13 55
Washington	16 00	Owego	9 65
Water Gap	15 15	Waverly	8 80
Stroudsburg	15 00	Elmira	8 10
Scranton	12 85	Atlanta	7 50
Pittston	13 25	Wayland	7 50
Kingston	13 55	Dansville	7 50
Wilkesbarre	13 55	Mount Morris	7 50

***EXCURSION NO. 44.—NIAGARA FALLS AND RETURN.**

Delaware, Lack. & Western R. R...to Buffalo.
N. Y. Cent. & Hudson River R. R. to Niagara Falls.
N. Y. Cent. & Hudson River R. R...to Albany.
Day Line Hud. River Steamers ...to New York.
From New York.........$16 15

***EXCURSION NO. 45.—NIAGARA FALLS AND RETURN.**

Delaware, Lack. & Western R. R. to Buffalo.
N. Y. Cent. & Hudson River R. R...to Niagara Falls.
N. Y. Cent & Hudson River R. R...to Schenectady.
Delaware & Hudson Canal Co......to Saratoga.
Delaware & Hudson Canal Co......to Troy.
N. Y. Cent. & Hudson River R. R...to New York.
From New York.........$18 70

***EXCURSION NO. 316.—NIAGARA FALLS AND RETURN.**

Delaware, Lack. & Western R. R...to Buffalo.
N. Y. Cent. & Hudson River R. R...to Niagara Falls.
N. Y. Cent. & Hudson River R. R...to Schenectady.
Delaware & Hudson Canal Co......to Saratoga.
Delaware & Hudson Canal Co......to Albany.
West Shore Railroad...............to New York.
From New York.......$18 80

***EXCURSION NO. 317.—NIAGARA FALLS AND RETURN.**

Delaware, Lack & Western R. R ..to Buffalo.
N. Y. Cent. & Hudson River R. R...to Niagara Falls.
N. Y. Cent. & Hudson River R. R...to Schenectady.
Delaware & Hudson Canal Co......to Saratoga.
Delaware & Hudson Canal Co......to Albany.
Day Line Hudson River Steamers..to New York.
From New York.......$17 70

***EXCURSION NO. 318.—NIAGARA FALLS AND RETURN.**

Del., Lack. & Western R. R....to Buffalo.
N. Y. Cent. & Hud. River R. R...to Niagara Falls.
N. Y. Cent. & Hud. River R. R...to Lewiston.
Rome, Watert'n & Ogdenb'g R. R. to Clayton.
Thousand Island Steamboat Co...to Alexandria Bay.
Thousand Island Steamboat...to Clayton.
Rome, Watert'n & Ogdenb'g R. R. to Utica.
N. Y. Cent. & Hud River R. R ...to New York.
From New York $23 60

***EXCURSION NO. 319.—NIAGARA FALLS AND RETURN.**

Del., Lack. & Western R. R.... ...to Buffalo.
N. Y. Cent. & Hud. River R. R....to Niagara Falls.
N. Y. Cent. & Hud. River R. R.
Rome, Watert'n & Ogdenb'g R. R. to Clayton.
Thousand Island Steamboat Co...to Alexandria Bay.
Thousand Island Steamboat Co...to Clayton.
Rome, Watert'n & Ogdenb'g R. R. to Utica.
West Shore Railroad........ ...to New York.
From New York $23 60

* NOTE.—Excursions Nos. 37, 44, 45, 46, 315, 316, 317, 318 and 319 may be sold from any Line Station on the Morris and Essex Division, Main Line or Buffalo Division, at the same rates as from New York. To make up round trip tickets from such Line Stations, agents will issue in connection with these tickets, Form C E, reading from "New York to Station stamped on back," which in connection with the tickets ending in New York, will make the complete round trip from the starting point.

These forms may be issued from other Line Stations in the same manner but agents will charge, in addition to the rates from New York, as follows: Pittston, 40c.; Kingston, 80c.; Wilkesbarre, 85c.; Plymouth, 90c.; Nanticoke, $1.05; Shickshinny, $1.45; Berwick, $1.85; Bloomsburg, $2.35; Danville, $2 85; Greene, 80c.; Oxford, $1.40; Norwich, $1.70; Cortland, $1.75, and Ithaca, $1.40.

EXCURSION NO. 40.—NIAGARA FALLS AND RETURN.

Del, Lack. & Western R. R.....to Buffalo.
N. Y. Cent. & Hud. River R. R...to Niagara Falls.
N. Y. Cent. & Hud. River R. R...to Utica.
Del., Lack. & Western R. R ....to Richfield Springs.
Del., Lack. & Western R. R.....to starting point.

EXCURSION NO. 41.—REVERSE OF THE PRECEDING.

THROUGH RATES.

New York	$19 15	Binghamton	$11 65
Paterson	19 15	Greene	11 65
Newark	19 15	Oxford	11 65
Morristown	18 85	Norwich	11 65
Dover	18 45	Sherburne	11 65
Hackettstown	17 65	Waterville	11 65
Washington	17 25	Owego	11 65
Water Gap	16 15	Ithaca	13 05
Stroudsburg	16 25	Waverly	11 65
Scranton	14 10	Elmira	11 65
Pittston	14 50	Corning	11 65
Kingston	14 60	Bath	11 65
Wilkesbarre	14 80		

EXCURSION NO. 42.—NIAGARA FALLS AND RETURN.

Delaware, Lack. & Western R. R...to Buffalo.
N. Y. Central & Hudson River R. R. to Niagara Falls.
N. Y. Central & Hud. River R. R...to Utica.
Delaware, Lack. & Western R. R...to starting point.

EXCURSION NO. 47.—REVERSE OF THE PRECEDING.

THROUGH RATES.

New York	$18 25	Binghamton	$10 75
Paterson	18 25	Greene	10 75
Newark	18 25	Oxford	10 75
Morristown	17 95	Norwich	10 75
Dover	17 45	Sherburne	10 75
Hackettstown	16 75	Waterville	10 75
Washington	16 35	Owego	10 75
Water Gap	15 55	Ithaca	12 10
Stroudsburg	15 35	Waverly	10 75
Scranton	13 20	Elmira	10 75
Pittston	13 60	Corning	10 75
Kingston	13 90	Bath	10 75
Wilkesbarre	13 90		

EXCURSION NO. 149.—NIAGARA FALLS AND RETURN.

Delaware, Lack. & Western R. R...to Buffalo.
N. Y. Central & Hud. River R. R...to Niagara Falls.
N. Y. Central & Hud. River R. R...to Syracuse.
Delaware, Lack. & Western R. R...to starting point.

EXCURSION NO. 150.—REVERSE OF THE PRECEDING.

THROUGH RATES.

New York	$16 00	Stroudsburg	$13 95
Paterson	16 00	Scranton	11 80
Newark	16 00	Pittston	12 20
Morristown	16 00	Kingston	12 50
Dover	16 00	Wilkesbarre	12 50
Hackettstown	15 30	Binghamton	9 35
Washington	14 95	Cortland	9 35
Water Gap	14 10		

DELAWARE, LACKAWANNA & WESTERN R. R.

EXCURSION No. 38.—NIAGARA FALLS AND RETURN.

Delaware, Lack. & Western R. R....to Buffalo.
N. Y. Central & Hud. River R. R...to Niagara Falls.
N. Y. Central & Hud. River R. R. } to Cayuga.
(via Clifton Springs)............ }
Cayuga Lake Steamer.............to Ithaca.
Delaware, Lack. & Western R. R....to starting point.

EXCURSION No. 39.—REVERSE OF THE PRECEDING.

New York	$17 00	Wilkesbarre	$12 70
Paterson	17 00	Binghamton	9 50
Newark	17 00	Greene	10 35
Morristown	16 80	Oxford	10 95
Dover	16 30	Norwich	11 25
Hackettstown	15 60	Sherburne	11 70
Washington	15 20	Waterville	12 55
Water Gap	14 35	Owego	8 70
Stroudsburg	14 20	Waverly	8 70
Scranton	12 10	Elmira	8 70
Pittston	12 40	Corning	8 70
Kingston	12 70	Bath	8 70

EXCURSION No. 48.—NIAGARA FALLS AND RETURN.

Delaware, Lack. & Western R. R....to Buffalo.
N. Y. Central & Hud. River R. R....to Niagara Falls
N. Y. Central & Hud. River R. R....to Geneva.
Seneca Lake Steamer............to Watkins.
Penn. R. R. (via Haven Glen)......to Elmira.
Delaware, Lack. & Western R. R....to starting point.

EXCURSION No. 49.—REVERSE OF THE PRECEDING.

THROUGH RATES.

New York	$17 00	Binghamton	$ 9 75
Paterson	17 00	Greene	10 55
Newark	17 00	Oxford	11 05
Morristown	16 75	Norwich	11 45
Dover	16 25	Sherburne	11 90
Hackettstown	15 50	Waterville	12 75
Washington	15 15	Owego	8 85
Water Gap	14 35	Ithaca	10 25
Stroudsburg	14 15	Waverly	7 85
Scranton	12 00	Elmira	7 00
Pittston	12 35	Corning	7 00
Kingston	12 65	Bath	7 00
Wilkesbarre	12 65		

EXCURSION No. 134.—NIAGARA FALLS AND RETURN.

Del., Lack & Western R. R.........to Buffalo.
N. Y. Cent. & Hud. River R. R...to Niagara Falls.
N. Y. Cent. & Hud. River R. R...to Lewiston.
Rome, Watert'n & Ogdenb'g R. R.to Clayton.
Thousand Island Steamboat Co...to Clayton.
Thousand Island Steamboat Co... to Alexandria Bay.
Thousand Island Steamboat Co....to Clayton.
Rome, Watert'n & Ogdenb'g R. R.to Utica.
Del., Lack. & Western R. R........to starting point.

EXCURSION No. 135.—REVERSE OF THE PRECEDING.

THROUGH RATES.

New York	$23 60	Oxford	$17 15
Paterson	23 60	Norwich	17 15
Newark	23 60	Sherburne	17 15
Morristown	23 60	Waterville	17 15
Dover	23 60	Owego	17 15
Hackettstown	23 15	Waverly	17 15
Washington	22 75	Elmira	17 15
Water Gap	21 95	Corning	17 15
Stroudsburg	21 75	Bath	17 15
Scranton	19 60	Atlanta	17 15
Pittston	20 05	Wayland	17 15
Kingston	20 30	Dansville	17 15
Wilkesbarre	20 30	Mount Morris	17 15
Binghamton	17 15	Buffalo	17 15
Greene	17 15		

EXCURSION No. 51.—NIAGARA FALLS AND RETURN.

Delaware, Lack. & Western R. R to Bath.
Bath & Hammondsport Railroad.to Hammondsport.
Lake Keuka Nav. Co.'s Steamers.to Penn Yan.
Pennsylvania Railroad........to Canandaigua.
N. Y. Cent. & Hud. River R. R...to Niagara Falls.
N. Y. Cent. & Hud. River R. R...to Buffalo.
Delaware, Lack. & Western R. R.to starting point.

EXCURSION No. 50.—REVERSE OF THE PRECEDING.

THROUGH RATES.

New York	$17 00	Wilkesbarre	$12 85
Paterson	17 00	Binghamton	9 70
Newark	17 00	Greene	10 50
Morristown	17 00	Oxford	11 10
Dover	16 50	Norwich	11 40
Hackettstown	15 55	Sherburne	11 85
Washington	15 35	Waterville	12 70
Water Gap	14 55	Owego	8 80
Stroudsburg	14 35	Ithaca	10 30
Scranton	12 20	Waverly	7 80
Pittston	12 55	Elmira	6 95
Kingston	12 25	Corning	6 95

EXCURSION No. 161.—NIAGARA FALLS AND RETURN.

Delaware, Lack. & Western R. R....to Buffalo.
N. Y. Central & Hud River R. R....to Niagara Falls.
N. Y. Central & Hud. River R. R....to Geneva.
F. B. C. Co.'s R.R. (via Watk's Glen).to Corning.
Del., Lack. & Western R. R.........to starting point.

EXCURSION No. 162.—REVERSE OF THE PRECEDING.

THROUGH RATES.

New York	$17 30	Binghamton	$ 9 80
Paterson	17 30	Greene	10 60
Newark	17 30	Oxford	10 10
Morristown	17 00	Norwich	10 45
Dover	16 50	Sherburne	11 90
Hackettstown	15 80	Waterville	12 75
Washington	15 40	Owego	9 00
Water Gap	14 55	Ithaca	10 35
Stroudsburg	14 40	Waverly	8 20
Scranton	12 25	Elmira	7 50
Pittston	12 65	Corning	6 90
Kingston	12 95	Bath	6 90
Wilkesbarre	12 95		

EXCURSION No. 163.—NIAGARA FALLS AND RETURN.

Delaware, Lack. & Western R. R....to Buffalo.
N. Y. Cent. & Hud. River R. R......to Niagara Falls.
N. Y. Cent. & Hud. River R. R......to Canandaigua.
Pennsylvania Railroad.........to Penn Yan.
F. B. C. Co. R. R. (via Wat, Glen).. to Corning.
Del., Lack. & Western R. R........to starting point.

EXCURSION No. 164.—REVERSE OF THE PRECEDING.

THROUGH RATES.

New York	$17 00	Binghamton	$ 9 65
Paterson	17 60	Greene	10 45
Newark	17 60	Oxford	10 95
Morristown	16 85	Norwich	11 30
Dover	16 40	Sherburne	11 75
Hackettstown	15 65	Waterville	12 60
Washington	15 25	Owego	8 85
Water Gap	14 40	Ithaca	10 20
Stroudsburg	14 25	Waverly	8 10
Scranton	12 10	Elmira	7 40
Pittston	12 50	Corning	6 75
Kingston	12 80	Bath	6 75
Wilkesbarre	12 80		

NORTH CONWAY, N. H.
(White Mountains.)

This village is situated on a terrace just above the intervale of the Saco. The valley is bounded on the west by the long Mote Mountains, on the East by the Rattlesnake Ridge, while on the North the Mountains part sufficiently to enable one to see the whole White Mountain range.

EXC. S T 44.—BOSTON TO NORTH CONWAY AND RETURN.

Boston & Maine R. R...to North Conway and Return
Sold only in connection with Summer Excursion Ticket to, or passing through Boston.
Rate $6 50

OAK BLUFFS, MASS.
(See COTTAGE CITY, MASS.)

OCEAN GROVE, (Asbury Park), N. J.

What is now the resort of hundreds of thousands of summer visitors was originally (and that but a few years since) a camp ground of members of the Methodist church. To-day it is a splendid summer city by the sea.

The rules prohibiting the sale of intoxicating liquors at any time, and forbidding driving, boating, bathing, etc., on Sunday are strictly enforced, and that a resting place with such moral observance is very popular with a large proportion of the people is amply attested by the unparalleled prosperity to be witnessed at Ocean Grove.

EXCURSION NO. 172.—OCEAN GROVE AND RETURN.

Delaware, Lack. & Western R. R....to New York.
Pennsylvania Railroad................to Ocean Grove.
Returning via same route.

EXCURSION NO. 23.—OCEAN GROVE AND RETURN.

Delaware, Lack. & Western R. R .. to New York.
Central R. R. of New Jersey Strs...to Sandy Hook.
Central Railroad of New Jersey ....to West End.
New York & Long Branch R. R.....to Ocean Grove.
Returning via same route.

*EXCURSION NO. 24.—OCEAN GROVE AND RETURN.

Delaware, Lack. & Western R. R....to New York.
Central Railroad of New Jersey ....to Perth Amboy.
New York & Long Branch R. R....to Ocean Grove.
Returning via same route.

THROUGH RATES FOR EITHER EXCURSION.

Morristown	$3 10	Plymouth	$8 75
Dover	3 60	Nanticoke	8 90
Hackettstown	4 30	Shickshinny	9 30
Washington	4 70	Berwick	9 70
Water Gap	5 55	Bloomsburg	10 20
Stroudsburg	5 70	Danville	10 70
Scranton	7 75	Binghamton	9 85
Pittston	8 25	Greene	10 65
Kingston	8 65	Oxford	10 85
Wilkesbarre	8 70	Norwich	10 85

Sherburne	$11 55	Elmira	$12 30
Waterville	11 85	Corning	12 75
Cortland	11 85	Bath	13 60
Syracuse	12 85	Atlanta	14 75
Oswego	13 85	Wayland	15 05
Owego	10 70	Dansville	15 55
Ithaca	12 35	Mount Morris	15 55
Waverly	11 45	Buffalo	17 85

EXCURSION NO. 22.—OCEAN GROVE AND RETURN.

Del., Lack. & Western R. R.........to New Hampton.
Central Railroad of New Jersey...to Perth Amboy.
New York & Long Branch R. R...to Ocean Grove.
Returning via same route.

THROUGH RATES.

Water Gap	$4 70	Sherburne	$11 55
Stroudsburg	4 85	Waterville	11 85
Scranton	7 00	Cortland	11 20
Pittston	7 35	Syracuse	11 85
Kingston	7 65	Oswego	11 85
Wilkesbarre	7 65	Owego	11 45
Plymouth	7 80	Ithaca	12 35
Nanticoke	7 95	Waverly	11 55
Shickshinny	8 30	Elmira	12 10
Berwick	8 75	Corning	12 75
Bloomsburg	9 25	Bath	13 60
Danville	9 70	Atlanta	14 75
Binghamton	9 85	Wayland	15 05
Greene	10 25	Dansville	15 55
Oxford	10 80	Mount Morris	15 55
Norwich	10 85	Buffalo	17 85

EXCURSION NO. 30.—OCEAN GROVE AND RETURN.

Del., Lack & Western R. R.........to New Hampton.
Central Railroad of New Jersey... to Perth Amboy.
New York & Long Branch R. R...to Ocean Grove.
New York & Long Branch R. R...to Perth Amboy.
Central Railroad of New Jersey...to New York.
Del., Lack. & Western R. R.........to starting point.

* EXCURSION NO. 274.—REVERSE OF THE PRECEDING.

THROUGH RATES.

Water Gap	$5 20	Syracuse	$12 00
Stroudsburg	5 35	Oswego	13 40
Scranton	7 50	Owego	10 60
Pittston	7 85	Ithaca	12 15
Kingston	8 15	Waverly	11 50
Wilkesbarre	8 15	Elmira	12 20
Binghamton	9 95	Corning	12 85
Greene	10 75	Bath	13 70
Oxford	11 30	Atlanta	14 50
Norwich	11 60	Wayland	14 70
Sherburne	12 05	Dansville	15 00
Waterville	12 90	Mount Morris	15 60
Cortland	11 70	Buffalo	18 10

* Good for passage between Ocean Grove and New York, either via the boat and trains of the Sandy Hook route, or the trains of either the Central Railroad of New Jersey or the Pennsylvania Railroad.

OLD ORCHARD BEACH, ME.

The name is derived from an old apple orchard a few miles from Saco, Me.

The beach, however, is the great attraction, being rated the finest in New England. Having an average width of three hundred feet at low tide, and extending about ten miles in length, it offers not only splendid bathing facilities but a charming drive.

EXCURSION S. T. 12.—BOSTON TO OLD ORCHARD BEACH AND RETURN.

Boston & Maine Railroad | to Old Orchard Beach and return.
Sold only in connection with Summer Excursion Ticket to, or passing through Boston.
Rate.............$4 00

OLD POINT COMFORT, VA.
(Fortress Monroe.)

Peace has here erected monumental reminders of her victories in the Soldier's Home, National Normal School, etc., interesting accompaniments to a sojourner, whether he hies him here to rest and recreation from business cares or in search of restored health. A mammoth hotel, of the first-class, supplies every creature comfort; the broad bay offers diversions that are competed for by the picturesque precincts of the fortress.

Music, the dance, bright uniforms, ships of war and peace, add life to the splendid picture, and though far away from the everyday activity of city life, monotony is unknown.

EXCURSION No. 170 Y.—OLD POINT COMFORT, VA.

Limited to three (3) months from date of sale.
Del., Lack. & Western R. R....to Manunka Chunk.
Pennsylvania Railroad.........to Delmar.
N. Y., Phila, & Norfolk R. R. to Old Point Comfort.
Returning *via* same route.

EXCURSION No. 168 Y.—OLD POINT COMFORT, VA.

Limited to three (3) months from date of sale.
Del., Lack. & Western R. R....to Manunka Chunk.
Pennsylvania Railroad........to Baltimore.
Baltimore Steam Packet Co...to Old Point Comfort.
Returning *via* same route.

THROUGH RATES.

Stroudsburg	$15 30	Syracuse	$21 45
Scranton	15 30	Fulton	22 45
Pittston	15 30	Oswego	22 85
Kingston	15 30	Owego	18 70
Wilkesbarre	15 30	Ithaca	20 05
Montrose	17 60	Waverly	18 70
Binghamton	17 80	Elmira	18 70
Greene	18 00	Corning	19 65
Oxford	19 15	Bath	20 90
Norwich	19 50	Atlanta	22 00
Sherburne	19 95	Wayland	22 40
Waterville	20 80	Dansville	22 80
Richfield Springs	21 95	Mount Morris	23 00
Utica	21 60	Buffalo	25 00
Cortland	19 55		

EXCURSION No. 171 Y.—OLD POINT COMFORT, VA.

Limited to three (3) months from date of sale.
Del., Lack. & Western R. R. to New York.
Pennsylvania Railroad........to Delmar.
N. Y., Phila. & Norfolk R. R..to Old Point Comfort.
Returning *via* same route.

EXCURSION No. 169 Y.—OLD POINT COMFORT, VA.

Limited to three (3) months from date of sale.
Del., Lack. & Western R. R....to New York.
Pennsylvania Railroad........to Baltimore.
Baltimore Steam Packet Co...to Old Point Comfort.
Returning *via* same route.

THROUGH RATES.

Summit	$16 40	Richfield Springs	$26 35
Morristown	16 85	Utica	24 85
Dover	17 35	Cortland	25 60
Hackettstown	18 05	Syracuse	26 60
Washington	18 45	Fulton	26 10
Stroudsburg	19 45	Oswego	27 60
Scranton	21 60	Owego	24 45
Pittston	22 00	Ithaca	26 10
Kingston	22 40	Waverly	25 20
Wilkesbarre	22 45	Elmira	26 05
Montrose	23 80	Corning	26 50
Binghamton	23 60	Bath	27 35
Greene	24 40	Atlanta	28 50
Oxford	24 60	Wayland	28 80
Norwich	24 60	Dansville	29 30
Sherburne	24 85	Mount Morris	29 30
Waterville	24 85	Buffalo	31 60

EXCURSION No. 382 Y.—OLD POINT COMFORT, VA.

Limited to three (3) months from date of sale.
Del., Lack. & Western R. R...to Manunka Chunk.
Pennsylvania Railroad.....to Washington.
Norfolk & Wash. D.C.Steamboat Co.............. | to Old Point Comfort.
Returning *via* same route.

THROUGH RATES.

Stroudsburg	$15 30	Syracuse	$21 00
Scranton	15 30	Fulton	22 00
Pittston	15 30	Oswego	22 40
Kingston	15 30	Owego	18 70
Wilkesbarre	15 30	Ithaca	20 05
Montrose	17 60	Waverly	18 70
Binghamton	17 80	Elmira	18 70
Greene	18 60	Corning	19 65
Oxford	19 15	Bath	20 90
Norwich	19 50	Atlanta	22 00
Sherburne	19 05	Wayland	22 40
Waterville	20 80	Dansville	21 80
Richfield Springs	21 95	Mount Morris	23 00
Utica	21 60	Buffalo	25 00
Cortland	19 55		

EXCURSION No. 383 Y.—OLD POINT COMFORT, VA.

Limited to three (3) months from date of sale.
Del., Lack. & Western R. R...to Washington.
Pennsylvania Railroad ......to Washington.
Norfolk & Wash.D.C.Steamboat Co............. | to Old Point Comfort.
Returning *via* same route.

THROUGH RATES.

Summit	$16 40	Norwich	$24 60
Morristown	16 85	Sherburne	24 85
Dover	17 35	Waterville	24 85
Hackettstown	18 05	Richfield Springs	26 35
Washington	18 45	Utica	24 85
Stroudsburg	19 45	Cortland	25 60
Scranton	21 60	Syracuse	26 60
Pittston	22 00	Fulton	26 10
Kingston	22 40	Oswego	27 60
Wilkesbarre	22 45	Owego	24 45
Montrose	23 80	Ithaca	26 10
Binghamton	23 60	Waverly	25 20
Greene	24 40	Elmira	26 05
Oxford	24 60		

EXCURSION No. 384 Y.—OLD POINT COMFORT, VA.

Limited to three (3) months from date of sale.
Del., Lack. & Western R. R...to Manunka Chunk.
Pennsylvania Railroad ......to Quantico.
Rich, Fred. & P. R. R.........to Richmond.
Ches & Ohio R. R.............to Old Point Comfort.
Returning *via* same route.

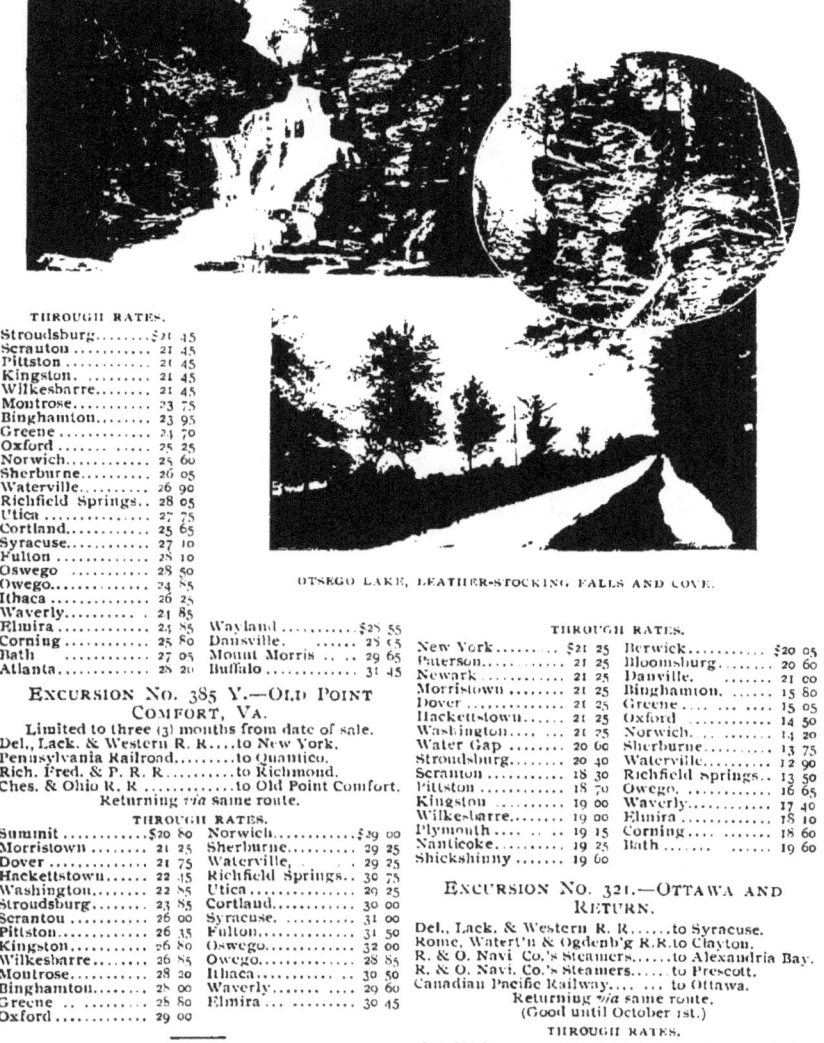

OTSEGO LAKE, LEATHER-STOCKING FALLS AND COVE.

THROUGH RATES.

Stroudsburg	$21 45
Scranton	21 45
Pittston	21 45
Kingston	21 45
Wilkesbarre	21 45
Montrose	23 75
Binghamton	23 95
Greene	24 70
Oxford	25 25
Norwich	25 60
Sherburne	26 05
Waterville	26 90
Richfield Springs	28 05
Utica	27 75
Cortland	25 65
Syracuse	27 10
Fulton	28 10
Oswego	28 50
Owego	24 85
Ithaca	26 25
Waverly	21 85
Elmira	24 85
Corning	25 80
Bath	27 05
Atlanta	28 20
Wayland	$28 55
Dansville	28 65
Mount Morris	29 65
Richfield Springs	30 75
Buffalo	31 45

EXCURSION NO. 385 Y.—OLD POINT COMFORT, VA.

Limited to three (3) months from date of sale.
Del., Lack. & Western R. R ... to New York.
Pennsylvania Railroad ... to Quantico.
Rich. Fred. & P. R. R ... to Richmond.
Ches. & Ohio R. R ... to Old Point Comfort.
Returning via same route.

THROUGH RATES.

Summit	$20 80
Morristown	21 25
Dover	21 75
Hackettstown	22 45
Washington	22 85
Stroudsburg	23 85
Scranton	26 00
Pittston	26 35
Kingston	26 80
Wilkesbarre	26 85
Montrose	28 20
Binghamton	28 00
Greene	28 80
Oxford	29 00
Norwich	$29 00
Sherburne	29 25
Waterville	29 25
Richfield Springs	30 75
Utica	29 25
Cortland	30 00
Syracuse	31 00
Fulton	31 50
Oswego	32 00
Owego	28 85
Ithaca	30 50
Waverly	29 60
Elmira	30 45

OTTAWA, ONT.
EXCURSION NO. 320.—OTTAWA AND RETURN.

Del., Lack. & Western R. R ... to Utica.
Rome, Watert'n & Ogdenb'g R. R. to Clayton.
R. & O. Navi. Co.'s Steamers ... to Alexandria Bay.
R. & O. Navi. Co.'s Steamers ... to Prescott.
Canadian Pacific R. R ... to Ottawa.
Returning via same route.
(Good until October 1st.)

THROUGH RATES.

New York	$21 25
Paterson	21 25
Newark	21 25
Morristown	21 25
Dover	21 25
Hackettstown	21 25
Washington	21 75
Water Gap	20 60
Stroudsburg	20 40
Scranton	18 30
Pittston	18 70
Kingston	19 00
Wilkesbarre	19 00
Plymouth	19 15
Nanticoke	19 25
Shickshinny	19 60
Berwick	$20 05
Bloomsburg	20 60
Danville	21 00
Binghamton	15 80
Greene	15 05
Oxford	14 50
Norwich	14 20
Sherburne	13 75
Waterville	12 90
Richfield Springs	13 50
Owego	16 65
Waverly	17 40
Elmira	18 10
Corning	18 60
Bath	19 60

EXCURSION NO. 321.—OTTAWA AND RETURN.

Del., Lack. & Western R. R ... to Syracuse.
Rome, Watert'n & Ogdenb'g R.R. to Clayton.
R. & O. Navi. Co.'s Steamers ... to Alexandria Bay.
R. & O. Navi. Co.'s Steamers ... to Prescott.
Canadian Pacific Railway ... to Ottawa.
Returning via same route.
(Good until October 1st.)

THROUGH RATES.

New York	$21 25
Paterson	21 25
Newark	21 25
Morristown	21 25
Dover	21 25
Hackettstown	21 20
Washington	20 80
Water Gap	20 00
Stroudsburg	19 80
Scranton	17 70
Pittston	18 05
Kingston	18 35
Wilkesbarre	$18 35
Plymouth	18 50
Nanticoke	18 60
Shickshinny	19 00
Berwick	19 40
Bloomsburg	19 95
Danville	20 40
Binghamton	15 20
Cortland	13 50
Owego	16 00
Waverly	16 50
Elmira	16 50

EXCURSION S. T. NO. 14.—PRESCOTT TO OTTAWA AND RETURN.

Canadian Pacific Railway. . . to Ottawa and return. Sold only in connection with Summer Excursion. Ticket to or passing through Prescott.
Rate................$3.50

PLATTSBURG, N. Y.
(Lake Champlain.)

EXCURSION NO. 432.—PLATTSBURG AND RETURN.

Del., Lack. & Western R. R.......to Binghamton.
Delaware & Hudson Canal Co....to Ft. Ticonderoga.
Delaware & Hudson Canal Co. or } to Plattsburg.
Lake Champlain Steamer.
Returning *via* same route.

THROUGH RATES.

Washington	$18 05	Waverly	$14 05
Water Gap	17 25	Elmira	14 75
Stroudsburg	17 15	Corning	15 30
Scranton	14 95	Bath	16 05
Pittston	15 35	Atlanta	16 80
Kingston	15 65	Wayland	17 15
Wilkesbarre	15 75	Dansville	17 55
Owego	13 30	Mount Morris	18 10
Ithaca	14 70	Buffalo	19 80

EXCURSION S. T. NO. 48—SARATOGA TO PLATTSBURG AND RETURN.

Delaware & Hudson Canal Co to Ft. Ticonderoga.
Delaware & Hudson Canal Co. or } to Plattsburg.
Lake Champlain Steamer.
Delaware & Hudson Canal Co. or } to Ft. Ticonderoga.
Lake Champlain Steamer.
Delaware & Hudson Canal Co....to Baldwin.
Lake George Steamer.........to Caldwell.
Delaware & Hudson Canal Co... to Saratoga.

EXCURSION S. T. 49.—REVERSE OF THE PRECEDING.

Rate for either Excursion $9.30

PLYMOUTH, MASS.

EXCURSION NO. 287.—PLYMOUTH AND RETURN.

Del., Lack. & Western R. R ....to New York.
Fall River Line Steamers..............to Fall River.
Old Colony Railroad.... .... to Plymouth.
Returning *via* same route.

THROUGH RATES.

Morristown	$ 8 25	Waterville	$17 00
Dover	8 75	Cortland	17 00
Hackettstown	9 45	Syracuse	18 00
Washington	9 85	Oswego	19 00
Water Gap	10 70	Owego	15 85
Stroudsburg	10 85	Ithaca	17 50
Scranton	13 00	Waverly	16 60
Pittston	13 40	Elmira	17 45
Kingston	13 80	Corning	17 90
Wilkesbarre	13 85	Bath	18 75
Binghamton	15 00	Atlanta	19 90
Greene	15 80	Wayland	20 25
Oxford	16 00	Dansville	20 60
Norwich	16 00	Mount Morris	20 70
Sherburne	16 70	Buffalo	23 00

POCASSET, MASS.

EXCURSION NO. 288.—POCASSET AND RETURN.

Del., Lack. & Western R. R............ to New York.
Fall River Line Steamers..............to Fall River.
Old Colony Railroad.............to Pocasset.
Returning *via* same route.

THROUGH RATES.

Morristown	$ 8 25	Waterville	$17 00
Dover	8 75	Cortland	17 00
Hackettstown	9 45	Syracuse	18 00
Washington	9 85	Oswego	19 00
Water Gap	10 70	Owego	15 85
Stroudsburg	10 85	Ithaca	17 50
Scranton	13 00	Waverly	16 60
Pittston	13 40	Elmira	17 45
Kingston	13 89	Corning	17 90
Wilkesbarre	13 85	Bath	18 75
Binghamton	15 00	Atlanta	19 90
Greene	15 80	Wayland	20 35
Oxford	16 00	Dansville	20 70
Norwich	16 00	Mount Morris	20 70
Sherburne	16 70	Buffalo	23 00

POCONO SUMMIT, PA.

LOCAL EXCURSION.

(Good for continuous passage only.)

THROUGH RATES.

*New York	$4 75	Shickshinny	$3 00
Passaic	4 50	Berwick	3 30
Paterson	4 35	Bloomsburg	3 60
Boonton	3 60	Danville	3 95
*Newark	4 75	Great Bend	3 20
*Roseville Ave	4 75	Binghamton	3 80
Orange	4 60	Greene	4 55
Mountain	4 50	Oxford	5 10
South Orange	4 45	Norwich	5 40
Milburn	4 30	Sherburne	5 85
Short Hills	4 25	Waterville	6 70
Summit	4 25	Richfield Springs	7 90
Chatham	4 05	Utica	7 60
Madison	3 95	Cortland	5 50
Morristown	3 80	Syracuse	6 95
Dover	3 30	Oswego	8 35
Hopatcong Station	2 85	Owego	4 60
Andover	3 10	Ithaca	5 95
Newton	3 30	Waverly	5 35
Franklin	3 80	Elmira	6 05
Hackettstown	2 60	Corning	6 65
Washington	2 20	Bath	7 50
Scranton	1 70	Atlanta	8 30
Pittston	2 10	Wayland	8 55
Kingston	2 45	Dansville	8 80
Wilkesbarre	2 45	Mount Morris	9 40
Plymouth	2 60	Buffalo	11 90
Nanticoke	2 75		

*Tickets good until used.

PROFILE HOUSE, N. H.
(White Mountains.)

The Profile House is the principal resort in the Franconian range, the feature in the locality being Mt. Lafayette (5,585 feet), Cannon, Bald, Liberty, Pleasant and others. Other peculiarities are Echo Lake, Eagle Cliff, Old Man of the Mountain, Profile Lake, the Flume, Pool, etc., etc. The house though immense in size and placed at an elevation of 2,000 feet above sea level, is sunk into comparative insignificance, so small is it compared with the almost perpendicular mountains which rise up from its doors.

What is particularly striking here is the magnitude of everything. The air is, of course, pure as can be obtained; the drives are perfect in their roadbed and penetrate romantic regions.

EXCURSION S. V. 45.—BETHLEHEM JUNCTION TO PROFILE HOUSE AND RETURN.

Profile & Franconia Notch (to Profile House and
Railroad...................... { return.
Sold only in connection with Summer Excursion Ticket to, or passing through Bethlehem Junction.
Rate...... ....$3.00

QUEBEC, P. Q.

Quebec, a great city of 75,000 inhabitants, is the only walled city in this country. It is triangular in form (St. Charles and St. Lawrence Rivers, and Plains of Abraham being the lines). There are really two towns—upper and lower—the former being strongly fortified and elevated nearly four hundred feet above the latter.

It is quaint and antique in the extreme and strangers are naturally surprised to find so ancient a city in this part of the world. The Citadel attracts every visitor to Quebec.

Within the battlements there are more than forty acres, the wall surrounding which is about three miles long.

EXCURSION No. 100 A.—TO QUEBEC.

Delaware, Lack. & Western R. R...to Buffalo.
N. Y. Central & Hud. River R. R....to Niagara Falls.
N. Y. Central & Hud. River R. R ...to Lewiston.
Niagara Navi. Co's Steamer.........to Toronto.
Canadian Pacific Railway............to Ottawa,
Canadian Pacific R'y, or Ottawa } to Montreal
 River Navi Co.'s Steamer....... }
Canadian Pacific R'y, or Richelieu } to Quebec.
 & Ontario Navi. Co.'s Steamer.. }

EXCURSION No. 430 A.—TO QUEBEC.

Delaware, Dack. & Western R. R....to Buffalo.
N. Y. Central & Hud. River R. R ..to Niagara Falls.
N. Y. Central & Hud. River R, R....to Lewiston.
Niagara Navi. Co.'s Steamer........ to Toronto.
Canadian Pacific R'y, or Richelieu } to Montreal.
 & Ontario Nav. Co.'s Steamer... }
Canadian Pacific R'y, or Richelieu } to Quebec.
 & Ontario Nav. Co.'s Steamer.. }

EXCURSION No. 102 A.—TO QUEBEC.

Delaware, Lack. & Western R. R...to Buffalo.
N. Y. Central & Hud River R. R....to Niagara Falls.
N. Y. Central & Hud River R. R....to Lewiston.
Niagara Nav. Co.'s Steamer.........to Toronto.
Grand Trunk R'y, or Richelieu & } to Kingston.
 Ontario Nav. Co.'s Steamer.... }
Grand Trunk R'y, or Richelieu & } to Prescott.
 Ontario Nav. Co.'s Steamer.... }
Grand Trunk R'y, or Richelieu & } to Montreal.
 Ontario Nav Co.'s Steamer..... }
Grand Trunk R'y, or Richelieu & } to Quebec.
 Ontario Nav, Co.' Steamer...... }

EXCURSION No. 255 A.—TO QUEBEC.

Del., Lack. & Western R. R....to Buffalo.
N. Y., Lake Erie & W. R. R....to Suspension Bridge.
Grand Trunk Railway ....to Port Dalhousie.
Steamer "Empress of India"..to Toronto.
Grand Trunk R'y, or Rich. & } to Kingston.
 Ontario Nav. Co.'s Steamer }
Grand Trunk R'y, or Rich. & } to Prescott.
 Ontario Nav. Co.'s Steamer }
Grand Trunk R'y, or Rich. & } to Montreal
 Ontario Nav. Co.'s Steamer }
Grand Trunk R'y, or Rich. & } to Quebec
 Ontario Nav. Co.'s Steamer }

EXCURSION No. 103 A.--TO QUEBEC.

Delaware, Lack. & Western R. R....to Buffalo.
N. Y. Central & Hud. River R. R....to Niagara Falls.
Grand Trunk Railway.... ....to Toronto.
Grand Trunk R'y, or Richelieu & } to Kingston.
 Ontario Nav. Co.'s Steamer..., }
Grand Trunk R'y, or Richelieu & } to Prescott
 Ontario Nav. Co.'s Steamer..... }
Grand Trunk R'y, or Richelieu & } to Montreal
 Ontario Nav. Co.'s Steamer..., }
Grand Trunk R'y, or Richelieu & } to Quebec
 Ontario Nav Co.'s Steamer..., }

EXCURSION No. 137 A.—TO QUEBEC.

Del. Lack & Western R. R.......to Buffalo.
N. Y. Cent. & Hud. River R. R....to Niagara Falls.
N Y Cent. & Hud. River R. R....to Lewiston.
Rome, Watert'n & Ogdenb'g R. R.to Clayton,
Rich. & Ontario Nav. Co.'s Strs...to Alexandria Bay.
Rich. & Ontario Nav. Co.'s Strs,..to Montreal.
Grand Trunk R'y, or Richelieu } to Quebec.
 & Ontario Nav. Co.'s Strs..... }
(Good until October 1st.)

THROUGH RATES,
FOR EXCURSIONS 100 A, 102 A, 103 A, 137 A, 255 A
AND 430 A.

New York..........	$22 25	Bloomsburg	$21 50
Paterson...........	22 25	Danville...........	21 75
Newark	22 25	Binghamton	19 25
Morristown	22 25	Greene.............	19 55
Dover	22 25	Oxford.......	.. 19 80
Hackettstown......	22 15	Norwich...........	19 95
Washington	21 95	Cortland...........	20 00
Water Gap........	21 55	Owego.............	18 70
Stroudsburg....	21 45	Ithaca	19 40
Scranton	20 35	Waverly...........	18 30
Pittston	20 55	Elmira.........	17 95
Kingston.........	20 70	Corning	17 90
Wilkesbarre......	20 70	Bath......	17 75
Plymouth	20 80	Atlanta...........	17 20
Nanticoke.........	20 85	Wayland...	17 10
Shickshinny.......	21 05	Dansville.........	16 90
Berwick...........	21 25	Mount Morris.....	16 55

EXCURSION No. 105 A.—TO QUEBEC.

Del., Lack & Western R. R.......to Utica.
Rome, Watert'n & Ogd'b'g R. R..to Clayton.
Rich. & Ontario Nav. Co.'s Strs ..to Alexandria Bay.
Rich. & Ontario Nav. Co.'s Strs... to Montreal.
Grand Trunk R'y, or Richelieu } to Quebec.
 & Ontario Nav. Co.'s Strs..... }
(Good until October 1st.)

THROUGH RATES.

New York..........	$16 50	Bloomsburg	$15 80
Paterson...........	16 50	Danville...........	16 00
Newark	16 50	Binghamton........	13 40
Morristown	16 50	Greene.............	13 05
Dover	16 50	Oxford...........	12 75
Hackettstown......	16 40	Norwich...........	12 60
Washington........	16 25	Sherburne.........	12 40
Water Gap........	15 80	Waterville..........	11 95
Stroudsburg.......	15 70	Richfield Springs..	12 25
Scranton	14 65	Cortland...........	13 85
Pittston	14 85	Owego.............	13 85
Kingston..........	15 00	Ithaca	14 50
Wilkesbarre	15 00	Waverly	14 20
Plymouth	15 10	Elmira.............	14 30
Nanticoke.........	15 15	Corning............	14 30
Shickshinny.......	13 30	Bath...............	14 90
Berwick....	15 55		

EXCURSION No. 106 A.—TO QUEBEC.

Del., Lack. & Western R. R.....to Richfield Springs.
Del., Lack, & Western R. R....to Utica.
Rome, Watert'n & Ogd'b'g R. R..to Clayton,
Rich. & Ont. Nav. Co.'s Strs....to Alexandria Bay.
Rich. & Ont. Nav. Co.'s Strs....to Montreal,
Grand Trunk R'y, or Rich. & } to Quebec.
 Ontario Nav. Co.'s Strs...... }
(Good until October 1st.)

DELAWARE, LACKAWANNA & WESTERN R. R.

THROUGH RATES.

New York	$17 40	Berwick	$16 45
Paterson	17 40	Bloomsburg	16 70
Newark	17 40	Danville	16 90
Morristown	17 40	Binghamton	14 30
Dover	17 40	Greene	13 95
Hackettstown	17 30	Oxford	13 65
Washington	17 15	Norwich	13 50
Water Gap	16 70	Sherburne	13 30
Stroudsburg	16 60	Waterville	12 85
Scranton	15 55	Cortland	14 75
Pittston	15 75	Owego	14 75
Kingston	15 90	Ithaca	15 40
Wilkesbarre	15 90	Waverly	15 10
Plymouth	16 00	Elmira	15 45
Nanticoke	16 10	Corning	15 80
Shickshinny	16 20	Bath	16 20

Excursion No. 185 A.—To Quebec.

Del., Lack. & Western R. R........to Syracuse.
Rome, Watertown & Ogdb'g R R..to Clayton.
R. & O. Navi. Co.'s Steamers......to Alexandria Day.
R. & O. Navi. Co.'s Steamers......to Montreal.
Grand Trunk Ry., or Richelieu } to Quebec.
 & Ontario Navi. Co.'s Strs... }

(Good until October 1st.)

THROUGH RATES.

New York	$17 40	Nanticoke	$14 95
Paterson	17 10	Shickshinny	15 15
Newark	17 40	Berwick	15 35
Morristown	16 80	Bloomsburg	15 65
Dover	16 65	Danville	15 85
Hackettstown	16 25	Binghamton	13 25
Washington	16 05	Greene	13 20
Water Gap	15 65	Oxford	13 45
Stroudsburg	15 55	Norwich	13 65
Scranton	14 50	Cortland	12 40
Pittston	14 70	Owego	13 30
Kingston	14 85	Waverly	13 30
Wilkesbarre	14 85	Elmira	13 30
Plymouth	14 90		

Excursion No. 157 A.—To Quebec.

Del., Lack. & Western R. R........to Oswego.
Rome, Watert'n & Ogdenb'g R.R..to Clayton.
R. & O. Navi. Co.'s Steamers......to Alexandria Bay.
R. & O. Navi. Co.'s Steamers......to Montreal.
Grand Trunk R'y, or Richelieu } to Quebec.
 & Ontario Nav. Co.'s Strs..... }

(Good until October 1st.)

THROUGH RATES.

New York	$17 70	Nanticoke	$15 25
Paterson	17 40	Shickshinny	15 45
Newark	17 70	Berwick	15 65
Morristown	17 50	Bloomsburg	15 95
Dover	16 95	Danville	16 15
Hackettstown	16 55	Binghamton	13 55
Washington	16 35	Greene	13 50
Water Gap	15 95	Oxford	13 75
Stroudsburg	15 85	Norwich	13 05
Scranton	14 80	Cortland	12 70
Pittston	15 00	Syracuse	11 95
Kingston	15 15	Owego	13 70
Wilkesbarre	15 15	Waverly	13 70
Plymouth	15 20	Elmira	13 70

Excursion S. T. 6.—Montreal to Quebec and Return.

Grand Trunk R'y, or Richelieu & } to Quebec and re-
 Ont. Navi. Co.'s Steamers...... } turn.
Sold only in connection with Summer Excursion
Ticket passing through Montreal.
Rate.............$5.00.

ROUTES RETURNING FROM QUEBEC.

Issued only in connection with routes to Quebec.
(See note to Routes returning from Montreal.)

*Excursion No. 304 X.—Quebec to New York.

Ferry.......................to Point Levis.
Grand Trunk Railway..........to Rouse's Point.
Del. & Hudson Canal Co.'s Lines.to Plattsburg.
Del. & Hud. Can Co.'s Lines, or } to Ft. Ticonderoga.
 Lake Champlain Steamer.... }
Del. & Hud. Canal Co.'s Lines....to Saratoga.
Del. & Hud. Canal Co.'s Lines... to Troy.
N. Y. Central & Hud. Riv. R. R...to New York.
Rate.................$12.00.

*Excursion No. 305 X.—Quebec to New York.

via same route as 304 X to Saratoga, thence
Delaware & Hudson Canal Co.'s Lines.to Albany.
Day Line Hudson River Steamers......to New York.
Rate.... ....$11.60.

*Excursion No. 306 X.—Quebec to New York.

via same route as 304 X to Saratoga, thence
Delaware & Hudson Canal Co.'s Lines.to Albany.
People's (Night) Line Hud. Riv. Strs....to New York.
Rate....................$10.95.

Excursion No. 307 X.—Quebec to New York.

Ferry.......................to Point Levis.
Grand Trunk Railway..........to Rouse's Point.
Del. & Hud. Canal Co.'s Lines .. to Plattsburg.
Del. & Hud. Canal Co.'s Lines, } to Ft. Ticonderoga.
 or Lake Champlain Steamer.. }
Del. & Hud. Canal Co.'s Lines .. to Baldwin.
Lake George Steamer...... ..to Caldwell.
Del. & Hud. Canal Co.'s Lines....to Saratoga.
Del. & Hud. Canal Co. s Lines....to Troy.
N. Y. Central & Hud. Riv. R. R...to New York.
Rate. ....$13 50.

*Excursion No. 308 X.—Quebec to New York.

via same route as 307 X to Saratoga, thence
Delaware & Hudson Canal Co.'s Line..to Albany.
Day Line Hudson River Steamers......to New York
Rate ....$13.10.

*Excursion No. 309 X.—Quebec to New York.

via same route as 307 X to Saratoga, thence
Delaware & Hudson Canal Co.'s Lines.to Albany.
People's (Night) Line Hud. Riv. Strs. .. to New York.
Rate. $12.45

*Excursion No. 310 X.—Quebec to New York.

Ferry.......................to Point Levis.
Grand Trunk Railway..........to St. John's.
Central Vermont Railroad..,... to Burlington.
Lake Champlain Steamer.........to Ft. Ticonderoga
Del & Hud. Canal Co.'s Lines ...to Baldwin.
Lake George Steamer......... to Caldwell.
Del. & Hud Canal Co.'s Lines...to Saratoga.
Del. & Hud. Canal Co.'s Lines,...to Troy.
N. Y. Central & Hud. Riv. R..to New York.
Rate.......... $13.50
* Not to be sold in connection with tickets to Quebec
via the Canadian Pacific Railroad.

*Excursion No. 311 X.—Quebec to New York.

via same route as 310 X to Saratoga, thence
Del. & Hudson Canal Co.'s Lines. .....to Albany.
Day Line Hudson River Steamers......to New York.
Rate............ $13.10

DELAWARE, LACKAWANNA & WESTERN R. R.

* EXCURSION No. 312 X.—QUEBEC TO NEW YORK.

via same route as 310 X to Saratoga, thence Delaware & Hudson Canal Co.'s Lines.to Albany. People's (Night) Line Hud. Riv. Strs...to New York.
Rate........ ......$12.45

*EXCURSION No. 121 X —QUEBEC TO NEW YORK.

Ferry.................................to Point Levis.
Grand Trunk Railway............to Sherbrooke.
Boston & Maine Railroad (Passumpsic Division)............. } to White River Jnc.
Central Vermont Railroad........to Windsor.
Boston & Maine R. R.........to Brattleboro.
Central Vermont Railroad........to South Vernon.
Boston & Maine R. R..... ....to Springfield.
N. Y., N. Hav. & Hartford R. R..to New York.
Rate..............$12.00

*EXCURSION No. 122 X.—QUEBEC TO NEW YORK.

Ferry. ....to Point Levis.
Grand Trunk Railway.. ....to Sherbrooke.
Boston & Maine Railroad (Passumpsic Division)............. } to St. Johnsbury.
St. Johnsbury & Lake Champl'n Railroad...................... } to Lunenburg.
Maine Central Railroad............ to Fabyan's.
Boston & Maine Railroad....... ....to Concord.
Boston & Maine Railroad.......... to Nashua.
Boston & Maine Rail'r'd (Lowell System).......................... } to Boston.
N. Y., N. H. & H. R. R.............to Fall River.
Fall River Line Steamers ....to New York.
Rate..............$15.50

EXCURSION No. 123 X.—QUEBEC TO NEW YORK.

Ferry........................to Point Levis.
Grand Trunk Railway............to Sherbrooke.
Boston & Maine R. R. (Passumpsic Division)................. } to St. Johnsbury.
St. Johnsbury & Lake Champl'n Railroad...................... } to Lunenburg.
Maine Central Railroad............to Fabyan's.
Maine Central Railroad (White Mountains Line)............. } to Crawford House.
Maine Central Railroad (White Mountains Line)...... } to North Conway.
Boston & Maine Railroad.........to Boston.
N. Y., N. H. & H. R. R.............to Fall River.
Fall River Line Steamers..........to New York.
Rate..............$15.50

*EXCURSION No. 124 X.—QUEBEC TO NEW YORK.

Same as Excursion 123 X to Fabyan's, thence
Boston & Maine Railroad....... } to Base Mount Washington.
Mount Washington Railway......to Summit.
Milliken's Stage Line.............to Glen House.
Milliken's Stage Line.............to Glen Station.
Maine Central Railroad (White Mountains Line)..... } to North Conway.
Boston & Maine Railroad.........to Boston.
N. Y., N. H. & H. R. R. ....to Fall River.
Fall River Line Steamers.........to New York.
Rate... ... .$25.30

*EXCURSION No. 148 X.—QUEBEC TO NEW YORK.

Same as Excursion 123 X to Fabyan's, thence
Maine Central Railroad (White Mountains Line).............. } to Portland.
Boston & Maine Railroad..........to Boston.
N. Y., N. H. & H. R. R. ....to Fall River.
Fall River Line Steamers........ to New York.
Rate..............$15.50

*EXCURSION No. 391 X.—QUEBEC TO NEW YORK.

Ferry.................. ....to Levis.
Quebec Central Railway...........to Sherbrooke.
Bos. & Me. R.R. (Passumpsic Div.).to White River Jc.
Central Vermont Railroad.........to Windsor.
Vermont Valley Railroad..........to Brattleboro.
Central Vermont Railroad.........to South Vernon.
Connecticut River Railroad........to Springfield.
N. Y., N. Hav. & Hartford R. R....to New York.
Rate..............$12.00

*EXCURSION No. 392 X.—QUEBEC TO NEW YORK.

Ferry ....to Levis.
Quebec Central Railway...........to Sherbrooke.
Boston & Maine Railroad. ......to Concord.
Concord & Montreal Railroad....to Nashua.
Boston & Maine Rail'r'd (Lowell System).......................... } to Fall River.
Old Colony Railroad..............to Fall River.
Fall River Line Steamers ... .to New York.
Rate..............$15.50

*EXCURSION No. 394 X.—QUEBEC TO NEW YORK.

Ferry...... ....to Levis.
Quebec Central Railway...........to Dudswell Junc.
Maine Central Railway...........to North Conway.
Boston & Maine Railroad.........to Boston.
Old Colony Railroad ....to Fall River.
Fall River Line Steamers ....to New York.
Rate..............$15.50

*EXCURSION No. 393 X.—QUEBEC TO NEW YORK.

Ferry.... .... to Levis.
Quebec Central Railway...........to Dudswell Junc.
Maine Central Railroad..........to Portland.
Boston & Maine Railroad.........to Boston.
Old Colony Railroad ....to Fall River.
Fall River Line Steamers.........to New York.
Rate..............$15.50

†EXCURSION No. 425 X.—QUEBEC TO NEW YORK.

Canadian Pac. Ry. or R. & O. Nav. Co..................... } to Montreal.
New York Central & Hudson R. R. R............... } to Albany.
People's Line (Night) H. R. St'rs..to New York.
Rate..............$11.70

†EXCURSION No. 427 X.—QUEBEC TO NEW YORK.

Canadian Pac. Ry. or R. & O. Nav C..................... } to Montreal.
New York Central & Hudson R.R.R.to Albany.
Hudson River Day Line Steamers.to New York.
Rate................ ....$12.00

†EXCURSION No. 426 X.—QUEBEC TO NEW YORK.

Canadian Pac. Ry. or R. & O. Nav. Co........ } to Montreal.
New York Central & Hudson R.R.R.to New York.
Rate..............$12.00

*Not to be sold in connection with tickets to Quebec *via* the Canadian Pacific Railway.
†Not to be sold in connection with tickets to Quebec *via* Grand Trunk Railway.

RICHFIELD SPRINGS, N. Y.

LOCAL EXCURSION.
(Good for continuous passage only.)

THROUGH RATES.

**New York......	$10 75	Pittston.......	$7 00
Passaic...........	10 75	Kingston.......	7 35
Paterson.........	10 75	Wilkesbarre....	7 35
Boonton..........	10 75	Plymouth.......	7 45
**Newark........	10 75	Nanticoke......	7 60
Roseville.........	10 75	Shickshinny....	8 00
Orange...........	10 50	Berwick.........	8 40
Mountain........	10 50	Bloomsburg.....	8 90
South Orange...	10 50	Danville.........	9 40
Milburn..........	10 50	Great Bend.....	4 75
Short Hills......	10 50	Binghamton....	4 00
Summit...........	10 50	Greene..........	3 40
Chatham.........	10 50	Oxford..........	2 85
Madison..........	10 50	Norwich.........	2 55
Morristown......	10 50	Sherburne......	2 05
Dover.............	10 50	Waterville......	1 20
Hopatcong Station	10 25	†Utica..........	1 50
Andover..........	10 60	*Utica...........	2 00
Newton...........	10 80	Cortland........	5 00
Franklin..........	11 30	Owego...........	5 00
Hackettstown...	10 15	Ithaca...........	6 35
Washington.....	9 80	Waverly.........	5 75
Portland.........	9 15	Elmira...........	6 45
Water Gap......	8 95	Corning.........	7 10
Stroudsburg.....	8 80	Bath.............	7 90
Scranton.........	6 65	Atlanta..........	8 70

†Rate for Excursion Tickets good for two days only, except that tickets purchased on a Saturday are good to return on the following Monday.
*Rate for Excursion Tickets good until October 31st.
**Good for stop-over.

EXCURSION S. T. 4.—UTICA TO RICHFIELD SPRINGS AND RETURN.

Del., Lack. & Western R. R. } to Richfield Springs and return.
Sold only in connection with Summer Excursion Ticket passing through Utica.
Rate........... $2 00

EXCURSION S. T. 27.—RICHFIELD JUNCTION TO RICHFIELD SPRINGS AND RETURN.

Delaware, Lackawana & } to Richfield Springs and Western Railroad...... } return.
Sold only in connection with Summer Excursion Ticket passing through Richfield Junction.
Rate................ 90 cents.

SARATOGA SPRINGS, N. Y.

Originally famous for the curative quality of its waters, Saratoga Springs has long been a leading resort for fashion.

The hotels are mammoth in their proportions, and on their piazzas and in their gardens the highest social figures of the day congregate to participate in the gayeties, which here are never ceasing. Justly celebrated for having the largest hotels in the world, conveying the idea of prohibitory rates to those of modest income, it should be understood that accommodations may be had in the town at rates satisfactory to all purses.

EXCURSION No. 5.—SARATOGA AND RETURN.

Delaware, Lack. & Western R. R...., to Binghamton.
Del. & Hud. C. Co. (via Howe's Cave) to Saratoga.
Returning via same route.

THROUGH RATES.

Washington.......	$12 90	Waverly.........	$8 85
Water Gap.......	12 10	Elmira...........	9 55
Stroudsburg.....	11 90	Corning.........	10 10
Scranton.........	9 25	Bath.............	10 85
Pittston..........	9 70	Atlanta.........	11 60
Kingston.........	10 05	Wayland........	11 95
Wilkesbarre.....	10 05	Dansville.......	12 40
Owego............	8 10	Mount Morris..	12 95
Ithaca............	9 50	Buffalo..........	14 35

EXCURSION No. 144.—SARATOGA AND RETURN.

Delaware, Lack. & Western R. R.....to Utica.
N. Y. Central & Hudson R. R. R....to Schenectady.
Delaware & Hudson Canal Co.......to Saratoga.
Returning via same route.

THROUGH RATES.

Washington.......	$14 15	Richfield Springs..	$6 25
Water Gap.......	13 35	Cortland.........	9 35
Stroudsburg.....	13 15	Owego...........	9 35
Scranton.........	11 00	Ithaca...........	10 75
Pittston..........	11 40	Waverly.........	10 15
Kingston.........	11 70	Elmira...........	10 80
Wilkesbarre.....	11 70	Corning.........	11 45
Binghamton.....	8 55	Bath.............	12 30
Greene...........	7 75	Atlanta.........	13 10
Oxford...........	7 20	Wayland........	13 35
Norwich..........	6 90	Dansville.......	13 60
Sherburne.......	6 45	Mount Morris..	14 15
Waterville.......	5 60	Buffalo..........	15 65

EXCURSION No. 145.—SARATOGA AND RETURN.

Delaware, Lack. & Western R. R....to Utica.
N. Y. Central & Hud. River R. R....to Schenectady.
Delaware & Hudson Canal Co.....to Saratoga.
D. & H. Canal Co. (via Howe's Cave).to Binghamton.
Delaware, Lack. & Western R. R..to starting point.

EXCURSION No. 146.—REVERSE OF THE PRECEDING.

THROUGH RATES FOR EITHER EXCURSION.

Washington.......	$13 55	Owego...........	$8 75
Water Gap.......	12 70	Ithaca...........	10 10
Stroudsburg.....	12 50	Waverly.........	9 50
Scranton.........	10 35	Elmira...........	10 20
Pittston..........	10 75	Corning.........	10 80
Kingston.........	11 05	Bath.............	11 65
Wilkesbarre.....	11 05	Atlanta.........	12 40
Binghamton.....	7 90	Wayland........	12 65
Greene...........	7 90	Dansville.......	12 95
Oxford...........	7 90	Mount Morris..	13 50
Norwich..........	7 90	Buffalo..........	16 00
Cortland.........	9 20		

EXCURSION No. 158.—SARATOGA AND RETURN.

Delaware, Lack. & Western R. R...to New York.
People's (N'g't) Line Hud. R. Strs..to Albany.
Delaware & Hudson Canal Co......to Saratoga.
Delaware & Hudson Canal Co......to Albany.
Day Line Hudson River Steamers to New York.
Delaware, Lack. & Western R. R..to starting point.

EXCURSION No. 159.—GOING via DAY LINE AND RETURNING via NIGHT LINE.

THROUGH RATES FOR EITHER EXCURSION.

Morristown.......	$7 00	Greene..........	$14 55
Dover.............	7 50	Oxford..........	14 75
Hackettstown...	8 20	Norwich.........	14 75
Washington.....	8 60	Sherburne......	15 45
Water Gap......	9 45	Cortland........	15 75
Stroudsburg.....	9 60	Syracuse........	16 75
Scranton.........	11 75	Oswego.........	17 75
Pittston..........	12 15	Owego...........	14 60
Kingston.........	12 90	Ithaca...........	16 25
Wilkesbarre.....	12 95	Waverly.........	15 35
Binghamton.....	13 75	Elmira...........	16 00

EXCURSION NO. 181.—SARATOGA AND RETURN.

Delaware, Lack. & Western R. R...to New York.
N. Y. Central & Hud. River R. R...to Troy.
Delaware & Hudson Canal Co......to Saratoga.
Delaware & Hudson Canal Co......to Troy.
N. Y. Central & Hud. River R. R...to New York.
Delaware, Lack. & Western R. R...to starting point.

THROUGH RATES.

Morristown	$8 75	Greene	$16 30
Dover	9 25	Oxford	16 50
Hackettstown	9 95	Norwich	16 50
Washington	10 35	Sherburne	17 20
Water Gap	11 20	Cortland	17 50
Stroudsburg	11 35	Syracuse	18 50
Scranton	13 50	Oswego	19 50
Pittston	13 90	Owego	16 35
Kingston	14 65	Ithaca	18 00
Wilkesbarre	14 70	Waverly	17 10
Binghamton	15 50	Elmira	17 75

SHARON SPRINGS, N. Y.

EXCURSION NO. 1.—SHARON SPRINGS AND RETURN.

Del., Lack. & Western R. R......to Binghamton.
Delaware & Hudson Canal Co....to Sharon Springs.
Returning via same route.

THROUGH RATES.

New York	$12 80	Cortland	$6 25
Paterson	12 20	Syracuse	7 70
Newark	12 80	Owego	5 45
Morristown	11 75	Ithaca	6 70
Dover	11 30	Waverly	6 20
Hackettstown	10 10	Elmira	6 90
Washington	10 10	Corning	7 45
Water Gap	9 30	Bath	8 20
Stroudsburg	9 10	Atlanta	8 95
Scranton	6 40	Wayland	9 30
Pittston	6 85	Dansville	9 60
Kingston	7 25	Mount Morris	10 15
Wilkesbarre	7 25	Buffalo	12 25

EXCURSION S. T. 13.—COBLESKILL TO SHARON SPRINGS AND RETURN.

Del & Hud. Canal Co..to Sharon Springs and return.
Sold only in connection with Summer Excursion.
Ticket passing through Cobleskill
Rate.............80 cents.

SHELDRAKE, N. Y.

Cayuga Lake is one of the finest inland lakes that make Central New York so famous as a summer resort. It is forty miles long and reposes between high hills that stretch along its entire length, and far beyond to the south. It is, also, one of the most magnificent lakes in this country, being clear and of great depth ; it abounds in most entrancing scenery. Lake fishing, which is always a delightful pastime, is here indulged in every season by many enthusiastic fishermen, who invariably catch sufficient trout, bass, etc., to convince one that old Cayuga Lake is the veritable Mecca of anglers.

Sheldrake, is a pretty little hamlet situated on the shore of the lake fifteen miles from Ithaca. The nights in this locality are cool and dry. Water is noted for its purity and medicinal qualities. Winding roads, under shade trees on the very shore of the lake, make this country noted for its drives.

Sheldrake can be reached by Robert L. Darragh's line of excursion steamers which run at frequent intervals between Sheldrake and Ithaca. These boats are new and have a speed of 18 knots an hour.

EXCURSION NO. 397.—SHELDRAKE AND RETURN.

Delaware, Lack. & Western R. R......to Ithaca.
Steamer "Laura A. Darragh"......to Sheldrake.
Returning via same route.

THROUGH RATES.

New York	$11 00	Plymouth	$6 00
Paterson	10 40	Nanticoke	6 15
Newark	11 00	Shickshinny	6 50
Orange	10 80	Berwick	6 95
Summit	10 30	Bloomsburg	7 55
Morristown	9 90	Danville	7 90
Dover	9 45	Binghamton	2 70
Hackettstown	8 70	Greene	3 50
Washington	8 50	Oxford	4 05
Water Gap	7 50	Norwich	4 35
Stroudsburg	7 30	Sherburne	4 80
Scranton	5 50	Waterville	5 70
Pittston	5 50	Utica	6 50
Kingston	5 90	Richfield Springs	6 85
Wilkesbarre	5 90		

SILVER LAKE, N. Y.

Silver Lake, famous for a brief, glorious period, a generation ago, because of its fabled sea serpent, has gained a less transitory fame in these latter days in that it has its devoted band of those who worship at Nature's shrine along its gravelly shores. Here, as at Conesus and Keuka and Seneca, yes, and as at Lake George, the cottage builder has adorned the leafy shores with his gay bungalow, and the tents of the campers gleam far across the sleeping waters.

The Geneseo Conference Camp Ground Association has thirty acres of improved grounds enclosed, on which are erected about sixty cottages, and the Silver Lake Temperance Assembly has a very extensive rendezvous upon the lake, meeting here annually.

Taken altogether, the grounds and surroundings are the handsomest to be found in Western New York, and are annually visited by over 30,000 people. There is a cabin, the first one of the kind ever erected in the United States, as a Pioneer Log Cabin Museum, and the collection within its walls could never be replaced should it by any means be destroyed.

164 DELAWARE, LACKAWANNA & WESTERN R. R.

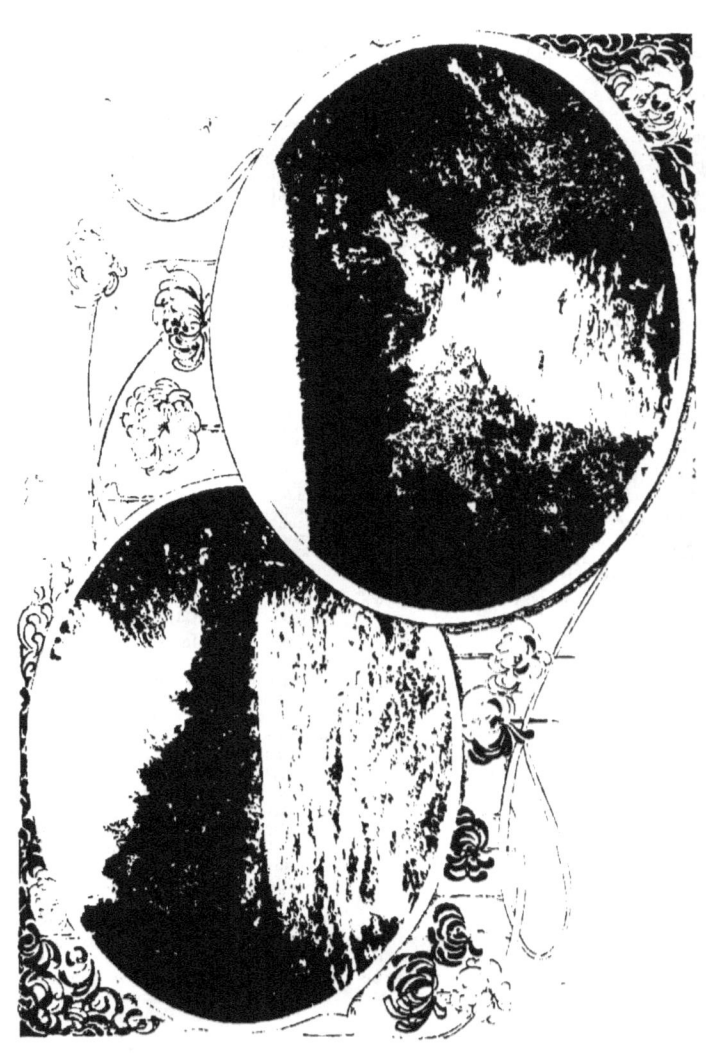

ALONG THE ANALOMINK, NEAR STROUDSBURG, PA.

EXCURSION No. 245.—SILVER LAKE AND RETURN.

Del., Lack. & Western R. R., to Buffalo, Rochester & Pittsburg Junction.
Buff., Roch. & Pittsburg R. R..to Silver Lake.
Returning *via* same route.

THROUGH RATES.

Corning	$3 70	Dansville	$2 30
Bath	3 60	Groveland	2 00
Kanona	3 45	Mount Morris	1 75
Avoca	3 30	Leicester	1 60
Wallace	3 20	Alexander	1 50
Cohocton	3 10	Darien	1 70
Atlanta	2 80	Alden	2 00
Wayland	2 60	Lancaster	2 35
Perkinsville	2 50	Buffalo	2 35

EXCURSION No. 245 L.—SILVER LAKE AND RETURN.

Same route as Excursion No. 245.
Limited to 30 days.

THROUGH RATES.

Bath	$2 65	Cohocton	$2 65
Kanona	2 65	Atlanta	2 65
Avoca	2 65	Wayland	2 55
Wallace	2 65		

SPRAGUEVILLE, PA.

LOCAL EXCURSION.

(Good for continuous passage only.)

THROUGH RATES.

*New York	$4 05	Shickshinny	$3 85
Passaic	3 65	Berwick	4 15
Paterson	3 50	Bloomsburg	4 45
Boonton	2 95	Danville	4 80
*Newark	4 05	Great Bend	3 90
*Roseville	4 05	Binghamton	4 45
Orange	3 75	Greene	5 25
Mountain	3 65	Oxford	5 80
South Orange	3 60	Norwich	6 10
Milburn	3 45	Sherburne	6 55
Short Hills	3 40	Waterville	7 40
Summit	3 40	Richfield Springs	8 60
Chatham	3 20	Utica	8 25
Madison	3 10	Cortland	6 20
Morristown	2 95	Syracuse	7 60
Dover	2 45	Oswego	9 00
Hopatcong Station	2 15	Owego	5 30
Andover	2 25	Ithaca	6 65
Newton	2 45	Waverly	6 00
Franklin	2 95	Elmira	6 75
Hackettstown	1 75	Corning	7 40
Washington	1 35	Bath	8 20
Scranton	2 55	Atlanta	9 00
Pittston	2 95	Wayland	9 20
Kingston	3 30	Dansville	9 55
Wilkesbarre	3 30	Mount Morris	10 10
Plymouth	3 45	Buffalo	12 55
Nanticoke	3 60		

*Tickets good until used.

STANHOPE, N. J.

(Station for Budd's Lake.)

LOCAL EXCURSION.

(Good for continuous passage only.)

THROUGH RATES.

*New York	$2 10	Mountain	$1 70
Passaic	1 55	South Orange	1 65
Paterson	1 40	Milburn	1 50
Boonton	85	Short Hills	1 40
*Newark	2 00	Summit	1 35
*Roseville	2 00	Chatham	1 20
Orange	1 80	Madison	1 10

Morristown	$ 90	Phillipsburg	$1 35
Dover	50	Easton	1 45
Andover	50	Portland	1 50
Newton	70	Water Gap	1 70
Franklin	1 20	Stroudsburg	1 90
Hackettstown	40	Scranton	3 90
Washington	80		

*Tickets good until used.

STROUDSBURG, PA.

LOCAL EXCURSION.

(Good for continuous passage only.)

THROUGH RATES.

*New York	$3 85	Shickshinny	$4 05
Passaic	3 45	Berwick	4 35
Paterson	3 30	Bloomsburg	4 65
Boonton	2 75	Danville	5 00
*Newark	3 85	Great Bend	4 05
*Roseville	3 85	Binghamton	4 60
Orange	3 55	Greene	5 40
Mountain	3 45	Oxford	5 95
South Orange	3 40	Norwich	6 30
Milburn	3 25	Sherburne	6 75
Short Hills	3 20	Waterville	7 60
Summit	3 20	Richfield Springs	8 80
Chatham	3 00	Utica	8 45
Madison	2 90	Cortland	6 35
Morristown	2 75	Syracuse	7 80
Dover	2 25	Oswego	9 20
Hopatcong Station	1 95	Owego	5 45
Andover	2 05	Ithaca	6 80
Newton	2 25	Waverly	6 20
Franklin	2 75	Elmira	6 90
Hackettstown	1 15	Corning	7 55
Washington	1 15	Bath	8 40
Scranton	2 75	Atlanta	9 20
Pittston	3 15	Wayland	9 40
Kingston	3 50	Dansville	9 70
Wilkesbarre	3 50	Mount Morris	10 25
Plymouth	3 65	Buffalo	12 75
Nanticoke	3 80		

*Tickets good until used.

TAUGHANNOCK FALLS, N. Y.

Halsey Creek has its rise upon the ridge dividing Seneca and Cayuga Lakes, and, flowing down the easterly watershed, finally reaches the latter by a prodigious plunge into a wild and romantic chasm, thus forming the Falls of Taughannock, the highest single cascade in the State, having a direct fall of two hundred and fifteen feet. The gorge is plainly visible from the decks of passing steamers, but its creamy, headlong cataract is deeply hidden by the environing foliage. About ten miles from Ithaca.

EXCURSION No. 133.—TAUGHANNOCK FALLS AND RETURN.

Del., Lack. & Western R. R..to Ithaca.
Cayuga Lake Steamer.... to Taughannock Falls.
Returning *via* same route.

THROUGH RATES.

New York	$11 00	Scranton	$5 50
Paterson	10 40	Binghamton	2 70
Newark	11 00	Greene	3 50
Morristown	9 80	Oxford	4 05
Dover	9 45	Norwich	4 35
Hackettstown	8 70	Sherburne	4 80
Washington	8 30	Waterville	5 70
Water Gap	7 50	Owego	2 00
Stroudsburg	7 30		

TOBYHANNA, PA.

LOCAL EXCURSION.
(Good for continuous passage only.)

THROUGH RATES.

*New York	$4 95	Shickshinny	$2 65
Passaic	4 85	Berwick	2 95
Paterson	4 70	Bloomsburg	3 25
Boonton	4 15	Danville	3 60
*Newark	4 95	Great Bend	3 00
*Roseville	4 95	Binghamton	3 60
Orange	4 95	Greene	4 35
Mountain	4 85	Oxford	4 90
South Orange	4 80	Norwich	5 20
Milburn	4 65	Sherburne	5 65
Short Hills	4 60	Waterville	6 50
Summit	4 60	Richfield Springs	5 70
Chatham	4 40	Utica	7 40
Madison	4 30	Cortland	5 30
Morristown	4 15	Syracuse	6 75
Dover	3 65	Oswego	8 15
Hopatcong Station	3 35	Owego	4 40
Andover	3 45	Ithaca	5 75
Newton	3 65	Waverly	5 15
Franklin	4 15	Elmira	5 85
Hackettstown	2 95	Corning	6 50
Washington	2 55	Bath	7 35
Scranton	1 35	Atlanta	8 10
Pittston	1 75	Wayland	8 35
Kingston	2 10	Dansville	8 60
Wilkesbarre	2 10	Mount Morris	9 20
Plymouth	2 25	Buffalo	11 70
Nanticoke	2 40		

* Tickets good until used.

TORONTO, ONT.

EXCURSION S. T. 15.—NIAGARA FALLS TO TORONTO AND RETURN.

N. Y. Central & Hud. River Railroad....to Lewiston.
Niagara Navigation Co.'s Steamer......to Toronto.
Returning via same route.
Sold only in connection with Summer Excursion Ticket to, or passing through Niagara Falls.
Rate........$2 25.

EXCURSION S. T. 36.—NIAGARA FALLS TO TORONTO AND RETURN.

Erie Railroad............to Suspension Bridge.
Grand Trunk Railway........to Port Dalhousie.
Steamer "Empress of India"..to Toronto.
Returning via same route.
Sold only in connection with Summer Excursion Ticket to, or passing through Niagara Falls.
Rate............$2.25.

TRENTON FALLS, N. Y.

Are on West Canada Creek, which flows into the Mohawk River—about fifteen miles north of Utica.

Slanting Water the Indians called them (Kuyahora).

A series of cascades—five in number—descend within a distance of two miles, over 300 feet. Deep channels have been worn in the limestone hills. The ravine formed by this incessant flow is very narrow, but deep, in some portions being two hundred feet below the level of the surrounding country. The names given to the principal falls are Sherman, High Mill-Dam, Alhambra and Rocky-Heart.

EXCURSION No. 25 —TRENTON FALLS AND RETURN.

Delaware, Lack. & Western R. R...to Utica.
Rome, Watert'n & Ogdensb'g R. R. to Trenton Falls.
Returning via same route.

THROUGH RATES.

New York	$10 25	Wilkesbarre	$10 70
Paterson	10 25	Binghamton	5 70
Newark	10 25	Greene	4 15
Morristown	10 25	Oxford	3 30
Dover	10 25	Norwich	3 20
Hackettstown	10 25	Sherburne	2 95
Washington	10 25	Waterville	1 90
Water Gap	10 25	Richfield Springs	2 50
Stroudsburg	10 25	Owego	6 95
Scranton	9 85	Waverly	7 10
Pittston	10 30	Elmira	7 65
Kingston	10 65		

EXCURSION S. T. 3.—UTICA TO TRENTON FALLS AND RETURN.

Rome, Watertown & Ogdensburg to Trenton Falls Railroad.............. and return.
Sold only in connection with Summer Excursion Ticket passing through Utica.
Rate............$1.00.

TULLY LAKE PARK, N. Y.

EXCURSION No. 351 L.—TULLY LAKE PARK AND RETURN.

(Good for continuous passage only.)
Del., Lack & Western R. R.....to Tully.
Tully Lake Park Transfer........to Tully Lake Park.
Returning via same route.

THROUGH RATES.

Binghamton	$2 60	Homer	$ 75
Chenango Bridge	2 40	Onativa	60
Chenango Forks	2 10	Jamesville	90
Whitney's Point	1 75	Syracuse	1 15
Lisle	1 65	Baldwinsville	1 65
Killawog	1 50	Lamsons	1 85
Marathon	1 40	Fulton	2 10
Messengerville	1 25	Oswego	2 55
Cortland	85		

WATCH HILL, R. I.

Years ago this charming site was selected as a site by a few families for their summer homes, but it was not long before others, appreciating the exceptional advantages and its picturesque situation, located here, until now Watch Hill, R. I., is as well known as any summer resort along the coast. It is situated on elevated ground, at the southwestern extremity of the State; while on the mainland it enjoys all the advantages of being out at sea. Eleven lighthouses and one lightship are visible from the town.

EXCURSION No. 70.—WATCH HILL, R. I., AND RETURN.

Delaware, Lack. & Western R. R......to New York.
Stonington Line Steamers.............to Stonington.
Steamer....................to Watch Hill.
Returning via same route.

EXCURSION No. 71.—WATCH HILL, R. I., AND RETURN.

Delaware, Lack. & Western R. R....to New York.
Norwich Line Steamers...............to New London.
Steamer Block Island................to Watch Hill.
Returning *via* same route.

THROUGH RATES FOR EITHER EXCURSION.

Morristown	$ 4 65	Waterville	$13 40
Dover	5 15	Cortland	13 40
Hackettstown	5 85	Syracuse	14 40
Washington	6 25	Oswego	15 40
Water Gap	7 10	Owego	12 25
Stroudsburg	7 25	Ithaca	13 90
Scranton	9 40	Waverly	13 00
Pittston	9 80	Elmira	13 85
Kingston	10 20	Corning	14 30
Wilkesbarre	10 25	Bath	15 15
Binghamton	11 40	Atlanta	16 30
Greene	12 20	Wayland	16 60
Oxford	12 40	Dansville	17 10
Norwich	12 40	Mount Morris	17 10
Sherburne	13 10	Buffalo	19 40

WATKINS GLEN, N. Y.

Here Dame Nature, outdoing herself, perfected a work that would reflect nothing but credit upon herself, for this wonderful piece of earthen architecture fills all humanity with amazement.

Of all places visited by those who go to enjoy themselves, and who love to investigate the wonders of this land, none has won such well-merited fame as Watkins Glen. From the very entrance of the Glen to its extreme limit there is something charming to be seen

GLEN MOUNTAIN HOUSE
WATKINS GLEN

The Glen is situated in the village of Watkins, Schuyler County, at the head of Seneca Lake. The village in itself is a pretty spot, but the Glen, of course, is the main attraction.

This Glen consists of a series of cascades, galleries and weird caves, and here and there silver cascades are to be found that impart a wonderfully romantic appearance to this romantic spot.

Here human art stepped in to assist Nature in exhibiting her marvelous store of wonders to the best advantage. Before any explorations could be made by tourists it became necessary to erect ladders, by means of which ascents could be made from one steep incline to another, and to cut pathways in the rock. This was done by the proprietor of the Glen Mountain House, who owns the Glen, and offers the best facilities of inspection to his guests.

Probably the most beautiful of the attractions of this spot is Rainbow Falls, so called, because at particular seasons when the sun is in a certain position, it shines through the mist which emanates from the waterfall, causing it to assume all the colors of the rainbow. The other great attractions are Entrance Cascade, Trout Pool, Glen Alpha, Stillwater Gorge, Minnehaha Cascade, Fairy Cascade, Neptune's Pool, Cavern Cascade, Cavern Gorge and the Labyrinth.

A delightful feature of the chasm is the wonderful coolness of the air. The sun never shines here, and very often on the hottest day a light wrap becomes a necessary adjunct to a tour of inspection.

EXCURSION No. 32.—WATKINS AND HAVANA GLENS AND RETURN.

Delaware, Lackawanna & Western R. R. to Elmira.
Pennsylvania R. R. (*via* Havana Glen)...to Watkins.
Returning *via* same route.

THROUGH RATES.

New York	$11 35	Norwich	$4 85
Paterson	10 85	Sherburne	5 30
Newark	11 35	Waterville	6 15
Morristown	10 40	Richfield Springs	7 35
Dover	9 90	Utica	7 00
Hackettstown	9 20	Owego	2 75
Washington	8 80	Ithaca	2 95
Water Gap	8 00	Waverly	1 75
Stroudsburg	7 80	Corning	75
Scranton	5 45	Bath	2 70
Pittston	5 45	Atlanta	3 50
Kingston	5 45	Wayland	3 75
Wilkesbarre	5 45	Dansville	3 85
Binghamton	3 65	Mount Morris	4 30
Greene	4 00	Buffalo	6 25
Oxford	4 50		

EXCURSION No. 244.—WATKINS GLEN AND RETURN.

Delaware, Lackawanna & Western R. R. to Corning.
Fall Brook Railway.... ....to Watkins.
Returning *via* same route.

THROUGH RATES.

New York	$11 65	Oxford	$5 00
Paterson	11 35	Norwich	5 30
Newark	11 65	Sherburne	5 75
Morristown	10 90	Waterville	6 65
Dover	10 40	Richfield Springs	7 85
Hackettstown	9 70	Utica	7 50
Washington	9 30	Owego	2 90
Water Gap	8 45	Ithaca	3 45
Stroudsburg	8 30	Waverly	2 15
Scranton	5 95	Bath	1 60
Pittston	5 05	Atlanta	2 40
Kingston	6 35	Wayland	2 65
Wilkesbarre	6 35	Dansville	2 95
Binghamton	3 70	Mount Morris	3 50
Greene	4 50	Buffalo	6 00

EXCURSION S. T. 1.—ELMIRA TO WATKINS GLEN AND RETURN.

Pennsylvania Railroad..to Watkins Glen and return.
Sold only in connection with Summer Excursion Ticket passing through Elmira.
Rate............90 cents.

EXCURSION S. T. 35.—CORNING TO WATKINS GLEN AND RETURN.

Fall Brook Railway.... to Watkins Glen and return.
Sold only in connection with Summer Excursion
Ticket passing through Corning.
Rate..............75 cents.

WEST BARNSTABLE, MASS.

EXCURSION NO. 289.—WEST BARNSTABLE AND RETURN.

Del., Lack. & Western R. R.,.....to New York.
Fall River Line Steamers........to Fall River.
Old Colony Railroad..............to West Barnstable.
Returning *via* same route.

THROUGH RATES.

Morristown.........	$ 8 85	Waterville..........	$17 60
Dover	9 35	Cortland..........	17 60
Hackettstown......	10 05	Syracuse	18 60
Washington	10 45	Oswego............	19 60
Water Gap.......	11 30	Owego............	16 45
Stroudsburg.......	11 45	Ithaca............	18 10
Scranton.........	13 60	Waverly..........	17 20
Pittston	14 40	Elmira............	18 05
Kingston..........	14 40	Corning..........	18 50
Wilkesbarre........	14 45	Bath..............	19 35
Binghamton........	15 60	Atlanta..........	20 50
Greene...........	16 40	Wayland..........	20 85
Oxford	16 60	Dansville.........	21 30
Norwich...........	16 60	Mount Morris.....	21 30
Sherburne.........	17 30	Buffalo..........	23 60

WINOLA LAKE, PA.

EXCURSION NO. 344.—WINOLA LAKE AND RETURN.

Delaware, Lack. & Western R. R...to Factoryville.
N. A. Gardner's Stage Line.........to Winola Lake.
Returning *via* same route.

THROUGH RATES.

New York..........	$7 40	Dover...........	$6 40
Paterson	7 40	Hackettstown......	5 60
Newark...........	7 40	Washington........	5 30
Morristown	6 90	Water Gap........	4 35
Stroudsburg......	4 15	Oswego...........	7 20
Scranton..........	3 35	Owego...........	3 50
Binghamton.......	2 65	Ithaca...........	4 90
Greene	3 45	Waverly...........	4 20
Oxford...........	3 95	Elmira............	4 95
Norwich..........	4 30	Corning	5 55
Sherburne.........	4 75	Bath..............	6 40
Waterville.....	5 60	Atlanta...........	7 20
Richfield Springs...	6 75	Wayland..........	7 40
Utica............	6 45	Dansville.........	7 75
Cortland..........	4 35	Mount Morris.	8 30
Syracuse	5 80	Buffalo	10 50

The above Excursion Tickets to Winola Lake go on sale July 1st. Sale to be discontinued August 31st.

YARMOUTH MASS.

EXCURSION NO. 290.—YARMOUTH AND RETURN.

Delaware, Lack. & Western R. R......to New York.
Fall River Line Steamers....... ......to Fall River.
Old Colony Railroad......... ....to Yarmouth.
Returning *via* same route.

THROUGH RATES.

Morristown	$ 9 15	Waterville..........	$17 90
Dover............	9 65	Cortland............	17 90
Hackettstown.....	10 35	Syracuse	18 90
Washington......	10 75	Oswego............	19 90
Water Gap	11 60	Owego............	16 75
Stroudsburg.......	11 75	Ithaca	18 40
Scranton........	13 90	Waverly............	17 50
Pittston	14 30	Elmira............	18 35
Kingston.........	14 70	Corning	18 80
Wilkesbarre......	14 75	Bath..............	19 65
Binghamton	15 90	Atlanta..........	20 80
Greene..........	16 70	Wayland..........	21 15
Oxford	16 90	Dansville	21 60
Norwich..........	16 90	Mount Morris......	21 60
Sherburne.....	17 60	Buffalo	23 90

CHAUTAUQUA THE SUMMER TOWN ON CHAUTAUQUA LAKE.

Offers a delightful life to all, amid ideal surroundings, charming scenery, pure air, pure water, perfect sanitary conditions, intellectual stimulus and congenial society. ✄ ✄ ✄ ✄ ✄
Lectures, Concerts, Readings, out of door amusements, etc. ✄ ✄ ✄ ✄ ✄ ✄ ✄ ✄
Free State School, July 13-30th.✄ ✄ ✄ ✄
Special low railway rates for 1897. ✄ ✄ ✄
Send for full particulars to✄ ✄ ✄ ✄ ✄ ✄

W. A. DUNCAN, Sec'y,

BOX A, CHAUTAUQUA, N. Y.

FERN ✢ HALL

CRYSTAL LAKE, PA. ❧ P. O. DUNDAFF, PA.
Near Carbondale, on Spur of Blue Ridge and Allegheny Mountains

........FINEST RESORT HOTEL IN PENNSYLVANIA.........

Opens June 1st under new and experienced hotel management. Cuisine of a high standard. Elevation 2,000, temperature always 15 degrees lower than New York or Philadelphia. Magnificent scenery, good fishing, fine roads for riding, driving and bicycling. Music, dancing and amusements of all kinds. Absolutely no mosquitos or malaria. Accommodations for 125; large airy rooms, broad piazzas. Telegraph and long distance telephone service in hotel. Tally-Ho twice daily from Carbondale to Fern Hall. Terms moderate. Send for illustrated booklet to

C. E. ATWOOD, Manager,

Fern Hall, Crystal Lake, Dundaff, Pa.

Delaware Lackawanna & Western R. R. Co.

FAMILY TICKET AND COMMUTATION TARIFF.

Commutation tickets will be furnished on application, at the several stations, and at 429 Broadway, New York City.

These tickets are subject to the rules and regulations of the Company, and must only be used by the persons named thereon. If offered by any other person, conductors will take up the ticket and collect fare.

Personal baggage will be checked on these tickets to the extent of 150 pounds.

These tickets will be valid for sixty (60) rides between the stations, and during the month named on face of ticket, and must be shown whenever required by conductors or ferry-masters.

They give the right of passage only on passenger trains that are advertised to stop at the stations named on ticket.

☞ Tickets are not valid for passage unless the ticket for preceding month is surrendered to conductor on first trip on which the ticket for the current month is used. School tickets good for 46 rides per month will be issued to scholars only, on presentation of certificate signed by the principal of the school or college which the scholar is attending. Printed form of certificates can be procured at the stations.

Fifty-trip tickets, valid for one year from date of sale, for use by purchaser, a member of, a visitor to, or a servant in the family of, the purchaser, are issued at rates given herein. These tickets may be purchased at the stations, or at 429 Broadway, New York City.

BETWEEN NEW YORK AND	RATES FOR CONSECUTIVE MONTHS.												Sum of Monthly Rates.	Yearly Rates.	Rates for 50-Trip Family Tickets.
	1st Month	2d Month	3d Month	4th Month	5th Month	6th Month	7th Month	8th Month	9th Month	10th Month	11th Month	12th Month			
Harrison	$5 50	$5 50	$5 50	$5 00	$5 00	$5 00	$5 00	$4 50	$4 50	$4 00	$3 50	$3 50	$55 00	$55 00	$5 00
Newark	5 50	5 50	5 50	5 00	5 00	5 00	5 00	4 50	4 50	4 00	3 50	3 50	55 00	55 00	5 00
Roseville Avenue	5 50	5 50	5 50	5 00	5 00	5 00	5 00	5 00	4 50	4 50	4 50	4 50	61 00	61 00	6 25
Grove Street	6 50	6 50	6 50	6 00	6 00	6 00	6 00	5 00	5 00	4 50	4 50	4 50	66 00	66 00	6 50
East Orange	6 50	6 50	6 50	6 00	6 00	6 00	6 00	5 00	5 00	4 50	4 50	4 50	66 00	66 00	6 50
Brick Church	6 50	6 50	6 50	6 00	6 00	6 00	6 00	5 00	5 00	4 50	4 50	4 50	66 00	61 00	7 00
Orange	6 50	6 50	6 50	6 50	6 00	6 00	6 00	5 00	5 00	4 50	4 50	4 50	68 00	63 00	7 50
Highland Avenue	7 00	7 00	7 00	6 50	6 00	6 00	6 00	5 00	5 00	4 50	4 50	4 50	68 00	64 00	8 75
Mountain	7 50	7 50	7 00	6 50	6 00	6 00	6 00	5 00	5 00	5 00	4 50	4 50	70 00	65 00	9 50
South Orange	8 00	8 00	7 00	6 50	6 00	6 00	6 00	5 00	5 00	5 00	4 50	4 50	70 00	65 00	10 00
Maplewood	8 50	8 50	8 00	7 00	6 50	6 00	6 00	5 00	5 00	5 00	4 50	4 50	73 00	68 00	11 25
Wyoming	9 00	9 00	9 00	7 00	6 50	6 00	6 00	5 00	5 00	5 00	4 50	4 50	75 00	70 00	12 50
Milburn	9 00	9 00	9 00	7 00	6 50	6 00	6 00	5 00	5 00	5 00	4 50	4 50	75 00	70 00	12 50
Short Hills	9 50	9 50	9 50	7 50	6 50	6 00	6 00	5 50	5 50	5 00	4 50	4 50	78 00	73 00	13 75
Huntly	9 50	9 50	9 50	7 50	7 50	6 50	6 00	5 50	5 50	5 00	4 50	4 50	78 00	73 00	13 75
Summit	9 50	9 50	9 50	7 50	6 50	6 00	5 50	5 50	5 00	4 50	4 50	4 50	79 00	74 00	15 00
New Providence	10 00	10 00	9 50	7 50	6 50	6 00	5 50	5 50	5 00	4 50	4 50	4 50	82 00	77 00	16 25
Chatham	10 00	10 00	10 00	8 00	7 00	6 50	6 00	5 50	5 50	4 50	4 50	4 50	85 00	80 00	17 50
Madison	10 50	10 50	10 50	8 50	7 50	7 00	6 00	5 50	5 50	4 50	4 50	4 50	85 00	83 00	18 75
Convent	11 00	11 00	11 00	9 00	8 00	7 50	6 50	6 00	5 50	5 50	4 50	4 50	91 00	85 00	20 00
Morristown	11 00	11 00	11 00	9 00	8 00	7 50	6 50	6 00	5 50	5 50	5 00	5 00	90 00	90 00	25 00
Mount Tabor	12 00	12 00	11 00	10 00	9 00	7 50	6 50	6 00	5 50	5 50	5 00	5 00	95 00	90 00	26 25
Denville	12 00	12 00	11 00	10 00	9 00	7 50	6 50	6 00	5 50	5 50	5 00	5 00	95 00	90 00	22 50
Morris Plains	13 50	11 50	11 50	9 50	8 50	8 00	6 50	6 00	5 50	5 50	4 50	4 50	93 00	88 00	26 25
Rockaway	13 00	13 00	13 00	10 00	9 00	8 50	6 50	6 00	5 50	5 50	5 00	5 00	110 00	95 00	27 50
Dover	14 00	14 00	13 50	11 00	10 00	9 50	8 00	7 00	6 50	6 00	5 50	5 00	115 00	105 00	28 75
Port Oram	15 00	15 00	13 50	11 00	10 00	9 50	8 50	7 00	6 50	6 00	6 00	6 00	120 00	110 00	31 25
Mount Arlington	16 50	15 50	13 50	11 50	11 00	10 50	8 50	7 50	7 00	6 50	6 00	6 00	120 00	115 00	31 25
Hopatcong Station	18 00	15 50	13 50	13 00	11 50	11 00	9 50	8 50	8 00	7 50	7 00	7 00	130 00	125 00	32 50
Stanhope	18 00	15 50	13 50	13 00	11 50	11 00	9 50	8 50	8 00	7 50	7 00	7 00	130 00	130 00	35 00
Waterloo	19 00	16 50	14 50	13 50	12 00	11 50	10 00	8 50	8 00	7 50	7 00	7 00	135 00	130 00	37 50
Hackettstown	20 00	17 00	15 00	14 00	12 50	12 00	10 50	9 00	8 50	7 50	7 00	7 00	140 00	135 00	41 25

DELAWARE, LACKAWANNA & WESTERN R. R. 171

NEWARK & BLOOMFIELD BRANCH.

BETWEEN NEW YORK AND	1st Month.	2d Month.	3d Month.	4th Month.	5th Month.	6th Month.	7th Month.	8th Month.	9th Month.	10th Month.	11th Month.	12th Month.	Sum of Monthly Rates.	Yearly Rates.	Rates for 50-Trip Family Tickets.
Ampere	$6 00	$6 00	$6 00	$5 50	$5 50	$5 50	$4 50	$4 50	$4 50	$4 00	$4 00	$4 00	$60 00	$55 00	$6 00
Watsessing	6 50	6 50	6 50	6 00	6 00	6 00	5 00	5 00	5 00	4 50	4 50	4 50	66 00	61 00	7 00
Bloomfield	6 50	6 50	6 50	6 00	6 00	6 00	5 00	5 00	5 00	4 50	4 50	4 50	66 00	61 00	7 50
Glen Ridge	6 50	6 50	6 50	6 00	6 00	6 00	5 00	5 00	5 00	4 50	4 50	4 50	66 00	61 00	8 25
Montclair	6 50	6 50	6 50	6 00	6 00	6 00	5 00	5 00	5 00	4 50	4 50	4 50	66 00	61 00	8 75

PASSAIC & DELAWARE BRANCH.

	1st	2d	3d	4th	5th	6th	7th	8th	9th	10th	11th	12th	Sum	Yearly	50-Trip
West Summit	10 00	10 00	9 50	7 50	6 50	6 00	5 50	5 50	5 00	4 50	4 50	4 50	79 00	74 00	16 25
Murray Hill	10 00	10 00	9 50	7 50	6 50	6 00	5 50	5 50	5 00	4 50	4 50	4 50	79 00	74 00	17 50
Berkeley Heights	10 50	10 50	10 00	8 00	7 00	6 50	6 00	6 00	5 50	5 00	5 00	5 00	85 00	80 00	18 75
Gillette	10 50	10 50	10 00	8 00	7 00	6 50	6 00	6 00	5 50	5 00	5 00	5 00	85 00	80 00	21 25
Stirling	11 00	11 00	10 50	8 50	7 50	7 00	6 50	6 50	6 00	5 50	5 00	5 00	90 00	85 00	22 50
Millington	11 50	11 50	11 00	9 00	8 00	7 50	7 00	7 00	6 50	6 00	5 00	5 00	95 00	90 00	23 75
Lyons	11 50	11 50	11 00	9 00	8 00	7 50	7 00	7 00	7 00	6 50	5 50	5 50	97 00	92 00	25 00
Basking Ridge	12 00	12 00	11 00	9 00	8 00	7 50	7 00	7 00	7 00	6 50	5 50	5 50	98 00	93 00	26 25
Bernardsville	12 00	12 00	11 00	9 00	8 00	7 50	7 00	7 00	7 00	6 50	5 50	5 50	98 00	93 00	27 50
Mine Brook	12 50	12 50	11 00	9 00	8 00	7 50	7 00	7 00	7 00	6 50	5 50	5 50	99 00	94 00	30 00
Far Hills	13 00	13 00	11 00	9 00	8 00	7 50	7 00	7 00	7 00	6 50	5 50	5 50	100 00	95 00	31 25
Peapack	14 00	14 00	13 50	11 00	9 50	9 00	7 50	7 00	7 00	6 50	5 50	5 50	110 00	105 00	33 75
Gladstone	14 00	14 00	13 50	11 00	9 50	9 00	7 50	7 00	7 00	6 50	5 50	5 50	110 00	105 00	35 00

BOONTON BRANCH.

	1st	2d	3d	4th	5th	6th	7th	8th	9th	10th	11th	12th	Sum	Yearly	50-Trip
Secaucus	6 00	6 00	5 50	5 00	5 00	5 00	4 50	4 50	4 50	4 00	4 00	4 00	58 00	55 00	3 75
Kingsland	6 00	6 00	5 50	5 00	5 00	5 00	4 50	4 50	4 50	4 00	4 00	4 00	58 00	55 00	6 25
Lyndhurst	6 50	6 50	6 00	5 50	5 50	5 00	5 00	5 00	5 00	4 50	4 50	4 50	64 00	60 00	7 50
Delawanna	6 50	6 50	6 00	6 00	5 50	5 50	5 00	5 00	5 00	4 50	4 50	4 50	65 00	61 00	8 75
Passaic	6 50	6 50	6 50	6 00	6 00	6 00	5 00	5 00	5 00	4 50	4 50	4 50	66 00	61 00	10 00
Clifton	6 50	6 50	6 00	6 00	6 00	6 00	5 50	5 50	5 00	4 50	4 50	4 50	67 00	62 00	11 25
Paterson	7 00	6 50	6 50	6 00	6 00	6 00	5 50	5 50	5 50	5 00	5 00	5 00	69 50	65 00	12 50
West Paterson	7 00	6 50	6 50	6 00	6 00	6 00	5 50	5 50	5 50	5 00	5 00	5 00	69 50	65 00	12 50
Little Falls	7 00	7 00	7 00	6 50	6 50	6 50	5 50	5 50	5 50	5 00	5 00	5 00	72 00	67 00	16 25
Mountain View	7 50	7 50	7 50	7 00	6 50	6 50	6 00	5 50	5 50	5 00	5 00	5 00	76 00	71 00	17 50
Lincoln Park	8 00	8 00	8 00	7 50	6 50	6 50	6 50	5 50	5 50	5 00	5 00	5 00	78 00	73 00	18 75
Whitehall	9 00	9 00	8 00	7 50	6 50	6 50	6 50	6 00	5 50	5 50	5 00	5 00	80 00	75 00	20 00
Montville	10 00	10 00	10 00	8 00	7 00	6 50	6 50	6 00	5 50	5 50	5 00	5 00	85 00	80 00	20 00
Boonton	11 00	11 00	10 50	9 00	8 00	7 00	6 50	6 00	5 50	5 50	5 00	5 00	90 00	85 00	20 00

CHESTER BRANCH.

	1st	2d	3d	4th	5th	6th	7th	8th	9th	10th	11th	12th	Sum	Yearly	50-Trip
Kenvil	15 50	14 50	13 50	12 00	11 00	10 50	9 00	7 50	7 00	6 50	6 00	5 00	118 00	113 00	31 25
Succasunna	16 00	15 00	14 00	12 50	11 00	10 50	9 00	7 50	7 00	6 50	6 00	5 00	120 00	115 00	32 50
Ironia	17 00	16 00	15 00	13 50	11 50	10 50	9 00	7 50	7 00	6 50	6 00	5 50	125 00	120 00	33 75
Chester	19 00	17 00	15 00	14 00	12 50	12 00	10 50	9 00	7 00	7 00	6 00	6 00	135 00	130 00	37 50

SUSSEX R. R.

	1st	2d	3d	4th	5th	6th	7th	8th	9th	10th	11th	12th	Sum	Yearly	50-Trip
Andover	20 00	17 00	15 00	14 00	12 50	12 00	10 50	9 00	8 50	7 50	7 00	7 00	140 00	135 00	43 75
Newton	22 00	18 00	16 00	14 50	13 00	12 00	10 50	9 00	8 50	7 50	7 00	7 00	145 00	140 00	47 50

W. F. HOLWILL,

General Passenger Agent.

The Hotel Bennett THE LEADING HOTEL

H. C. HAYT, Prop'r.   GEORGE HAYT, Mgr.

Centrally Located, with all Modern Improvements
Elegant Turkish and Russian Baths Connected   Free Omnibuses

BINGHAMTON, N. Y.

The Rathbun House, Elmira, N. Y.   H. C. HAYT, PROPRIETOR

Elmira and Horseheads Ry Co.

Cars to all parts of the City of Elmira and all Depots. Direct line between Elmira and Horseheads, and shortest line to Eldredge Park

NEW CARS NEW TRACK ON TIME

POLITE EMPLOYES

F. W. Devoe & C. T. Raynolds Co.

MANUFACTURERS OF

PAINTS, VARNISHES, BRUSHES

ARTISTS' MATERIALS   MATHEMATICAL INSTRUMENTS

FULTON AND WILLIAM STREETS

NEW YORK

DIRECTORS

F. W. Devoe	E. L. Molineux	G. A. Meyer	C. C. Barrett
J. Seaver Page	E. H. Raynolds	G. W. Betts	I. W. Drummond

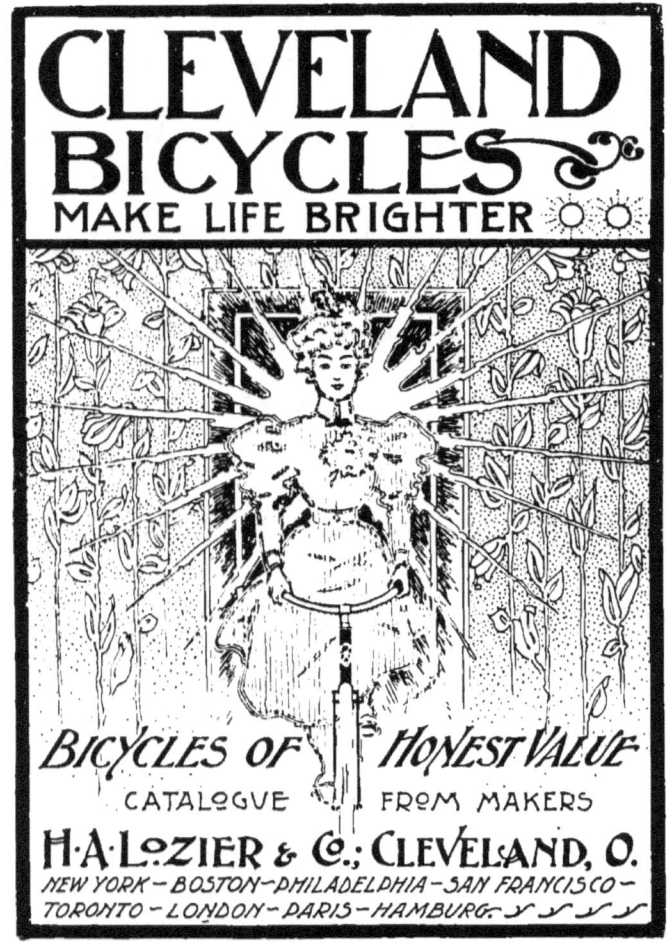

HEFT LUBRICATING OIL CO.

EASTON, PA.

....MANUFACTURERS OF....

Lubricating Oils and Greases

RAILROAD OILS AND GREASES

A SPECIALTY

ALSO THE NEW PROCESS AXLE GREASE

The New York State Fair

WILL BE HELD AT

SYRACUSE, NEW YORK

AUGUST 23D TO 28TH, INCLUSIVE

THE GREATEST EXHIBITION OF AGRICULTURAL AND
MECHANICAL PRODUCTS IN THE COUNTRY

GREAT TROTTING AND PACING RACES

FAMOUS HORSES AND NOTED CATTLE FROM THE
LEADING STOCK FARMS

Make your arrangements to attend the great Fair and Exposition
of the Empire State

Full information from D., L. & W. Ticket Agents

"Rathbun Villas" Snug Harbor on Lake Keuka, Steuben Co., New York

FINE FISHING, BOATING AND BATHING

Steam Yacht for the use of Guests of the House

....RATES ON APPLICATION TO THE PROPRIETOR.....

SIMEON B. RATHBUN
HAMMONDSPORT
NEW YORK

J. ROGERS MAXWELL, Pres. JOSE F. DE NAVARRO, Vice-Pres
ALFONSO DE NAVARRO, 2d Vice-Pres. HOWARD W. MAXWELL, Treas.
HENRY GRAVES, Jr., Sec'y.

ATLAS PORTLAND CEMENT

WARRANTED EQUAL TO ANY AND SUPERIOR TO MOST OF THE FOREIGN BRANDS

Official Tests, Nos. 3567 and 3568, made by the Department of Docks, New York, March 31, 1894, being part of contract No. 464 for 8,000 barrels

Tensile Strength, 7 days, neat cement............................. 622 lbs.
" " 7 days, 2 parts sand to 1 of cement................. 332 lbs.
Pats steamed and boiled... Satisfactory

All our product is of the first quality, and is the only American Portland Cement that meets the requirements of the U. S. Government and the New York Department of Docks. We make no second grade or so-called improved cement.

ATLAS CEMENT COMPANY

143 LIBERTY STREET NEW YORK CITY

GENEVA

BICYCLES

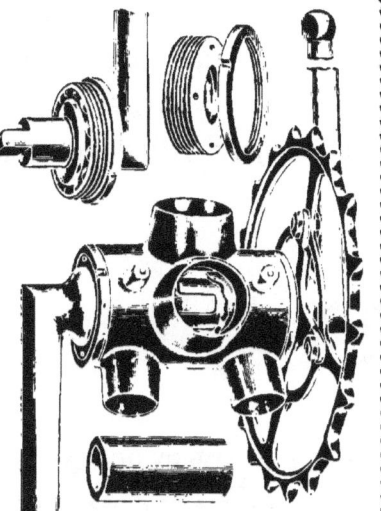

Patent Two-Piece Crank Hanger, used in "Geneva Special."

Met with unparalleled success in 1894, 1895 and 1896. Decided improvements made in 1897 enables us to say that

THE GENEVA LEADS THE WORLD

Full line to meet the requirements of all. The OHIO, as a medium price machine, defies competition. Write for prices.

**New York Office
92 Reade Street**

A. M. SCHEFFEY & CO.
General Eastern Sales Agents

JANNEY, SEMPLE & CO.
Minneapolis, Minn.
Agents for Northwest

WYETH HDW. MFG. CO.
St. Joseph Mo.
Agents for the Central West

The Geneva Cycle Co.
Geneva, Ohio, U. S. A.

DO NOT ❧ ❧

BUY A CHEAP AND POORLY CONSTRUCTED BICYCLE. ❧ ❧ ❧ IT WILL AFFORD YOU NO PLEASURE AND BE A CONSTANT SOURCE OF EXPENSE. ❧ ❧ ❧ ❧ ❧ ❧ ❧ ❧ ❧ ❧ ❧ IF YOU WANT TO ENJOY YOUR VACATION BUY A

"PACKER" WHEEL.

THE PACKER IS HIGH GRADE INSIDE AS WELL AS OUT. MADE OF THE FINEST MATERIALS, AND CONTAINS ALL THE LATEST IMPROVEMENTS INCLUDING LARGE SPROCKETS, LARGE BALLS AND PERFECT BEARINGS. ELEGANT ENAMEL AND NICKEL. EASY RUNNING. ❧ ❧

MANUFACTURED BY ❧ ❧ ❧ ❧ ❧
THE PACKER CYCLE CO.
READING, PA. ❧ ❧ ❧ ❧ ❧ ❧ ❧ ❧   WRITE FOR CATALOGUE

GOLD CRANK
FALCON
......BICYCLE
$75.00

This wheel stands as a representative of the degree of excellence which may be attained at the popular price. There is nothing better at any price. It embodies the highest possible grade of construction, even to the smallest detail. Send for Catalogue.

THE YOST MFG. CO.

YOST STATION   TOLEDO, O.

LIST OF HOTELS, BOARDING AND FARM HOUSES TAKING SUMMER BOARDERS
ON OR NEAR THE LINES OF THE
DELAWARE, LACKAWANNA & WESTERN RAILROAD.

Post Office.	Railway Station.	Hotel or Boarding House.	Name of Proprietor.	Miles from Station.	Capacity.	Price per Day.	Price per Week.	Altitude above Sea.	How Reached from Railway Station.
Paterson, N. J.	Paterson	U. S. Hotel	A. A. Van Voorhees		75	E. P. Europ. plan.			Electric cars.
Boonton, N. J.	Boonton	Mansion House	D. Bowden		55	2.00	8.00 to 12.00	700 ft.	
Netcong, Morris Co., N. J.	Stanhope	Rockwood Farm							
Budd's Lake, N. J.	"	Forrest House	A. Chamberlain	1	15	1.00	6.00	1200	Stages meet all trains, fare 15c.
"	"	Lansons Cottage	F. M. Duryea	2	250	2.50	8.00 to 12.00	1200	Hotel stages meet all trains.
Newton, Sussex Co., N. J.	Newton	Hotel Newton	A. F. Juergens	1½	30	2.00	6.00 to 8.00	1200	Stages meet all trains.
"	"	Cochran House	S. R. Jensen	¾		2.00	7.00 to 10.00		Hotel stages meet all trains.
"	"		R. H. Snook	¾			7.00 & upwds		"
Swartswood, Swartswood Lake, N. J.	"	Emmon's Grove Farm House	James Emmons	5	15	1.50	8.00	480	For further particulars write.
Delaware Water Gap, Monroe Co., Pa.	Water Gap	The Kittatinny	W. A. Broadhead & Sons		350	3.00to 4.00	16.00 to 27.00	800	Hotel stages meet all trains.
"	"	Cataract House	L. M. Tucker	2	100	2.00	7.00 to 10.00	1600	"
"	"	River Farm House	E. T. Croasdale	1	35	2.00	8.00 to 10.00	500	Carriages if notified.
"	"	Woodside Cott'ge	A. J. Doughty	¾	15	1.00	6.00	616	"
"	"	The Central	S. D. Oserfield	¾	75	2.00	8.00 to 10.00	1600	Hotel stages meet all trains.
"	"	Mountain House	Mrs. Theo Hauser & Son						
"	"	River View	Mrs. T. L. LeBarre	½	80	2.00	10.00 to 12.00	800	"
"	"	Glenwood	P. R. Johnson	¾	140	2.00	7.00 to 9.00	500	One minute's walk from station.
"	"				200	2.00to 2.50	8.00 to 14.00	1500	Stage or carriage.
"	"	The Arlington	Louise A. Dutot	½	60	2.00	6.00 to 10.00	1600	Carriage meets all trains.
"	"	Forrest House	A. L. Marsh	¼	40	1.50	6.00 to 10.00	690	Carriage meets trains.
"	"	Far View	Aaron Transul	¾	100	1.50	6.00 to 8.00		Carriage if notified.
"	"	Delaware House	Jno. M. Hill		25	1.00	6.00 to 8.00	1200	Opposite station.
"	"	Caldeno Cottage	Frank Edinger	½	15		6.00	1200	Carriage if notified.
"	& Ninsi	Gap View	Samuel Overfield	1½	60	1.00	6.00 to 7.00	1300	"

Post Office.	Railway Station.	Hotel or Boarding House	Name of Proprietor.	Miles from Station.	Capacity.	Price per Day.	Price per Week.	Altitude above Sea.	How Reached from Railway Station.
Delaware Water Gap........	Water Gap.......	BridgeViewCt'ge	Grant Edinger...	1/3	20	—	6.00	1300 ft.	Stage if notified.
Swift Water, Monroe Co., Pa.	Mt. Pocono.......	The Swift Water	The Swift Water	—	125	3.00 to 3.50	12.00 to 20.00	1800 "	References exchanged with strangers.
Mt. Pocono, Monroe Co., Pa	Mt. Pocono.......	The Wiscasset..	I. D. Iverson, Manager	1 1/4	125	3.50	14.00 to 22.50	1700 "	References requested of strangers.
Gouldsboro, Wayne Co., Pa	Gouldsboro.......	Simons House....	W. L. Haven.....	–	25	1.50	7.00	1970 "	Opposite D., L. & W. station.
Sherburne, Chen'go Co., N.Y.	Sherburne.	Hotel Daniels....	Ferguson & Nash	—	75	2 00	7.00 to 10.00	1040 "	Near station.
" "	"	Spring House ..	C. H. Reynolds..	1	50	2.00	8.00 to 12.00	1040 "	Free carriage if notified.
Cortland, Cortland Co., N. Y.	Cortland.........	Cortland House..	D. C. Smith.....	1/3	60	2.00 to 2.50	10.50	297 "	Bus and electric cars.
Richfield Springs, Otsego Co., N. Y.	Richfield Springs	Spring House	T. R. Proctor .	1/8	300	4.00	according to room, etc.	1750 "	Hotel stages meet all trains.
" "	" "	Kendalwood. ..	G. W. Tunnicliff.	1/4	200	3.00	16.00 to 21.00	" "	Free bus to all trains. Illustrated book on application.
" " "	" "	Cary Cottage....	Edward Cary....	1/4	200	2.00	10.00 to 15.00	" "	Bus to all trains.
" " "	" "	The National....	S. P. Barker.....	1/4	200	2.00	7.00 to 14.00	" "	" "
" " "	" "	Schuyler.	Fred Feldman..	—	200	2.00	10.00 to 15.00	" "	Opposite D., L. & W. depot.
Utica, N. Y..................	Utica........	Bagg's Hotel. ..	W. T. Johnson...	acr's str'et	150	4.00	according to room, etc.	—	Across the street. Uniformed porters meet all trains.
" "	"	The Butterfield..	C. A. Nott & Co..	1/4	200	3.00 to 4.00	according to room		Bus to all trains.
" "	"	St. James........	F.K.McLaughlan	—	90	2.00 to 2.50	14.00	—	One block. Porter meets all trains.
Oswego, N. Y................	Oswego...........	Doolittle House..	Kelts & Rector...	1/8	500	3.00	14.00 to 18.00	819 "	Free carriage meets all trains.
" "	"	Lake Shore Ho'se	C. E. Keyes......	opp.	200	2.00 to 3.00	7.00 to 14.00	" "	
" "	....	Waldorf Hotel...	Larry Hayes.....	1/8	20	2.00	8.00 to 10.00	" "	Free carriage meets all trains.
Dansville, Livingston Co., N. Y.	Dansville..........	Sanatorium......	J.ArthurJackson	3/4	300	3.50	17.50 to 49.00	1400 "	Bus meets all trains.
Binghamton, N. Y...........	Binghamton......	Binghamton	S. B. Dugan......	1/4	250	2.00	10.50	—	Free bus.
Elmira, N. Y................	Elmira......	Delaware House.	M. Crocker.......	—	—	2.00	—	—	Electric cars.
" "	"	TheFrasier Ho'se	J. A. Steck.......	—	—	2.00	—	—	Below Union depot.
Corning, N. Y................	Corning...........	Hotel............	Fuller Bros......	1	100	2.00	....	—	Hotel bus meets all trains.
" "	"	Hotel.	J. W. Fuller.. .	1	100	2.00	10.00	—	" "
Bath, N. Y....................	Bath...............	Messerschmitt...	J. M. Messerschmitt	1/4	45	A-EP 150up	9.00 to 12.00	—	
Owego, N. Y................	Owego............	Ah-wa-ga........	B. J. Davis.......	—	75	2.00	10.50	—	Bus.

The Gleason Sanitarium
─┤ 1852 - 1897 ┝──
ELMIRA, N. Y.

A real **home** for those seeking health, rest or recreation. Under care of regularly graduated physicians of long experience in this special line of practice.

Location high and airy, fine views of city, river and hills, beautifully wooded glen at rear of house, cool and shady.

Skilled attendant to give all forms of baths, electricity, massage, Swedish movements, etc. **Cuisine,** home-like and dainty.

All modern improvements, steam heat, open fires, safety hydraulic elevator, gas, electric bells, telephone and livery, daily papers, and all the comforts of a well-appointed home.

Send for illustrated booklet to   **EDWARD B. GLEASON, Mgr.**

American Bank Note Company,
78 TO 86 TRINITY PLACE, NEW YORK.

BUSINESS FOUNDED 1795.

JAMES MACDONOUGH, *President.*
AUG. D. SHEPARD,) *Vice-Presidents.*
TOURO ROBERTSON,)
THEO. H. FREELAND, *Secretary & Treasurer.*
JNO. E. CURRIER, *Assistant Secretary.*
J. K. MYERS, *Assistant Treasurer.*

ENGRAVERS AND PRINTERS OF BONDS AND STOCK CERTIFICATES,

And all other documents requiring security.
Safety Colors—Safety Papers.
Work executed in fire-proof buildings.

RAILWAY PRINTING OF ALL DESCRIPTIONS.

Railway Tickets, Maps, Folders and Illuminated Show Cards of the most approved styles. Numbered, Local and Coupon Tickets of any Size, Pattern, Style or Device, with Steel Plate Tints.

LITHOGRAPHIC AND TYPE PRINTING OF ALL KINDS.

Lake Keuka, Eight hundred feet above Sea level.

STEUBEN COUNTY, NEW YORK.

Absolutely free from Malaria, Miasma, Hay Fever and Mosquitoes.

THE FAVORITE FISHING GROUNDS OF THE LATE SETH GREEN.

Salmon, Trout, Black Bass, Pickerel.

EXCELLENT HOTEL ACCOMMODATIONS

FOR OVER ONE THOUSAND GUESTS AT VARIOUS LOCATIONS AND PRICES.

COMPRISING

HOTELS AND ADJACENT COTTAGES, AND BOARDING HOUSES.

NUMEROUS EXCELLENT MEDICINAL SPRINGS.

Nine hours ride from New York, Philadelphia, Baltimore, Washington and Boston, via Delaware, Lackawanna & Western, and Bath & Hammondsport Railways, on the direct route to Niagara Falls. The finest steamboats and the lowest rates of fare to be found upon any of the inland lakes of this country. Steamboats make sixteen trips per day, the entire length of the lake, 22 miles.

Lake Keuka is in the heart of the great grape growing and champagne manufacturing districts of the United States. Its scenery is unsurpassed.

Excellent locations are set apart for excursion parties, including groves and play grounds.

For full particulars on all questions, address

THE LAKE KEUKA NAVIGATION CO.,
HAMMONDSPORT,
NEW YORK.

ESTABLISHED 1856.

Henry Maurer & Son,

MANUFACTURERS OF

FIRE-PROOF

Building Materials

OF EVERY DESCRIPTION.

ISOMETRICAL VIEW.

"Excelsior" End Construction Flat Arch. [Patented July 21st, 1801.]
25 per cent. lighter and stronger than any other method.

POROUS TERRA COTTA OF ALL SIZES.

FLUE LININGS, FLOOR ARCHES, PARTITIONS, FURRING, ROOFING, &c.

Fire Brick of all Shapes and Sizes.

CLAY RETORTS FOR GAS WORKS.

OFFICE AND DEPOT:

420 EAST 23D ST., NEW YORK.

WORKS: MAURER, N. J. P. O. Box No. 1.

(ON CENTRAL R. R. OF N. J.)   Send for Catalogues.

DELAWARE, LACKAWANNA & WESTERN R. R. 185

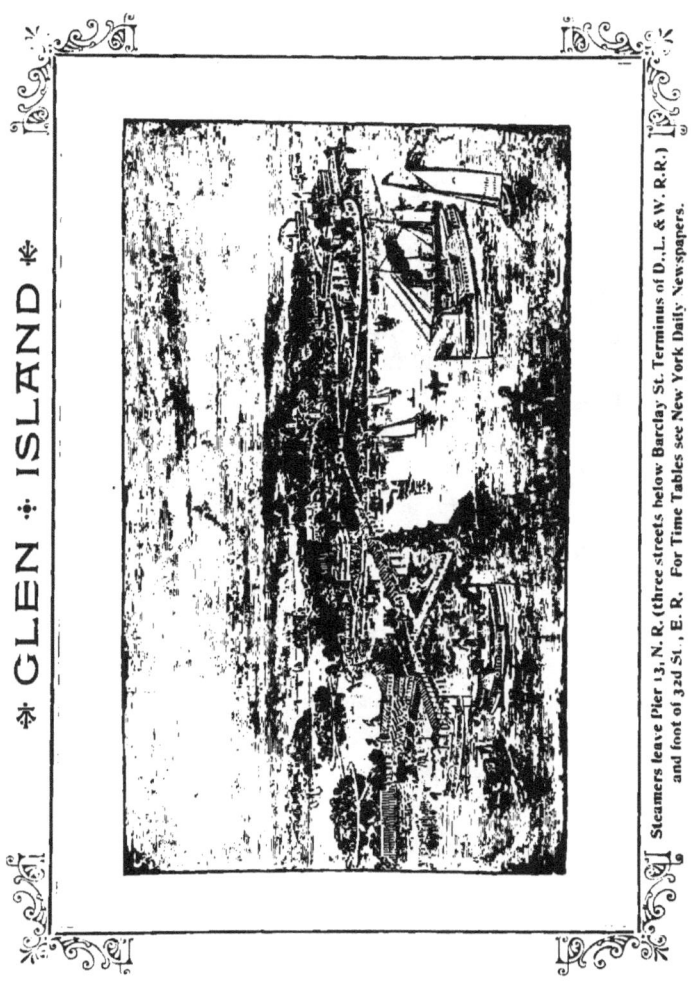

GLEN ISLAND

Steamers leave Pier 13, N. R. (three streets below Barclay St. Terminus of D.,L. & W. R.R.) and foot of 32d St., E. R. For Time Tables see New York Daily Newspapers.

1875—1897.   Twenty-third Season.

✤ SPRING HOUSE ✤
RICHFIELD SPRINGS,   -   -   -   NEW YORK.

✤ ✤ ✤

THE new Bathing Establishment furnishes all the accepted European methods of treatment (by sulphur water) of Rheumatism, Gout, Catarrh and Skin Diseases.

It contains Sulphur Baths, Turkish and Russian Baths (with sulphur vapor), Douche, Massage, Inhalation and Pulverization rooms, Swimming Bath, Gymnasium, Sun Room, Resting Rooms and other conveniences.

Skilled Masseurs of both sexes.

A full corps of competent attendants.

✤ ✤ ✤

THE SPRING HOUSE (Hotel) and BATH HOUSES
OPEN EVERY YEAR FROM JUNE TO OCTOBER.

New York Office, - - Windsor Hotel,
From May 1st to June 20th.

Illustrated pamphlet on application.   T. R. PROCTOR.

The Fuller House and Cottages,
N. D. JEWELL, Proprietor.

RICHFIELD SPRINGS, N. Y.

30th Season, under one management. May to October.

Main Street, opposite Springs and Park and the new Baths.

ACCOMMODATES 150 GUESTS.

Excellent Cuisine. Evening Dinners Electric Lights. Sanitary conditions perfect. A liberal discount for months of May, June and September. For terms or circulars address the proprietor.

SCHAEFER BROTHERS

ORNAMENTAL GLASS AND MIRRORS

464 WEST BROADWAY

LOUIS SCHAEFER
FREDERICK SCHAEFER.   *NEW YORK*

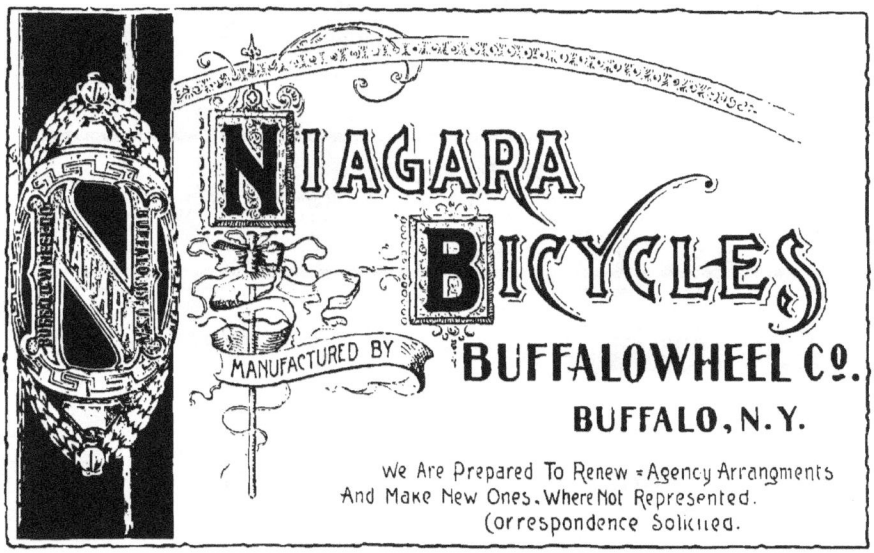

NIAGARA BICYCLES

MANUFACTURED BY **BUFFALOWHEEL CO.**

BUFFALO, N.Y.

We Are Prepared To Renew Agency Arrangements And Make New Ones. Where Not Represented. Correspondence Solicited.

THE ONLY WAY TO SEE THE.........
FALLS, RAPIDS AND RIVER
IS BY TAKING THE
GREAT GORGE ROUTE American Side

New Line Through NIAGARA'S WONDERLAND

All points of interest seen without leaving car seats

FARE, ROUND TRIP   -   -   -   ONLY 60 CENTS

Cars pass through main streets at Niagara, pass all Hotels and Depots

J. M. BRINKER, PRES. AND GEN. MGR.   D. B. WORTHINGTON, GEN. PASS. AGT.

DELAWARE, LACKAWANNA & WESTERN R. R.

"THE JEFFERSON"   WATKINS, NEW YORK

TABLE AND SERVICE UNSURPASSED
First-Class in Every Respect

O. S. LEVIS   FREE 'BUS TO THE GLEN   RATES, $2.00 PER DAY

JUST LIKE THE D., L. & W.

Always on time, finest equipment; nothing too good for our patrons, best service, and highly recommended as the D., L. & W. leading Funeral Director, F. L. ZIMMERMAN, Office open Day and Night, 218 E. Water St. Telephone 465.

The Millard   J. E. Markel and Son, Proprietors

OMAHA, NEBRASKA

....LEADING HOTEL IN THE CITY....

American and European Plan

M. B. Heller & Co.

Hardware, Stoves, Tinware, Etc.

126 West Water Street, Elmira, N. Y.

AGENTS FOR
The Monroe Range
Red Cross Range
Red Cross Heating Stoves
Hood Furnaces
Leonard Refrigerator

SEND FOR PRICES

W. M. HINDS & CO.

Plumbing, Steam Heating and Gas Fitting

DEALER IN

Fine Plumbing Goods, Gas Fixtures, Brass Goods for Steam and Water Works. Well and Cistern Pumps, Sinks, etc., etc., Lead and Iron Pipe. Salt Glazed, Vitrified and Cement Sewer Pipe and Fittings.

129 WEST WATER STREET

Telephone No. 314.   ELMIRA, N. Y.

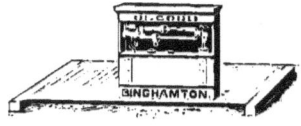

OSGOOD'S U.S. STANDARD SCALES
BINGHAMTON, N. Y.

CATALOG FREE

DALRYMPLE

ELMIRA'S FINEST SUBURB

Is the name selected for what is to become Elmira's finest suburb. *It is a beautiful name, indeed,* and one that will be found well suited to the place. The name is taken from that of the old and honorable family that has so long resided upon this property. It is true that the Queen City of the Southern Tier has no rival in its wealth of magnificent and charming suburban territory. Dalrymple will excel. Elmira, as is well known, is, and for many years has been, the most promising city of the Southern Tier. Whatever doubt there may at any time have been upon this point has been forever dispelled by the triumphant manner in which Elmira has passed through the perilous, panicky times of the last four years.

SIZE AND PRICE OF LOTS

All lots, except those fronting on Pennsylvania Avenue, have a frontage of 50 feet and are from 137½ to 140 feet deep. These lots are offered for a limited time at $200 each. *The title of this property* is of the best, and has passed the inspection of the most skillful conveyancers within a year. *Payments* are $10.00 down at the time of purchase and the balance in monthly, semi-monthly, or weekly instalments at the rate of not less than $5.00 per month, payable at the home office, Elmira, N. Y.

Situated 100 miles from Syracuse and from Rochester and 150 miles from Buffalo, Elmira is the only city of her class in a large circle of territory, and is the main center of distribution for the counties of Chemung, Tioga, Tompkins, Schuyler, Yates, Steuben and Allegany in New York State, and Bradford, Wyoming, Sullivan, Tioga and Potter, in Pennsylvania. Four of the great trunk lines of the continent—the Erie, the Lackawanna, the Lehigh and the Pennsylvania—enter Elmira, furnishing unsurpassed facilities for transportation.

NATHAN SKINNER, Proprietor, Elmira, N. Y.

C. E. ROOD

Manufacturer of

MALLEABLE IRON

QUALITY GUARANTEED

RAILROAD WORK A SPECIALTY

OFFICE AND WORKS, LANCASTER, NEW YORK

STATE MAPS   *RAILWAY GUIDES*

FINE STATIONERY

FAINE'S DUPLICATE WHIST TRAYS

JEANNETTE ADAMS
POST OFFICE, BOOK AND NEWS STAND
ELMIRA, N. Y.

The New Fairchild House

Hammondsport
New York

Newly Furnished Throughout
Very Best of Accommodations
At the Head of Keuka Lake
Rates, $2.00 per day
Only Hotel commanding full
view of Lake
Boating, Bathing and Fishing

AUGUST HAFFNER
Proprietor

GIBSON HOUSE ......ON LAKE KEUKA

NOW OPEN
For the Season of
1897

NO MOSQUITOES

Finest Trout and Bass
Fishing Grounds
on the Lake

Rates very moderate, and conveniences up to date

W. H. TAYLOR, Manager
P. O. Catawba, N. Y.

Something New

An advertisement that will take every time. ❧ ❧ ❧ ❧ Fotografic designs, original and artistic. ❧ ❧ ❧ ❧ ❧ ❧ Send the article you wish to advertise, or description of same and I will submit to you, **on approval** something catchy and out of the common line of ads. Don't fail to give this due consideration, should it prove satisfactory its cost is but nominal and is the way to advertise

GULICK ❧ ❧
Artist and Fotografer
126 N. Main Street   Elmira, N. Y.

STUDY—TAKEN FROM LIFE

THE ELLSWORTH ❧ ❧

ALBERT BUNDY
Proprietor

115-121 West Water Street
ELMIRA, N. Y.

❧

Rate $1.50 to $2.00 per day

❧

Headquarters for Societies and Conventions

FIRST-CLASS IN ALL ITS APPOINTMENTS

❧

Electric Cars from all Depots

❧

Steam Heat and Electric Bells

MOUNTAIN VIEW HOUSE

F. MÜLLER
Proprietor

Lake Hopatcong
New Jersey

P. O. Address
Landing, N. J.

THIS HOTEL is situated on the west side of Lake Hopatcong 1 1-4 miles from the Delaware, Lackawanna & Western Railroad Station and 45 miles from New York City. The Hotel is a distance of 350 feet from the lake, on a beautiful elevation of 200 feet above the lake level and 1,500 feet above the level of the sea; and commands a picturesque and extensive view of the wonderful Hopatcong. Since last season the Hotel has been greatly enlarged and improved, also by Electric Lights. Special parties, Outings or Excursions, only taken in June and September. This first-class Hotel contains the highest, largest and best ventilated rooms of any house at the lake. These rooms are furnished throughout with entirely new Oak Bed-room Sets, Hair Mattresses, Steel Springs, and all the latest improvements, and are able to accommodate 125 guests. All modern improvements

American Railway Supply Co.

(Successors to Hoole Manufacturing Co.)

24 PARK PLACE,   **NEW YORK.**

Manufacturers of

Baggage, Hotel and Time Checks,

Badges, Medals, Uniform Caps and Buttons.

Uniform Buttons for Corporations

A SPECIALTY

Knowles Mining Pumps

...... THE STANDARD!

Send for Special Catalogue, descriptive of all types of
Steam and Electric driven Mine Pumps

KNOWLES STEAM PUMP WORKS

93 LIBERTY STREET   NEW YORK

DICKSON LOCOMOTIVE WORKS
SCRANTON, PA.

BUILDERS OF

Standard and Narrow Gauge Locomotives

C. H. ZEHUDER, Prest.

L. F. BOWER, Sec'y and Treas.   DeCOURCY MAY, Gen. Mgr.   J. D. CAMPBELL, Mgr.

W. H. BLIGHT, Pres. L. S. KINGBURY, Sec. JOHN E. NICKS, V.-P.

The Nicks Tobacco Co.
Successors to John I. Nicks

Manufacturers of the Celebrated

JOHN I. NICKS LONG SMOKING AND CHEWING TOBACCO

The John I. in Tin Foil — the Oronoco

Jobbers in Fine Chewing and Smoking Tobaccos

615 Railroad Avenue   ELMIRA, N. Y.

We All Patronize
HASTING'S LAUNDRY, ELMIRA, N. Y.
Because it is the Best

Agents wanted everywhere. Write for Terms

W. J. BROWN
161 BALDWIN STREET
ELMIRA, N. Y.

Art Works
Art Worker
Pictures and Frames
Artistic Picture Frames Made to Order
Crayons, Water Colors & Pastel Portraits

HOTEL GARDNER,
DANSVILLE, N. Y.

One of the most popular hotels in western New York. Electric Lights. Electric bells. Commercial men's home. Large sample room on first floor. Free bus. Rates $2.00 per day and up. For particulars write

CHAS. H. GARDNER, Prop.,
Dansville, N. Y.

SMITH & WESSON REVOLVERS

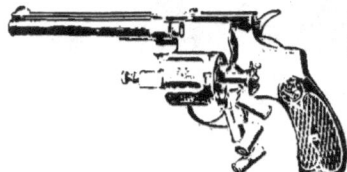

Unequalled for Accuracy, Durability and fine workmanship.

Three Calibres
32 and 38 and 44

Single Action
  Double Action
    and Hammerless

Hand Ejector Revolver

SEND FOR ILLUSTRATED CIRCULAR TO

M. W. ROBINSON COMPANY
79 Chambers Street, New York

Trade Mark Stamped on each Revolver

1866...... 1897

T. BRIGGS & CO.
Manufacturers of ALES AND PORTER
INDIA PALE ALE A SPECIALTY
ELMIRA, N. Y.

SCHOMACKER PIANOS

THE...

GOLD STRING PIANO

IS THE MOST BEAUTIFUL
TONED PIANO MADE...

CALL OR WRITE FOR CATALOGUE AND PRICES

H. R. HARRIS, Agent
410 MAIN STREET, ELMIRA, N. Y.

DANIEL SMITH & SON,
Largest Wholesale Dealers in

Confectionery and Fancy Candies   IN SOUTHERN TIER.
No. 327 Carroll Street, Elmira, N. Y.

JOS. F. WEBBER
MAKER OF   D., L. & W., WEST SHORE and HUDSON RIVER LINE   UNIFORMS
65 FIFTH AVE., NEW YORK

BILLS OF FARE...   For Banquets, Sundays and every-day use.
Largest and Best Line of Menus on the Market. Send for Samples.

Headquarters for   QUEEN CITY PRINTING CO.,
HOTEL STATIONERY.   115-117 East Henry St., ELMIRA, N. Y.

DELAWARE, LACKAWANNA & WESTERN R. R.

FOUNDED 1837.

THEO. W. MORRIS & CO.,
GLASS

Window Glass, Polished and Crystal Plate, French and German Mirror Plates, Rough and Ribbed Glass, Cathedral Ondoyant, Florentine, Opalescent, Ornamental, Cut and Colored Glass.

WIRE GLASS.
474, 476 and 478 GREENWICH STREET, NEW YORK.

Passaic Rolling Mill Co.,
PATERSON, N. J.

Structural Steel for...
Buildings and Bridges.

New York Office,   45 BROADWAY.

BRADLEY & SMITH
MANUFACTURERS OF BRUSHES

For Railroads, Painters and Families.

ALSO FOR EXPORT TRADE

251 Pearl Street, New York.

A. WYCKOFF & SON, 110 *EAST CHEMUNG PLACE, ELMIRA, N. Y.*
PATENT STEAM-PIPE CASING   Manufacturers of
For Underground Steam Pipes.   **WOOD WATER PIPE**
For Coal and Iron Mines, Coke Works and General Water Supply.

Two staves removed to show the lining between the inside and outside staves.

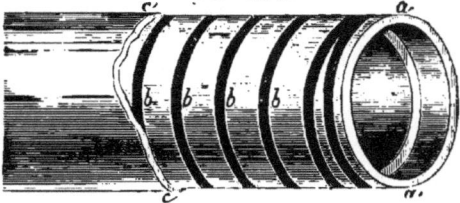

Send for Catalogues and Price List.

DELAWARE, LACKAWANNA & WESTERN R. R.

FLORIDA VIA CLYDE LINE

FINEST STEAMSHIPS IN THE COASTWISE SERVICE
The Fleet comprises the following Elegant Steamships
"Comanche" (new)
"Algonquin" "Iroquois" "Seminole" "Cherokee"
Superb Passenger Accommodations. Tables supplied with the best to be had in Northern and Southern Markets
TRI-WEEKLY SAILINGS FROM PIER 29 E. R., NEW YORK

Write for new descriptive matter, rates schedules, etc.
W. P. CLYDE & CO., General Agents,
12 South Delaware Ave., Phila.   5 Bowling Green, N. Y.
M. H. CLYDE, Asst. Traf. Mgr.   W. H. WARBURTON, East. Pass. Agt.   THEO G. EGER, Traf. Mgr.
5 Bowling Green, N. Y.

J. HENRY HAGGERTY,

HIGH OILS GRADE

RAIL ROAD OILS AND GREASES.

50 South Street, - - New York.

VANDERBILT & HOPKINS,
126 LIBERTY ST.,   NEW YORK.

YELLOW PINE, WHITE PINE, OAK
AND CYPRESS SAWED TO ORDER.

RAILROAD TIES FOR STEAM AND
ELECTRICAL ROADS.

CAR AND
RAILROAD
LUMBER.
CYPRESS
SHINGLES.

YELLOW PINE
AND
CYPRESS LUMBER
Dressed and delivered
in car-load lots,
all rail.

The Jackson & Woodin Mfg. Co.

BERWICK, PA.,

MANUFACTURERS OF

CAR WHEELS FOR FREIGHT OR MINE CARS, ALL SIZES AND WEIGHTS.

FREIGHT CARS

Of all Descriptions and Gauges for Export and Domestic use.

CAST IRON PIPE CAST VERTICALLY FOR GAS OR WATER.

FORGINGS FOR CARS OR SPECIALTIES.

CASTINGS OF EVERY DESCRIPTION.

Branch Castings, Pipe and Bar Iron kept in stock, and all other material furnished promptly at lowest market prices.

WORKMANSHIP AND QUALITY ALWAYS GUARANTEED.

GOLD CAR HEATING CO.

NEW YORK ADDRESS:

N. E. Cor. Frankfort and Cliff Sts.

CHICAGO OFFICE:

668 The Rookery, E. H. GOLD, Representative.

Upwards of 10,000 Cars and Locomotives equipped with our Systems of Car Heating; also adopted on some of the largest railroads in Europe.

Gold's "Universal" Straight Port Coupling,

which couples with Sewall, is the only one extant, having an adjustable brass-faced seat. Supplied with Gold's Automatic Gravity Relief Traps, which are a positive preventive against freezing.

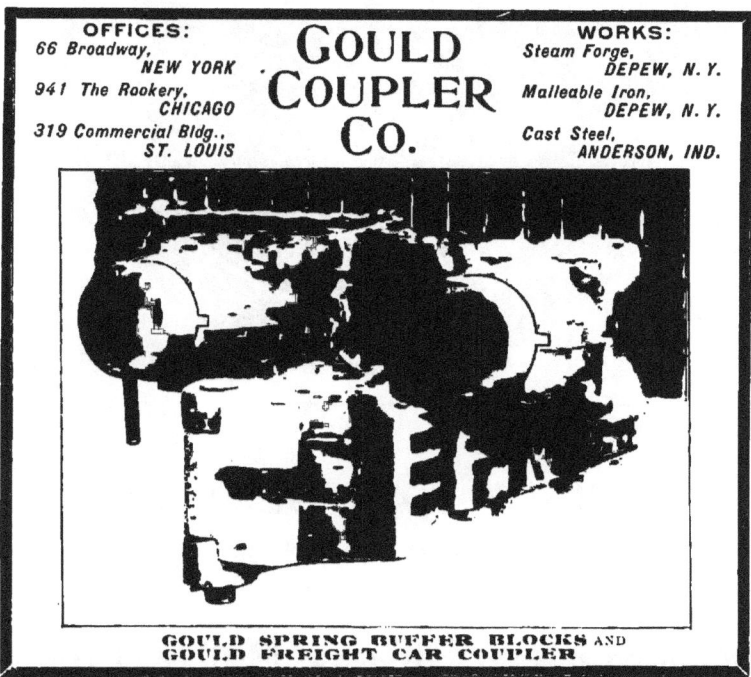

A. A. DAME, President.   O. T. SUMNER, Secretary.

DAME & TOWNSEND CO.,

(Successors to JAMES O. MORSE.)

ESTABLISHED 1849.

Wrought Iron Pipe AND Boiler Tubes,

Manufacturers of all kinds of Brass and Iron Fittings
for Steam, Gas and Water,

STEAM and WATER GAUGES, STEAM TRAPS, GATE VALVES,
RADIATORS, RAILWAY, MILL and ENGINEERS' SUPPLIES.

Gas and Steam Fitters' Tools, Etc.

76 JOHN, and 29, 31 & 33 PLATT STREET,
NEW YORK.

DELAWARE, LACKAWANNA & WESTERN R. R.

THEODORE IRWIN, President. GEO. B. SLOAN, JR., Sec'y and Treas.
EDWARD CLIFF, Superintendent.

NATIONAL RAILWAY SPRING CO.

OSWEGO, N. Y.

Manufacturers of

Elliptic and Spiral Car Springs

SPECIAL SPRINGS MADE TO SPECIFICATIONS

NEW YORK OFFICE, 39 CORTLANDT ST.

THE UNION CAR CO.,

MANUFACTURERS OF FREIGHT CARS.

CAR WHEELS AND CASTINGS.

Estimates on all kinds of Freight Equipment furnished promptly.

Works: DEPEW, N. Y.   *Office: BUFFALO, N. Y.*

EDWARD CLIFF, President and Manager.   LYMAN D. JONES, Secretary and Treasurer.

Vose & Cliff Manufacturing Co.,
Room 108, No. 39 Cortlandt Street, New York.

MANUFACTURERS OF

KING'S FLEXIBLE SIDE BEARING.

Pat. Nov. 8, '81; Mar. 6, '83.

This device secures reduced wear for wheel flanges; greater durability for trucks; longer life for cars; economy in freight service.

Adopted as standard by most of the largest Railway systems of the United States.

Sample and Trial Set Furnished if Desired.

DELAWARE, LACKAWANNA & WESTERN R. R.

THE BURNET CO.,
115 MAIDEN LANE, NEW YORK.

Manufacturers of **BURNET IMPROVED CABLE COATING,**
A Wire Rope Lubricant and Preservative for Mine Haulage and Hoists.

Also GUM OLEO FOR ELEVATOR USE.

☞ Descriptive Circulars and Prices on application.

THE WYOMING SHOVEL WORKS
WYOMING, PA.

MANUFACTURERS
OF

Shovels

Spades

and

Scoops

LAPPIN BRAKE SHOES.
✦ CAST IN ONE PIECE ✦
WITH ALTERNATE SPACES OF CHILLED AND SOFT IRON

They Preserve the Tires and Outwear all other Shoes.

Sample Sets of Flanged or Plain Shoes for Locomotives or Cars furnished for test free of charge.

THE LAPPIN BRAKE SHOE CO.,
39 & 41 Cortlandt St., - - - NEW YORK.
Works: BLOOMFIELD, ESSEX CO., N. J.

YACHT HARDWARE

TOPPING BROTHERS
92 Chambers Street

Tel. 1393 Cortlandt   Tel. 2878 Cortlandt   **NEW YORK**

BRASS AND GALVANIZED HARDWARE, YACHT, BOAT,
CANOE AND STEAM LAUNCH FITTINGS

Aluminum, Aluminum Bronze and Lignumvitae Blocks, Steering
Gear, Anchors, Chafus, Oars, Rope, &c.

SEND FOR CATALOGUE

JERSEY CITY SPIKE WORKS.

W. AMES & CO.,
MANUFACTURERS OF

Splice Bars, Boat and Ship Spikes, Screw Bolts, Track Bolts, Horse R. R. Spikes, R. R. Spikes, Dock Spikes and Hot Pressed Nuts. Bar Iron.

ROLLING MILL AND FACTORY:
WASHINGTON, MORGAN & STEUBEN STREETS,
JERSEY CITY, N. J.

Maloney Oil & Manufacturing Co.
M. W. COLLINS, Manager

Manufacturers and Wholesale Dealers in

BURNING, LUBRICATING AND CYLINDER OILS

ALSO SHAFTING AND JOURNAL GREASES
WHITE AND COLORED COTTON WASTE

OFFICE AND WAREHOUSE, 141 to 149 MERIDIAN ST.
SCRANTON, PA.

H. W. JOHNS'
ASBESTOS
LIQUID PAINTS

SUGGESTIONS FOR "EXTERIOR DECORATION" MAILED FREE

WE ALSO MANUFACTURE H. W. JOHNS' ASBESTOS ROOFING, FIRE-PROOF PAINTS, BUILDING FELT, STEAM-PIPE AND BOILER COVERINGS, ASBESTOS STEAM PACKINGS, GASKETS, ETC.

VULCABESTON MOULDED RINGS, WASHERS, ETC.

H. W. JOHNS MANUFACTURING CO.
100 WILLIAM ST., NEW YORK

CHICAGO   PHILADELPHIA   BOSTON

ACME LAMP BRACKET.
Nickel Plated.
Price, . . 5 Cents Each.
Postage, 2 Cents.

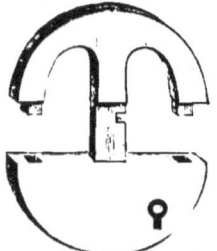

UNION LOCK.
Attaches to sprocket and chain.
Bronze finish.
Price, . . 25 Cents Each.
Postage, 5 Cents.

STAR FORK.
Made for right or left fork.
Nickel-plated and polished.
Price, . . 25 Cents Each.
Postage, 3 Cents.

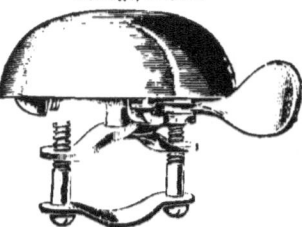

O. K. SINGLE STROKE.
Price, . . 15 Cents Each.
Postage 5 Cents.

DOUBLE STROKE.
Nickel-plated. 2½ inches.
Price, . . 25 Cents Each.
Postage, 5 Cents.

NONPAREIL TOE CLIP.
Tempered Steel. Nickel Polished.
Price, . . 15 Cents Pair.
Postage, 5 Cents.

H. & M. LAMP.
Made on an entirely new principle; detachable oil well; colored side lights; full nickeled.
Price, ... $1.25 Each.
Postage, 13 Cents.

VEST POCKET CUP.
Collapsing. Nickeled.
Price, No. 1, 8 Cents Each.
Postage, 2 Cents.
Price, No. 2, Large, 20 Cts. Each.
Postage, 5 Cents.

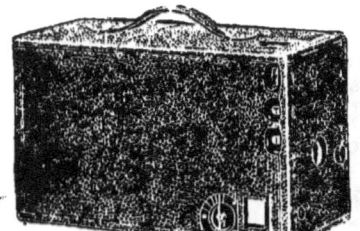

POCO, 4 x 5, SPECIAL CAMERA.

It is covered with morocco grain leather, and has a leather handle. All working parts are flush with side of camera box.
It has two large brilliant view-finders, two tripot plates, and large panel at the back of focus on the ground-glass. The focussing scale is accurately marked for each lens that accompanies the camera.
It has a high grade Rapid Achromatic Lens and a Rochester Shutter.

Price, complete with one Holder, $6.00.

Our 100-page Catalogue illustrating and describing everything pertaining to the Bicycle Cameras and Supplies mailed free.

Manhattan Electrical Supply Co., 32 CORTLANDT STREET, NEW YORK.

RESULTS MAKE REPUTATION......

HIGHEST GRADE VARNISHES AND JAPANS

COACH AND CAR
PIANO AND CABINET
HOUSE PAINTERS'
AND JAPANNERS'

......MANUFACTURED BY......

MINETT VARNISH CO.

1210 Ridge Avenue
PHILADELPHIA

Works: DELAWANNA, N. J.

60 Pearl Street
NEW YORK

......ESTABLISHED 1844

Made with the No. 4 Cartridge Kodak.

For 4 x 5 Pictures.

Price,

$25.⁰⁰

The Cartridge Kodak

combines our Film Cartridge System by which the camera Loads in Daylight, with a Folding Kodak of the highest type. It embodies in an instrument 3½ inches in thickness, every feature which the skilled amateur desires in his camera. It uses either film cartridges or glass plates and is

PERFECTLY ADAPTED TO USE A WHEEL.

"Bicycle Kodaks" booklet free at agencies or by mail.

EASTMAN KODAK CO.
ROCHESTER, N. Y.

$2,853.00 in Prizes for Kodak Pictures. $1,475.00 in Gold. Send for "Prize Contest" Circular.

$2,853.00

In Prizes for Kodakers

THE EASTMAN

AMATEUR PHOTOGRAPHIC CONTEST

$1,475.00 in Gold
$1,308.00 in Cameras
$70.00 in Lantern Slide
Plates and Film

130 Prizes

The conditions are easy to comply with—the prizes valuable. Prizes for contact prints, enlargements and lantern slides. Special classes for Pocket Kodak Prints and Pocket Kodak Enlargements. Circular giving conditions and enumerating prizes free at Kodak agencies or by mail.

EASTMAN KODAK CO.

Kodaks
Kodets
Bullets
Bulls-Eyes } $5.00 to $100.00

Rochester, N. Y.

BATH OFFICE.

MILLER'S
TURKISH, ELECTRIC
and ROMAN BATHS.

41 W. 26th St., New York City.

HOT-AIR, ELECTRO-THERMAL,
GALVANISM, MASSAGE.

Best Ventilated, Best Conducted and
Most Carefully Administered
Baths in the Country.

QUIET, CLEANLINESS,
CULTURE, REFINEMENT.

HOURS:
Gentlemen—Week-days, 6 to 8 A. M.,
2 to 11 P. M.; Sundays,
6 A. M. to 6 P. M.
Ladies—Every week-day,
9 A. M. to 2 P. M.

Massage treatment given at residence.

Rooms with or without meals can
be had in connection with the Baths.

C. H. HAYNES, Proprietor.

Arrange to take your Summer Vacation

While the Y. P. S. C. E. State Convention is in
Session at Elmira, N. Y., Oct. 4, 5, 6, 1887

BEST SPEAKERS   ENTHUSIASTIC SINGING
SPLENDID ENTERTAINMENT

For Rates, Time Tables, etc., send to

J. L. BOAK, Elmira, N. Y.
Chairman Committee on Transportation

N. B.—The Lackawanna is the best Route in and out of Elmira

Y. P. S. C. E.
Christian Endeavorers' Greeting ✢ ✢ ✢

If you are going to attend the convention of the great Christian armies at San Francisco or Elmira, you are invited cordially to use the Lackawanna Route. All its resources will be placed at your disposal to give you the most comfortable service possible. For information as to rates, routes, reservations, etc., apply to the nearest D., L. & W. R. R. agent. For maps, guides and printed matter of all kinds, write to the General Officers of the Passenger Department, or to FRED P. FOX, G. P. A., Elmira, New York. Correspondence solicited and promptly answered.

www.ingramcontent.com/pod-product-compliance
Lightning Source LLC
Chambersburg PA
CBHW020904230426
43666CB00008B/1313